IMAGES
of America

THE BEVERLY YACHT CLUB

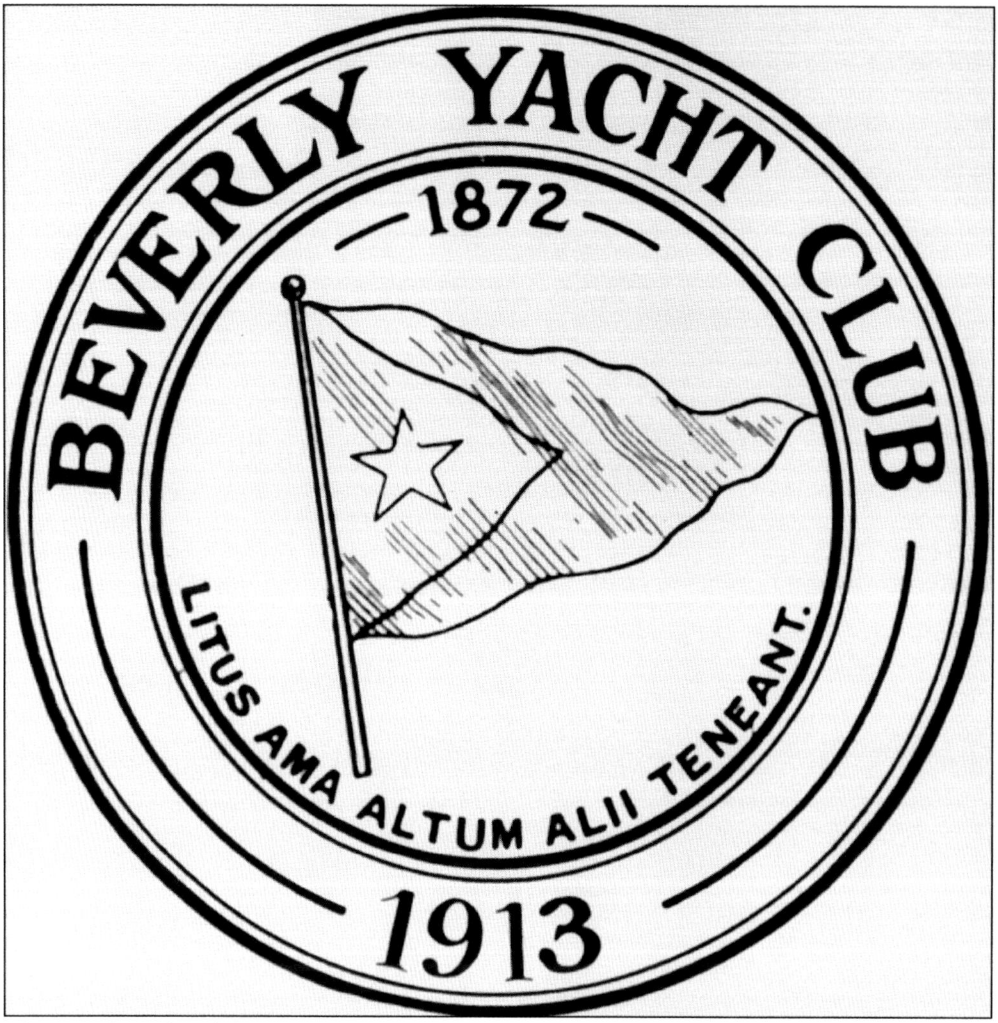

The Beverly Yacht Club was founded in 1872. The seal was adopted in 1913, when the club was incorporated. The Latin inscription, *litus ama altum alii teneant*, translates, "Others seek the deep, I like the shallow water."

On the cover: Audrey and Leslie Goodwin sail their Beverly dinghy in 1951 near the Beverly Yacht Club. The Beverly dinghy was designed in 1951 by Sydney Herreshoff (the son of Nathanael Herreshoff) for the Beverly Yacht Club. It is still being built today by Cape Cod Shipbuilding Company, where Gordon Goodwin is president. The Beverly dinghy was the last in a long line of Beverly Yacht Club boats carrying the Herreshoff name. (Courtesy of the Beverly Yacht Club archives, donated by Gordon Goodwin.)

IMAGES
of America

THE BEVERLY YACHT CLUB

Judith Westlund Rosbe

ARCADIA
PUBLISHING

ISBN 978-0-7385-4515-8

Published by Arcadia Publishing
Charleston, South Carolina

Printed in the United States of America

Library of Congress Catalog Card Number: 2006925665

For all general information contact Arcadia Publishing at:
Telephone 843-853-2070
Fax 843-853-0044
E-mail sales@arcadiapublishing.com

Visit us on the Internet at www.arcadiapublishing.com

For my grandson,
Benjamin Neil Auerbach,
born October 17, 2002.

Contents

ACKNOWLEDGMENTS

Most of the early images in this book are from the Beverly Yacht Club's historical collection. The most complete record of the early years came from massive scrapbooks kept from 1872 to 1892 by one of the founding members of the Beverly Yacht Club, Walter Lloyd Jeffries. His scrapbooks contain newspaper and magazine clippings not only about yachting in general throughout America but also every Beverly Yacht Club racing circular and race results reported in the *Boston Herald* and other periodicals. In addition, he included in the front of each scrapbook an alphabetical list of all yachts mentioned in the newspaper articles and referenced the pages in the scrapbooks where the yacht was mentioned. In many ways, the scrapbooks are a comprehensive history of yachting in America in its early stages. Jeffries was the commodore of the Beverly Yacht Club for 3 years, from 1879 to 1882, its secretary and treasurer for 11 years, its measurer for 5 years, and the chairman and a member of the Racing Committee for almost 30 years. He was born in 1854 in Boston and died in 1898. I wish I could have known such a diligent and conscientious historian and record keeper of the Beverly Yacht Club's early history. To think that he was only 18 years old when he began his role as Beverly Yacht Club historian is truly remarkable.

Many of the Beverly Yacht Club members also shared their photographs with me, as well as their recollections about their sailing experiences at the club. Special thanks go to past commodore John Buckley, who appointed me to the position of Beverly Yacht Club historian, and to past commodore Linda Goodwin, under whose encouragement this project began. Present commodore Brian Ladouceur and his council have continued that support in numerous ways, as have club manager Joe Odachowski, who called me whenever he found something in the clubhouse that he thought I might be interested in, and member services coordinator Kelly Darmetko, who assisted me in countless ways. I especially thank my husband, Bob Rosbe, who shared his extensive nautical library and knowledge with me for this project.

—Judith Westlund Rosbe
Beverly Yacht Club Historian

INTRODUCTION

According to an account left by Walter Burgess, a younger brother of the famous yacht designer Edward Burgess, the idea of forming the Beverly Yacht Club began when he and two of his summer neighbors, Franklin Dexter and William F. Whitney, were riding their horses in Beverly in the fall of 1871. The three commiserated that the Eastern Yacht Club, which had been founded in 1870 in Marblehead, had refused to permit smaller yachts under 26 feet in length on the waterline (this number was subsequently raised to 30 feet) to enter its yacht races. At the suggestion of Walter's father, Benjamin F. Burgess, they invited their young friends on the north shore to a supper party at their home at 62 Beacon Street in Boston on the evening of February 24, 1872, and the Beverly Yacht Club was formally launched for the racing of smaller yachts. Dues were set at $5 a year.

Besides Edward, Sidney, Arthur, and Walter Burgess, there were present at this initial meeting Count Nicola Altrochi, John F. Andrew, William Appleton, Perry Belmont, T. Dennie Boardman, Arthur W. Cabot, Abbott W. Cobb, Edward W. Codman, Franklin Dexter, Edward Everett, George Fiske, George A. Gibson, William A. Jeffries, Walter Lloyd Jeffries, Henry W. Lamb, William Lawrence, Lewis Cass Ledyard, William Caleb Loring, Harrison Gray Otis, William F. Otis, Dudley M. Pickman, Edward B. Russell, David Sears Jr., Alanson Tucker, Frank M. Weld, George West, Edward F. Whitney, William F. Whitney, and Charles H. Williams. Edward Burgess, who was closely connected with the Eastern Yacht Club, consented to act as commodore of the newly formed Beverly Yacht Club for two years.

The first regatta was held at Beverly on June 22, 1872, where 11 boats, 10 catboats, and a sloop started in three classes. Only yachts under 30 feet on the waterline were eligible to enter the Beverly Yacht Club races. The first class was for boats between 21 and 30 feet in length on the waterline, the second class was for boats between 17 and 20 feet, and the third class was for boats under 17 feet. Most of the boats were catboats, which were of various custom designs, so a formula was devised to handicap the yachts, adding or subtracting time to the actual racing time of each boat to determine the winners of each race on corrected time. Pennants were also given for best actual times in addition to corrected time winners.

Because of the problems connected with handicap racing, some of the members decided to investigate commissioning a one-design boat for the members to race against each other. In 1898, Nathanael Herreshoff designed a gaff-rigged sloop called the one-design 15 footer, or the Herreshoff 15 (also the E class or *Es*), especially for members of the Beverly Yacht Club. The class became very popular, and approximately 70 boats were eventually built. The most popular of all classes to be raced at Beverly Yacht Club has been the Herreshoff 12 footer, which was designed by Nathanael Herreshoff in 1914.

Over the years, many additional one-design classes have been included in the fleet of boats racing at the Beverly Yacht Club. The club motto written on the club seal in Latin, *litus ama altum alii teneant* (Others seek the deep, I like the shallow water), still reflects the club's strong tradition in small-boat racing.

One

Beginnings
1872

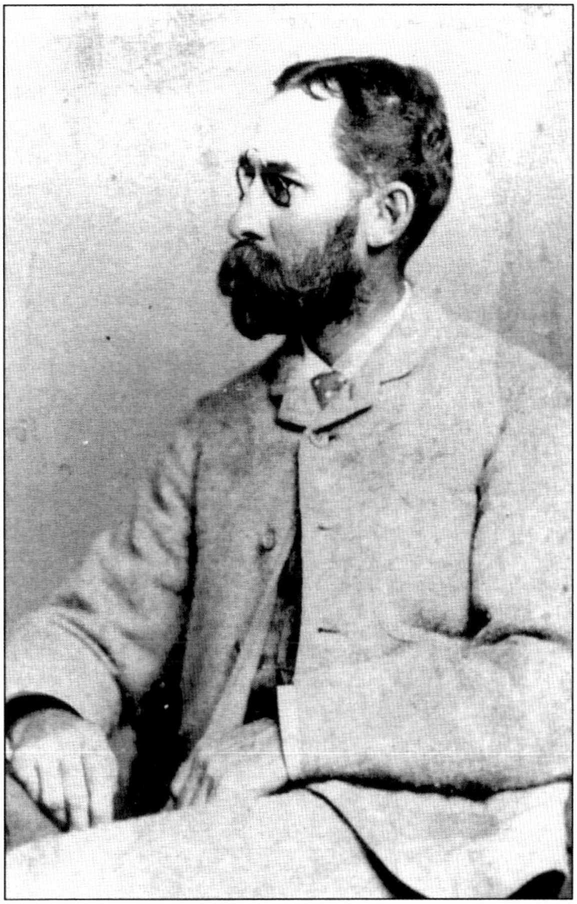

Edward Burgess was the first commodore of the Beverly Yacht Club, serving from 1872 to 1874. At the suggestion of his father, Benjamin F. Burgess, Edward and his brother Walter invited their young friends to launch a new club for racing small yachts that were under 26 (later raised to 30) feet on the waterline. Another brother, Arthur Burgess, was commodore from 1877 to 1879.

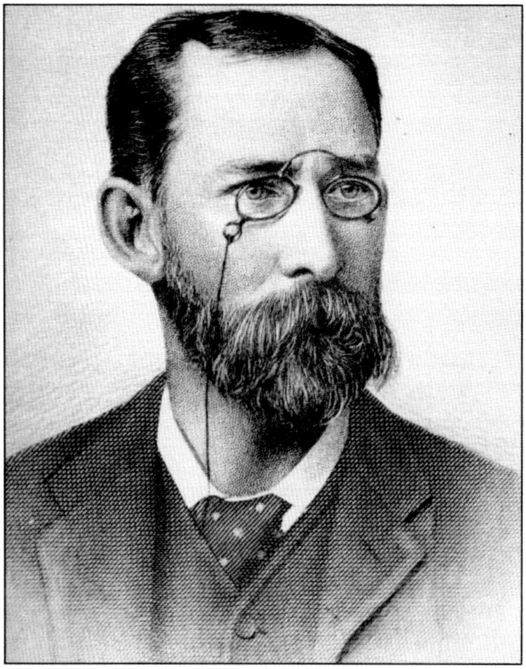

This is another photograph of Edward Burgess, who became the leading American yacht designer in the 1880s and designed three successive America's Cup winners (in 1885, 1886, and 1887) and 207 vessels in only seven years. Edward Burgess began his career as a professor of entomology at Harvard. The 1883 failure of his family's company forced Edward to turn his passion for mathematics and design into a practical career. In 1885, his firm was asked by a Boston group to design a yacht to enter the America's Cup and Burgess's design, the *Puritan*, won the America's Cup in 1885.

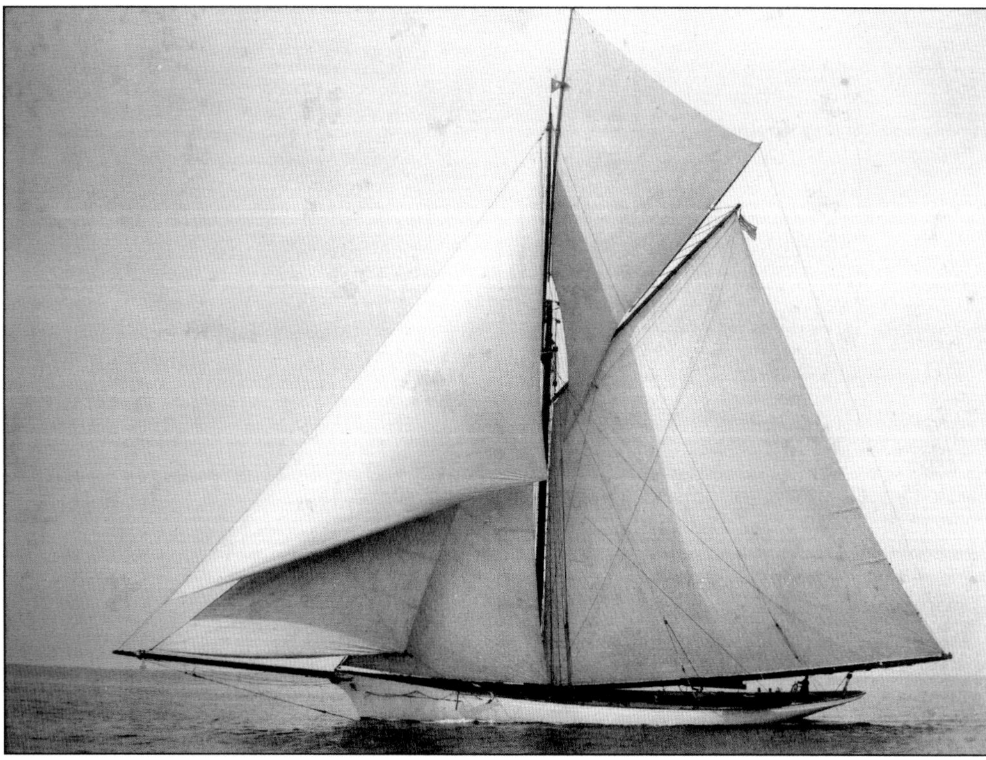

The *Volunteer*, shown above, was designed by Edward Burgess. It defeated the *Thistle* in the 1887 America's Cup series and brought home the coveted cup. The prior year, in 1886, Edward Burgess designed the *Mayflower*, which also won the America's Cup. Burgess died at age 43 at the height of his career. His son, W. Starling Burgess, carried on with a successful yacht designing career.

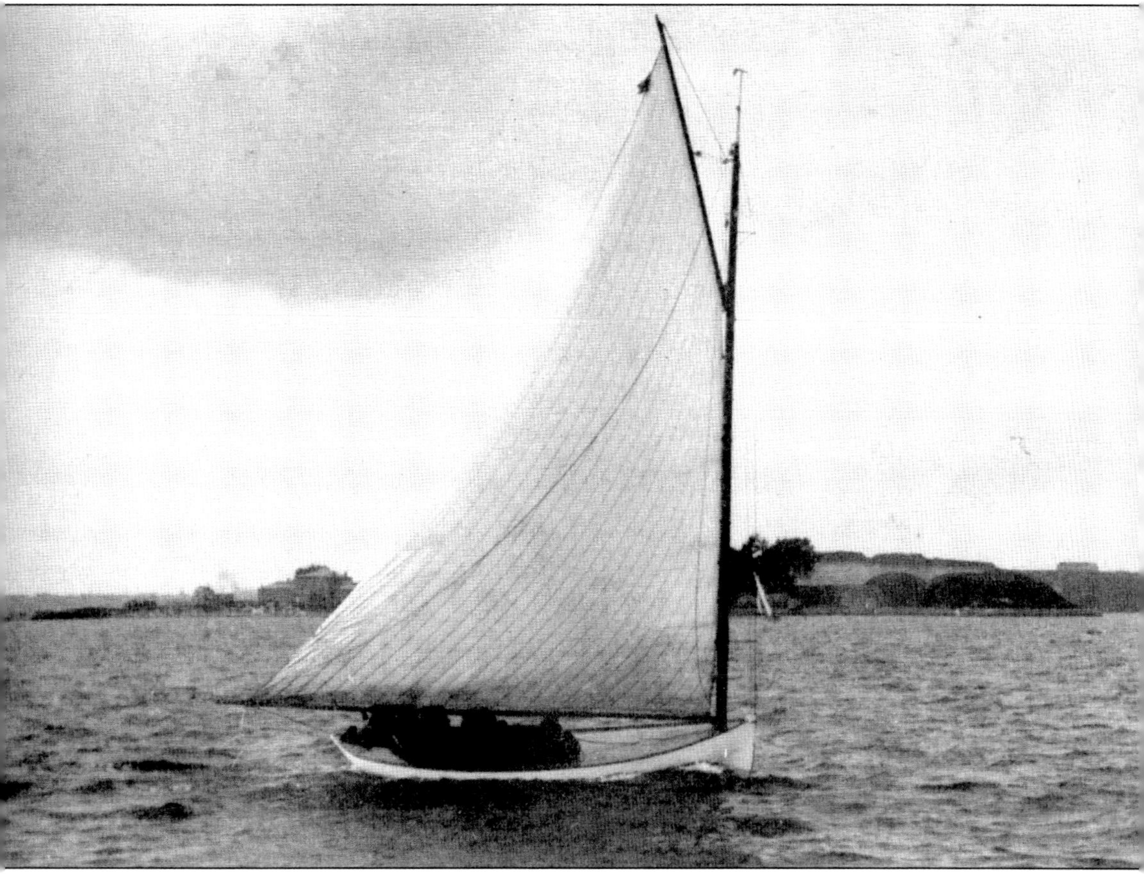

This centerboard catboat (*Nora*) raced in the first regatta run by the Beverly Yacht Club off Beverly on June 22, 1872, where 11 boats, 10 catboats, and a sloop started in three classes based on boat length: 21 to 30 feet on the waterline, 17 to 21 feet on the waterline, and 17 feet and under on the waterline. The *Nora* was owned by original Beverly Yacht Club member Franklin Dexter. It was 16 feet 4 inches in length, with a beam of 7 feet 4 inches, and was built by J. B. Herreshoff in Bristol, Rhode Island. It raced in the third class of boats, which were under 17 feet in length on the waterline. It came in third in its class, behind Edward Burgess's *Bluebell* and his brother Arthur Burgess's *Rose*.

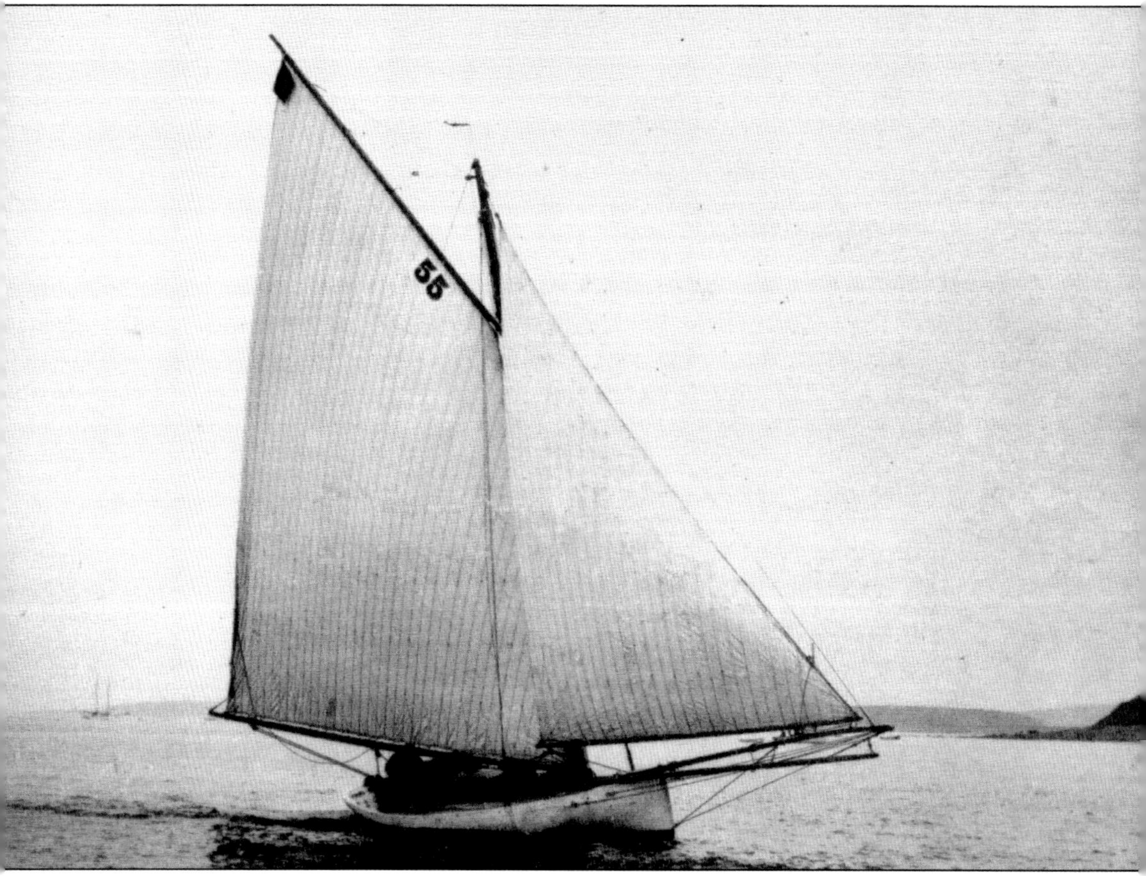

The *Posy*, a catboat 21 feet 4 inches in length, was also raced in the Beverly Yacht Club's first regatta, held in Beverly on June 22, 1872. The *Posy* was owned by N. T. Allen and raced in the first class for yachts between 21 feet and 30 feet in length on the waterline. In 1872, most American yachts were wide, shallow boats with inside ballast.

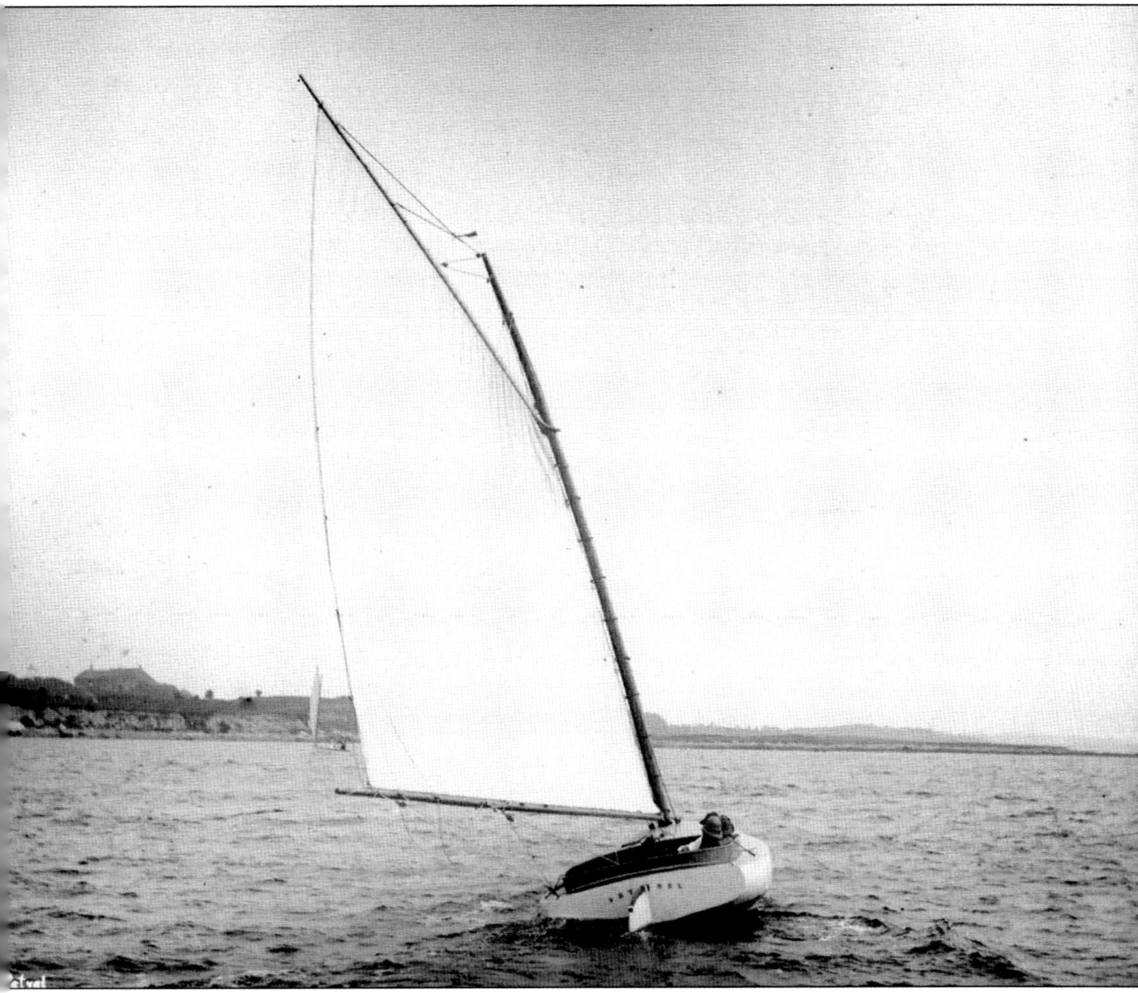

The *Petrel* won first place in the second class in the second regatta run by the Beverly Yacht Club in Boston Harbor on June 6, 1872.

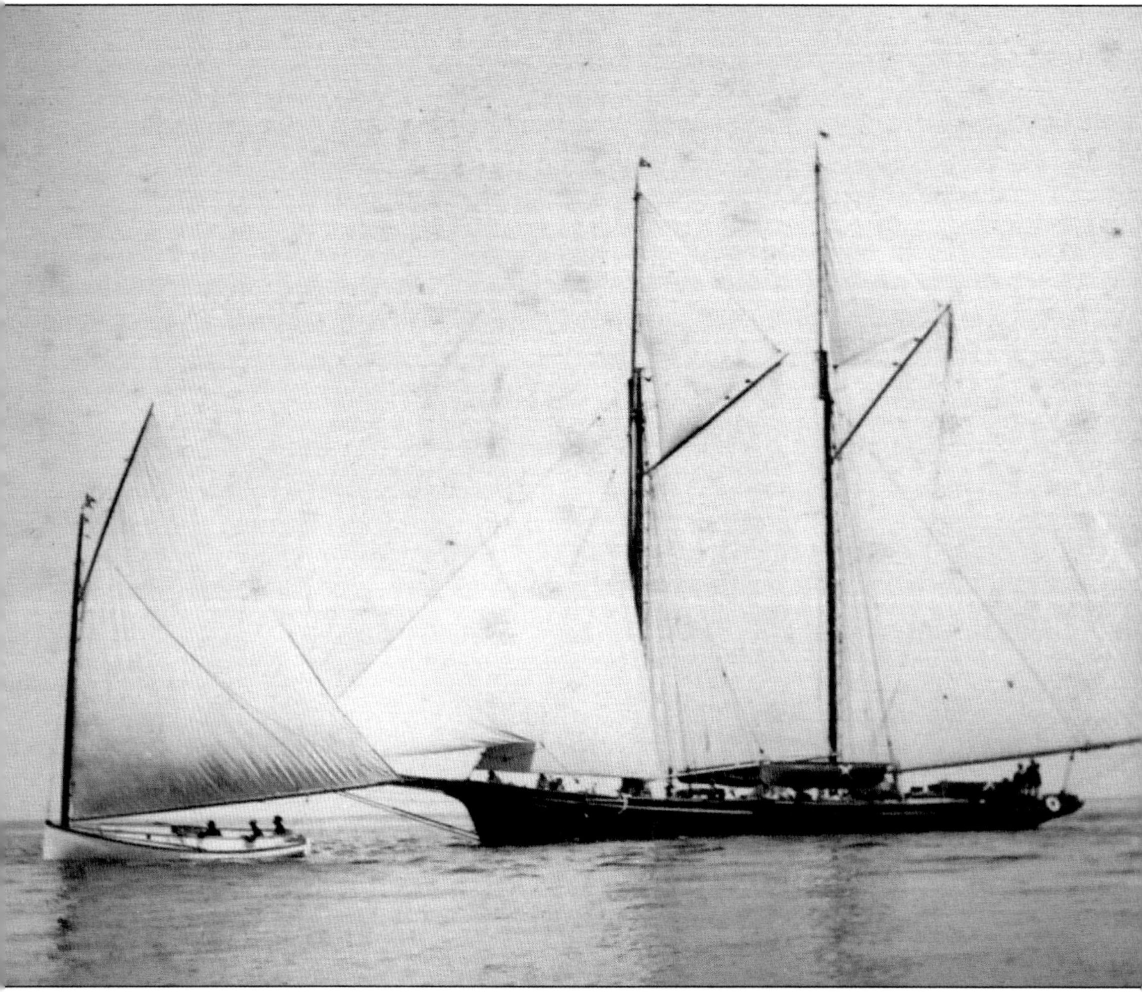

The *Rebecca*, on the right, was a schooner owned in 1875 by Beverly Yacht Club member F. E. Peabody of Boston. It was too large to enter the Beverly Yacht Club races. The *Violet*, on the left, was owned by Beverly Yacht Club member G. H. Richards.

Two

CATBOATS 1872–1895

Beverly Yacht Club.

Officers for 1874.

COMMODORE,
WILLIAM C. LORING.

VICE COMMODORE,
SAMUEL S. GRAY.

SECRETARY,
WALTER BURGESS.

MEASURER,
HENRY W. LAMB.

REGATTA COMMITTEE,
CHAS. H. WILLIAMS, EDW. B. RUSSELL,
W. D. HODGES, W. L. JEFFRIES.
WALTER BURGESS.

Secretary's Office, 23 Merchants' Exchange.
P. O. Address, Box 1078, Boston.

The Beverly Yacht Club officers in 1874 were William C. Loring (commodore), Samuel S. Gray (vice commodore), Walter Burgess (secretary), and Henry W. Lamb (measurer). The Regatta Committee consisted of Charles H. Williams, E. B. Russell, W. D. Hodges, Walter Lloyd Jeffries, and Walter Burgess. During the season, 40 Beverly Yacht Club yachts were raced; 33 were catboats, and seven were sloops.

BEVERLY YACHT CLUB.

SPECIAL REGATTA.

Beverly, Monday, July 13, 1874.

WM. SOHIER, ESQ., having kindly offered a set of Prizes to be sailed for by Yachts belonging to the Beverly Yacht Club and under its Rules and Regulations, a Regatta will be sailed on July 13th The Prizes are a Silver Cnp for each of the regular Classes, and also one as a "Consolation Prize," for the last boat in.

The start will be a flying one; Yachts will cross the line between Judges' Yacnt and a Stakeboat moored off Hospital Point.

Four guns will be fired for the start, at intervals of five minutes. The first a preparatory gun, at 12 o'clock. The First Class will start between the 2d and 3d guns; the Second Class between the 3d and 4th guns; and the Third Class at the 4th gun, also being allowed five minutes for starting. Yachts on their return will pass BETWEEN THE JUDGES' YACHT AND THE STAKEBOAT. Yachts are requested to carry their private signals at the peak.

As soon as the courses are decided on, white flags bearing their number will be displayed on the Judges' Yacht.

Courses. — For all Classes.

No. 1. From Starting Point,
Leaving Stakeboat off Woodbury's Point on port hand,
" Buoy on Archer's Rock [off Lowell Is.] on port hand,
" R. Buoy. No. 8 [off Misery Is.] on port hand,
To Judges' Boat.

No. 2. From Starting Point,
Leaving R. Buoy No. 8 [off Misery Is.] on starboard hand,
" Buoy on Archer's Rock [off Lowell Is.] on starboard hand,
" Stakeboat off Woodbury's Point on starboard hand,
To Judges' Boat.

In case of bad weather the Regatta will be postponed until the first favorable day.

CHAS. H. WILLIAMS,
E. B. RUSSELL,
W. D. HODGES,
W. L. JEFFRIES,
WALTER BURGESS.
Regatta Committee.

This July 13, 1874, racing circular announced a special regatta for three classes of yachts off Beverly. The first class included all boats between 21 to 30 feet on the waterline, the second class included all boats measuring over 17 feet and not over 21 feet, and the third class consisted of all boats under 17 feet. During the early years of racing, most of the boats racing were catboats, and the winner was chosen by a handicap system of rating the boats. The first class was won by the *Eva*, the second class was won by the *Peri*, and the third class was won by the *Pink*.

BEVERLY YACHT CLUB.

1874.

FOURTH REGATTA.

Nahant, Saturday, July 25, at 12 o'clock.

PRIZES.

The first prize for each Class will be of solid silver A second prize will also be given. These prizes will be sailed for with the time allowance. A Champion Pennant will be awarded to the first Yacht, without allowance, in each Class, to be held by the winner until the following Regatta, and to become the property of the Yacht winning it the greatest number of times during the season.

The start will be flying Yachts crossing a line between the Judges' Yacht and Stakeboat moored off the Yacht Anchorage, near the Steamboat wharf.

Four guns will be fired for the start, at intervals of five minutes. The first, a preparatory gun, at 12 o'clock. The First Class will start between the 2d and 3d guns; the Second Class between the 3d and 4th guns; and the Third Class at the 4th, also being allowed five minutes for starting.

Yachts on their return will *pass between the Judges' Yacht and the Stakeboat.*

Yachts are requested to carry their private signals at the peak.

As soon as the Courses are decided on, white flags bearing their numbers will be displayed on the Judges' Yacht.

In case of unfavorable weather, the regatta will be sailed on the following Monday.

Courses for First Class.

No. 1.

From Starting Point.
  Leaving Red Buoy No. 2, off Winthrop Head on port hand,
  " Bell Buoy, off Graves, on port hand.
To Judges' Yacht.

No. 2.

From Starting Point.
  Leaving Bell Buoy, off Graves, on starboard hand.
  " Red Buoy No. 2, off Winthrop Head, on starboard hand.
To Judges' Yacht.

Courses for Second and Third Classes.

No. 3.

From Starting Point,
  Leaving a *Stake* bearing a flag, off Shag Rocks, on starboard hand.
  " a *Stakeboat*, anchored two miles to the southward of Nahant, on starboard hand.
  " the Steamboat Mark (a black barrel) off Bass Point, on starboard hand.
  " the Steamboat Mark (a red barrel) off Bailey's Hill, on the port hand.
To Judges' Yacht.

No. 4.

From Starting Point,
  Leaving Steamboat Mark off Bailey's Hill, on starboard hand.
  " Steamboat Mark off Bass Point, on port hand.
  " *Stakeboat* on port hand.
  " *Flag Stake*, off Shag Rocks on port hand.
To Judges' Yacht.

F. B. Russell,
W. D. Hodges,
W. L. Jeffries,
Walter Burgess,
Chas. H. Williams, } Regatta Committee.

The fourth regatta of the Beverly Yacht Club was held off Nahant on July 25, 1874. The *Sunday Herald* reported on the event: "Of all the many regattas of this club none have been blessed with more propitious weather than that of yesterday—clear sky, warm sun, a good breeze, a full attendance of members and boats, a fine sail with no mishaps—all tending to render the fourth regatta one of unexcelled and rarely equaled merit. . . . In the first class the *Eva* (W. H. Bangs Jr.) took the first prize, a silver inkstand, and the *Fire Fly* (G. H. Balch) the second, a silver goblet. The first prize in the second class was awarded to the *Peri* (S. W. Burgess), and the second to the *Avon* (F. R. Sears Jr.). In the third class the *Tulip* (W. Burgess) took the first and the *Pink* (J. B. Mills Jr.) the second."

Beverly Yacht Club

1874.

UNION REGATTA.

Open to ALL Yachts not over 30 feet on the Water Line.

BEVERLY, Saturday, Aug. 29, at 12 M.

The first Prize for each Class will be of Solid Silver. A second Prize will also be given. These Prizes will be sailed for with the time allowance of the Club. The Champion Pennants will be awarded to Yachts of the Club only.

In case of unfavorable weather the Regatta will be sailed the first fair day.

The start will be a flying one; Yachts will cross the line between the Judges' Yacht and a Stakeboat, moored off Curtis' Point.

Four guns will be fired for the start, at intervals of five minutes. The first, a preparatory gun at 12 o'clock. The first Class will start between the 2d and 3d guns; the second Class between the 3d and 4th guns; and the third Class at the 4th, also, being allowed five minutes for starting.

Yachts on their return will pass *between the Judges' Yacht and the Stakeboat*

Yachts are requested to carry their private signals at the peak.

As soon as the Courses are decided on, white flags bearing their number will be displayed on the Judges' Yacht.

Extracts from the Sailing Regulations.

RULE I. Yachts shall be divided into three Classes.

The First Class shall include all Yachts measuring over 21 feet on the water line.

The Second Class shall include all Yachts measuring over 17 feet, and not over 21 feet on the water line.

The Third Class shall include all Yachts not measuring over 17 feet on the water line.

RULE III. Yachts contending for a prize may carry sail as follows:

SCHOONERS, - -	Mainsail, Foresail and Jib.
SLOOPS, - - -	Mainsail and Jib.
CAT BOATS, - -	Mainsail.

And no means but sails shall be used to propel a Yacht.

RULE IV. Yachts during a Regatta are allowed to carry men as follows:—

Not over 13 feet - - -	2 men,
Over 13 feet and not over 17 feet, -	3 "
" 17 " 21 "	4 "
" 21 " 26½ "	5 "
" 26½ - - - - -	6 "

On August 29, 1874, the Beverly Yacht Club held a union regatta off Beverly in Salem Harbor. *Field and Stream* magazine reported, "The race was very successful, though the wind was light. The entries were free to all yachts not over thirty feet on the water line. Nineteen yachts started in three classes. They were all centre-board sloops and cat-boats, and among them many known as the fastest boats in their respective classes. The *Eva*, *Mabel* and *Tulip* had easy work in their classes in holding a good lead from the start. The first prizes were won by the *Eva* (W. H. Bangs Jr.)

RULE VI, of the sailing regulations requiring a Member of the Club to be in and sail each Yacht, will be *waived* for this Regatta.
RULE VII. No change shall be made in the weight of ballast on the day of a race, and no trimming by dead weight allowed during a race.
RULE VIII. No race shall be made unless the course shall have been sailed over by one boat of the 1st class, at a rate not less than two and three-fourths miles an hour, and by a boat of the 2d and 3d class respectively, at a rate not less than two and one half miles an hour.

COURSES.

For 1st and 2d Classes:

No. 1.

From Starting Point.
Leaving Stakeboat, off Woodbury's Point, on port hand.
" Buoy, on Archer's rock, (off Lowell Is.,) on port hand.
" R. Buoy, No. 8, (off Misery Is.,) on port hand.
" Stakeboat, off Woodbury's Point, on starboard hand.
To Judges' Boat.

No. 2.

From Starting Point.
Leaving Stakeboat, off Woodbury's Point, on port hand.
" R Buoy, No. 8, (off Misery Is.,) on ~~port~~ hand.
" Buoy, on Archer's rock, (off Lowell Is.,) on ~~port~~ hand. stb
" Stakeboat, off Woodbury's point, on starboard hand.
To Judges' Boat.

For 3d Class:

No. 3.

From Starting Point.
Leaving Black Buoys, Nos. 7, 5 and 3, (off Haste and Coney Is.,) on starboard hand.
" Striped Buoy, on Chapel's Ledge, on port hand.
" Red Buoy, No. 8, (off Misery Is.) on port hand.
To Judges' Boat.

No. 4.

From Starting Point.
Leaving Red Buoy, No. 8, (off Misery Is.) on starboard hand.
" Striped Buoy, on Chapel's Ledge, on starboard hand.
" Black Buoys, Nos. 3, 5 and 7, (off Haste and Coney Is.) on port hand.
To Judges' Boat.

REGATTA COMMITTEE.

CHAS. H. WILLIAMS, E. B. RUSSELL,
W. L. JEFFRIES, W. D. HODGES,
WALTER BURGESS.

in the first class, *Mabel* (J. N. Roberts) in the second, and the *Tulip* (Walter Burgess) in the third. The second prizes were won by *Posey* (J. M. McKee), *Water Lily* (P. Grant Jr.) and *Pink* (J. B. Mills Jr.), in the first, second and third class respectively. . . . The judges were Messrs. T. D. Boardman, G. D. Howe and C. H. Williams on board the yacht *Foam*, which Mr. Boardman kindly offered as judges' yacht."

Beverly Yacht Club

1874.

SIXTH REGATTA.

BEVERLY, Wednesday, Sept. 16, At 12, M.

The first Prize for each Class will be of Solid Silver. A sec nd Prize will also be given. These Prizes will be sailed for vith the time allowance of the Club. The Champion Pennants vill be awarded to Yachts in the first and second Classes.

In case of unfavorable weather the Regatta will be sailed the irst fair day.

The start will be a flying one; Yachts will cross the line be-ween the Judges' Yacht and a Stakeboat, moored off Curtis' Point.

Four guns will be fired for the start, at intervals of five min-ıtes. The first, a preparatory gun at 12 o'clock. The first Class will start between the 2d and 3d guns; the second Class between the 3d and 4th guns; and the third Class at the 4th, also, being allowed five minutes for starting.

Yachts on their return will pass *between the Judges' Yacht and the Stakeboat.*

Yachts are requested to carry their private signals at the peak.

As soon as the Courses are decided on, white flags bearing their number will be displayed on the Judges' Yacht.

The sixth regatta of the Beverly Yacht Club was held on September 16, 1874, off Beverly with a flying start. The *Boston Daily Globe* reported, "The breeze was so slight as to very much resemble a calm, and but few boats participated. The *Mona* and *Water Lily* started in the second class, but did not return within the time and their time was not taken." The first-class winners were (first) the *Eva* (W. H. Bangs Jr.), (second) the *Surf* (W. C. Loring), and (third) the *Ariel* (W. D.

COURSES.

For 1st and 2d Classes:

No. 1.

From Starting Point.
Leaving Stakeboat, off Woodbury's Point, on port hand
" Buoy, on Archer's rock, (off Lowell Is..) on port hand
" R. Buoy, No. 8, (off Misery Is.,) on port hand.
" Stakeboat, off Woodbury's Point, on starboard hand
To Judges' Boat.

No. 2.

From Starting Point.
Leaving Stakeboat, off Woodbury's Point, on port hand.
" R Buoy, No. 8, (off Misery Is..) on starboard hand.
" Buoy, on Archer's rock, (off Lowell Is ,) on starboard hand.
" Stakeboat, off Woodbury's point, on starboard hand.
To Judges' Boat.

For 3d Class:

No. 3.

From Starting Point.
Leaving Black Buoys, Nos. 7, 5 and 3, (off Haste and Coney Is., on starboard hand
" Striped Buoy, on Chapel's Ledge, on port hand.
" Red Buoy, No. 8, (off Misery Is.) on port hand.
To Judges' Boat.

No. 4.

From Starting Point.
Leaving Red Buoy, No. 8, (off Misery Is.,) on starboard hand
" Striped Buoy, on Chapel's Ledge, on starboard hand
" Black Buoys, Nos. 3, 5 and 7, (off Haste and Coney Is., on port hand
To Judges' Boat.

REGATTA COMMITTEE.

CHAS. H. WILLIAMS,
W. L. JEFFRIES,
E. B. RUSSELL,
W. D. HODGES,
WALTER BURGESS.

Sohier). The second-class winners were (first) the *Peri* (W. H. Burgess) and (second) the *Ibis* (H. S. Leeds), and the third-class winners were (first) the *Tulip* (W. Burgess) and (second) the *Pink* (J. B. Mills Jr.). "The Regatta Committee were Messrs. Charles H. Willliams, W. L. Jeffries, E. B. Russell, W. D. Hodges and Walter Burgess."

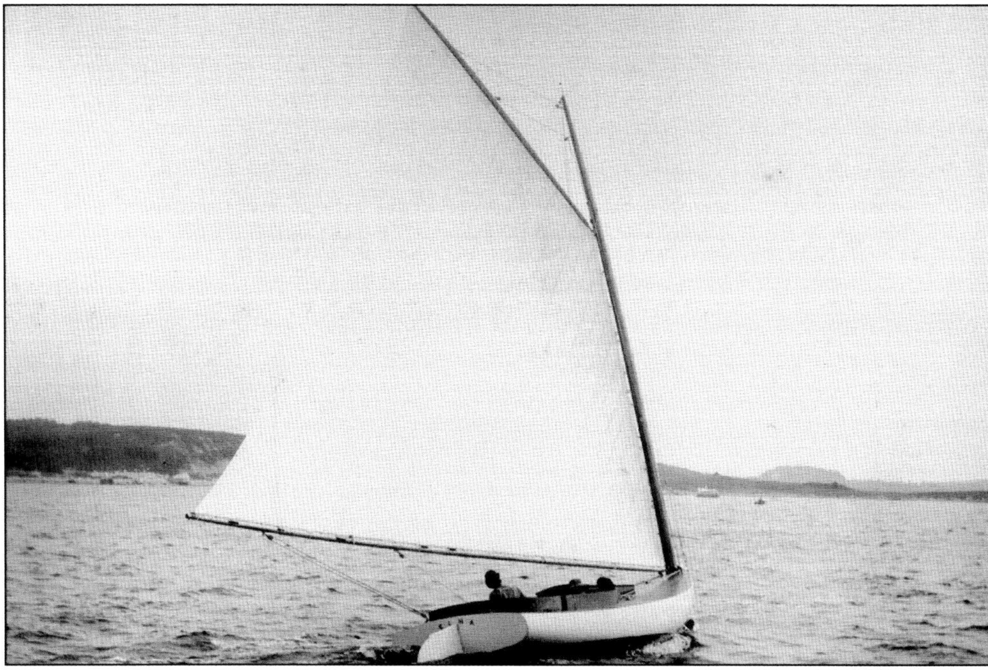

The *Eina* was built in 1889 for John Parkinson by builder C. C. Hanley of Monument Beach.

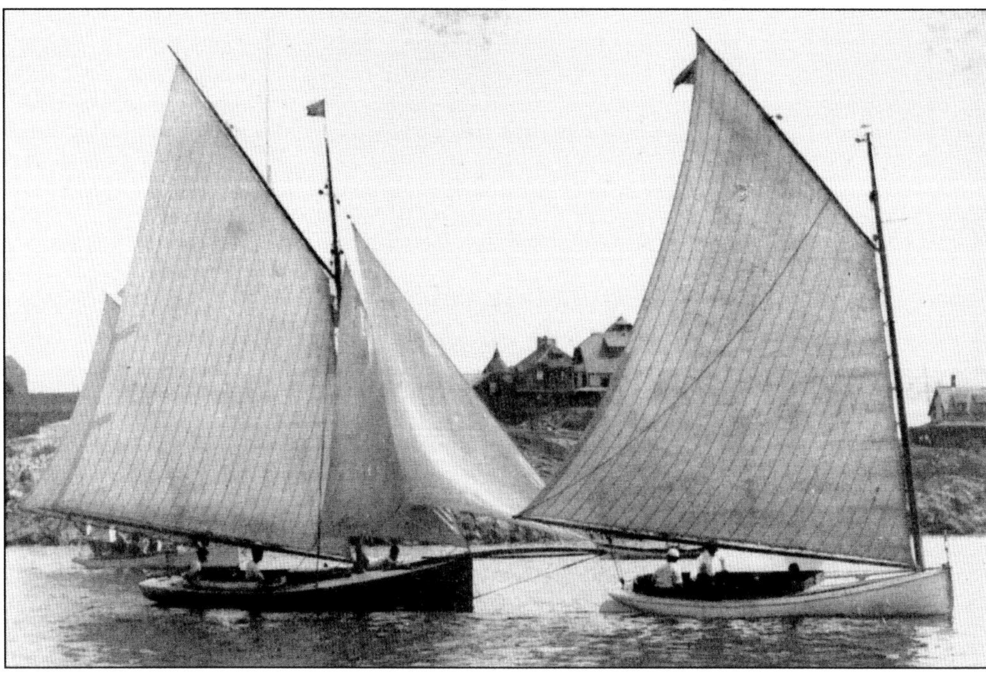

The catboat on the right is the *Dolphin*, owned by Royal Robbins of Marblehead. It was designed and built by J. B. Herreshoff and was 18.8 feet overall, 16.10 feet on the waterline. Its beam was 7.6 feet, and its draft was 2.6 feet. Because the Eastern Yacht Club of Marblehead refused to run races for boats under 30 feet in length, the Beverly Yacht Club provided about all the good and official small-boat racing that there was. This culminated in Marblehead in August 1883 when 176 boats crossed the starting line, a world's record that stood for 40 years.

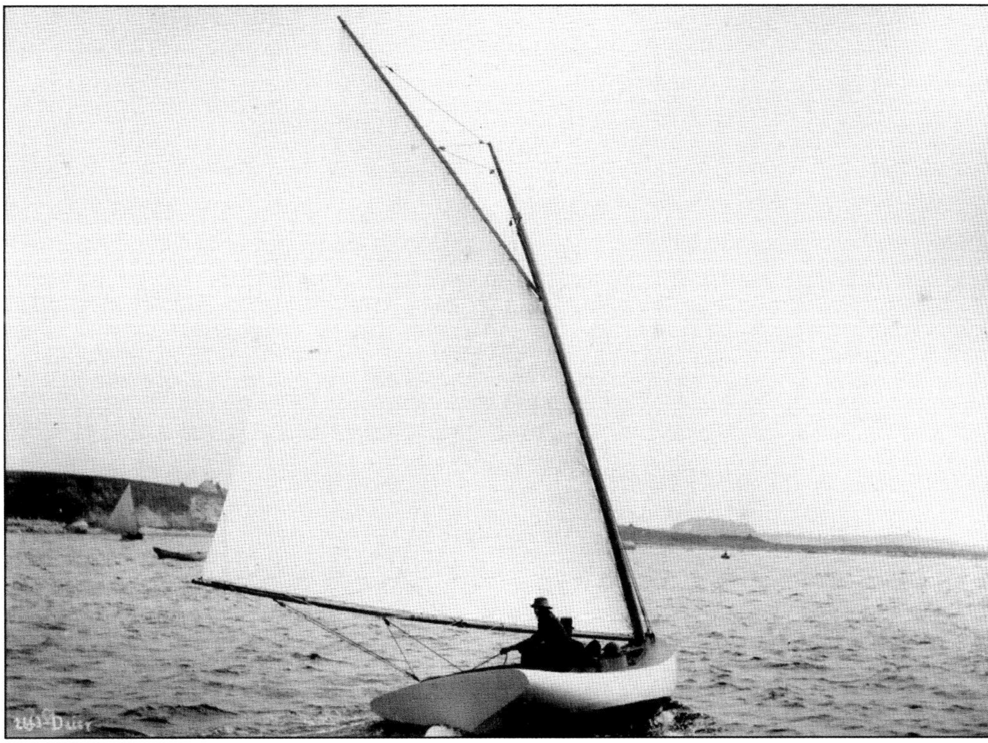

The *Daisy* was owned by Howard Stockton, vice commodore. It was built in 1888 by F. J. Dunn of Monument Beach. Its length overall was 20.9 feet, and its length on the waterline was 18.2 feet. It won 10 first places and two seconds in 1888.

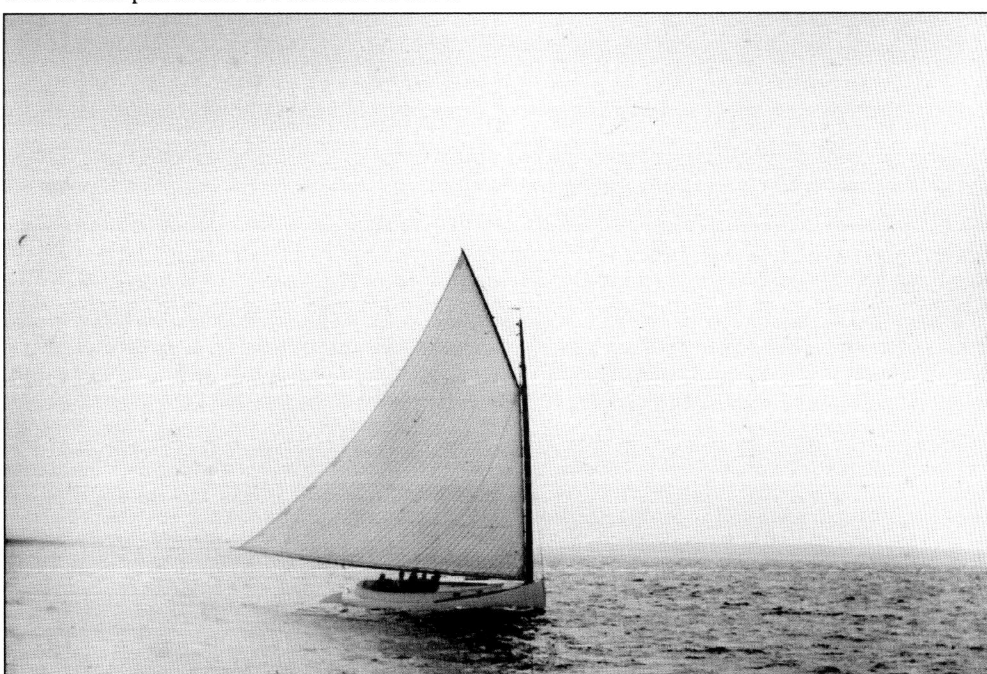

This photograph shows the *A. P. E.*, an early catboat, racing off Wing's Neck in 1889.

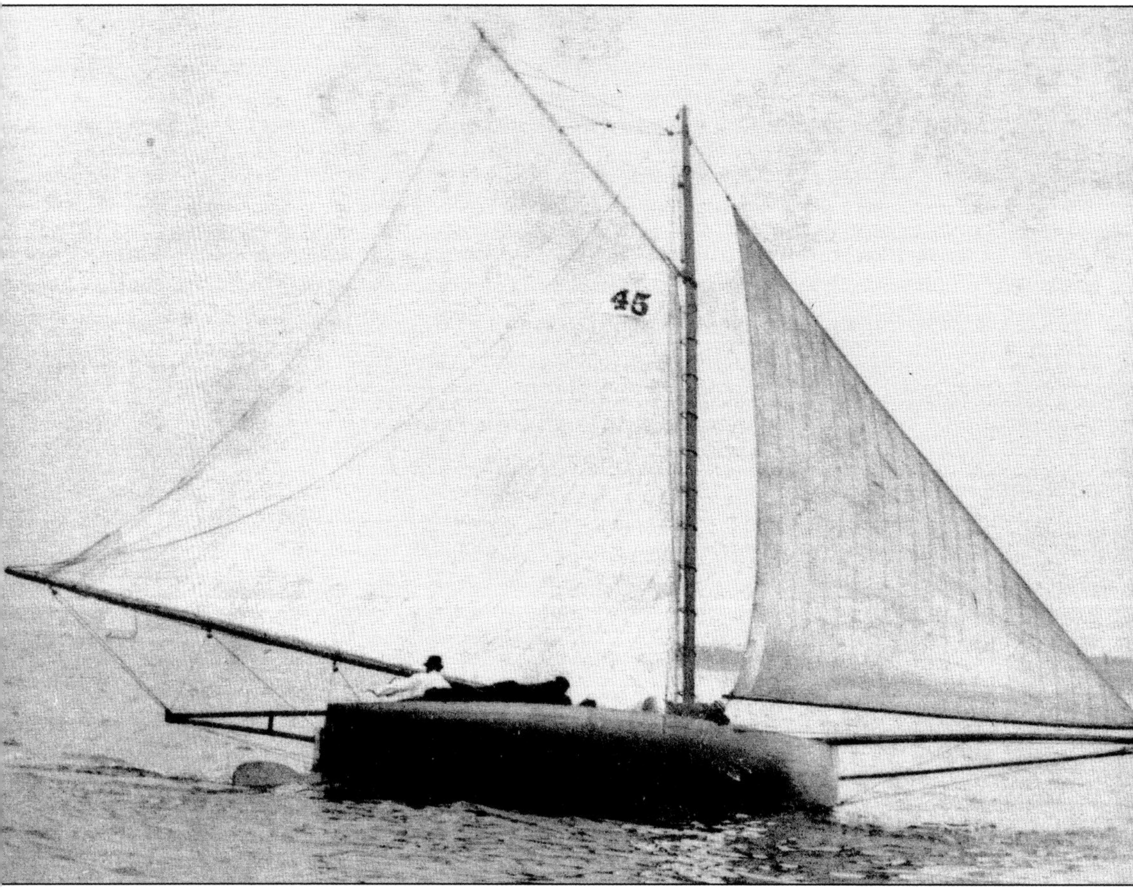

The *Coyote*, owned by Walter Abbott of Boston, was designed by Edward Burgess and built by G. Lawley and Son in 1886. It was 20.6 feet on the waterline.

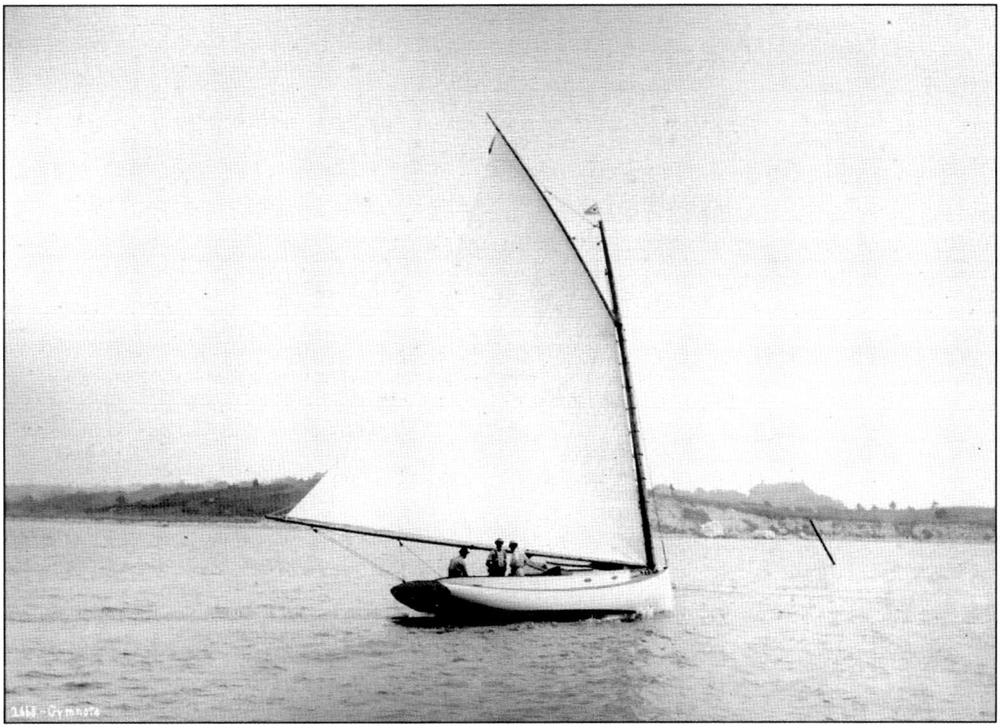

The *Gymnote* was built in 1889 for W. E. C. Eustis and won the Beverly Yacht Club Championship in 1892. Its length overall was 27.3 feet, its length on the waterline was 23.3 feet, and its beam was 11.3 feet.

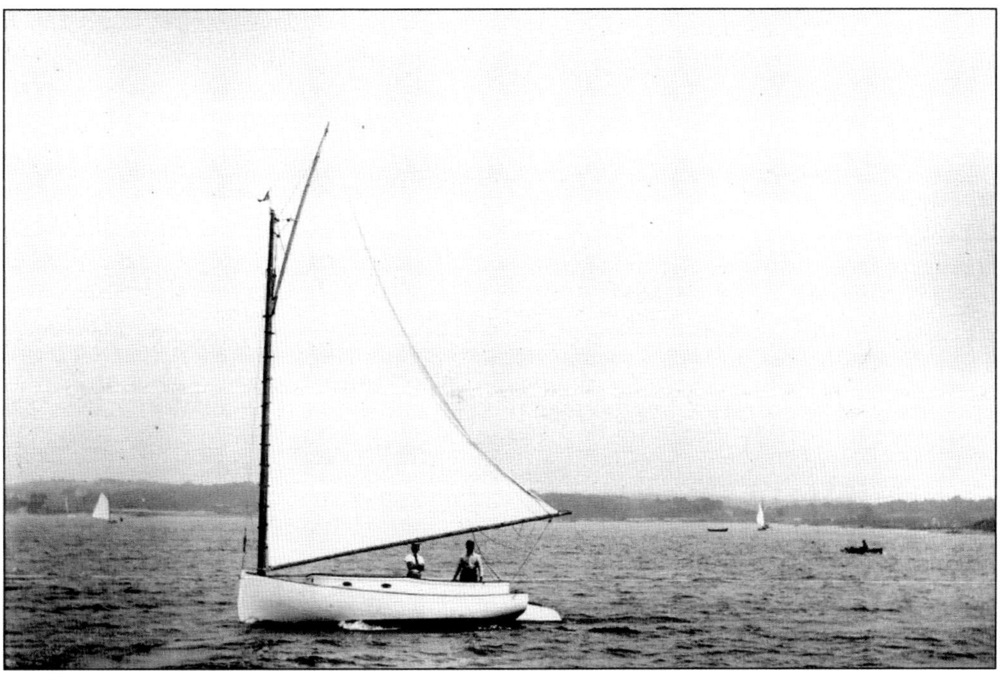

The *Hera* was a Holmes cat built in 1889 for Louis Bacon. Its length overall was 19.9 feet, its length on the waterline was 19.5 feet, and its beam was 9 feet.

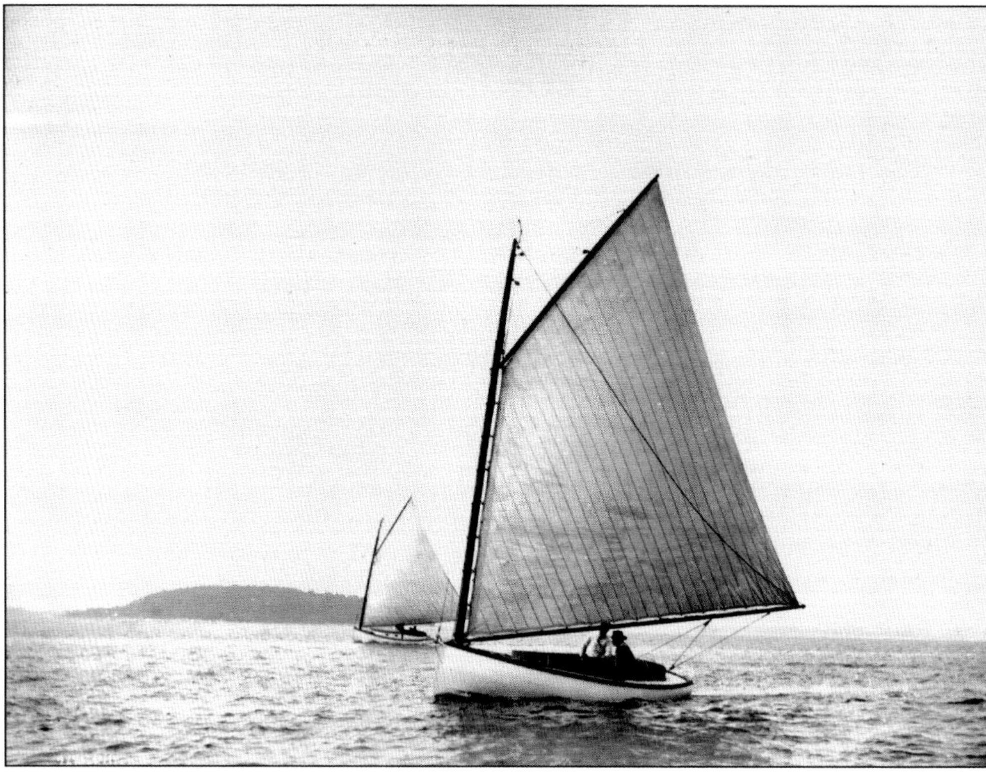

The *Kitten* was a Hauley cat built in 1889 for G. H. Richards. Its length overall was 17.5 feet, length on the waterline was 17 feet, and its beam was 8 feet.

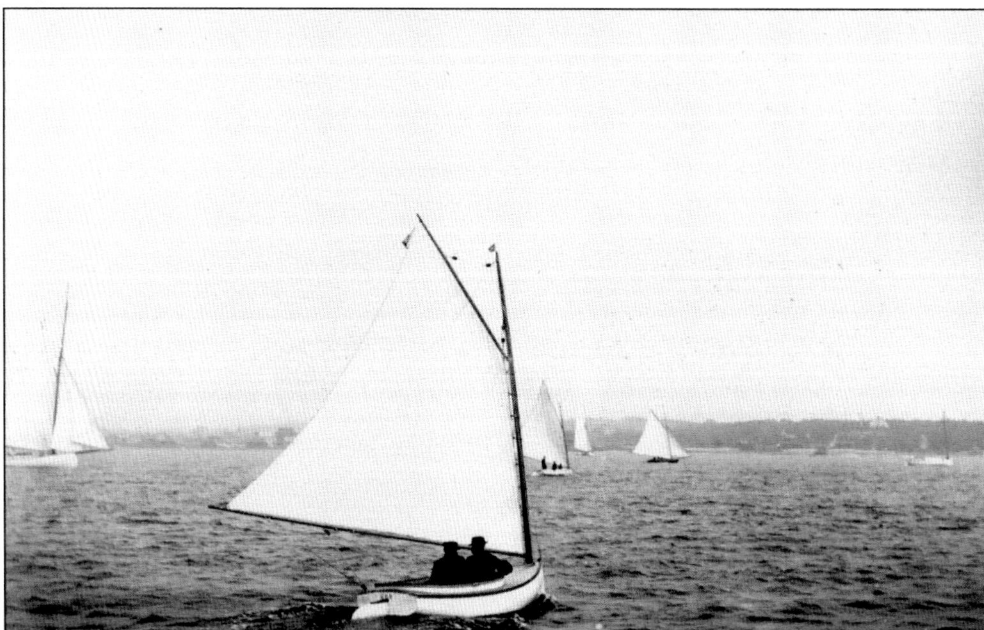

The *Mab* was a Clark cat built in 1888 for F. B. Beaumont. Its length overall was 12.4 feet, length on the waterline was 12.3 feet, and its beam was 5.5 feet.

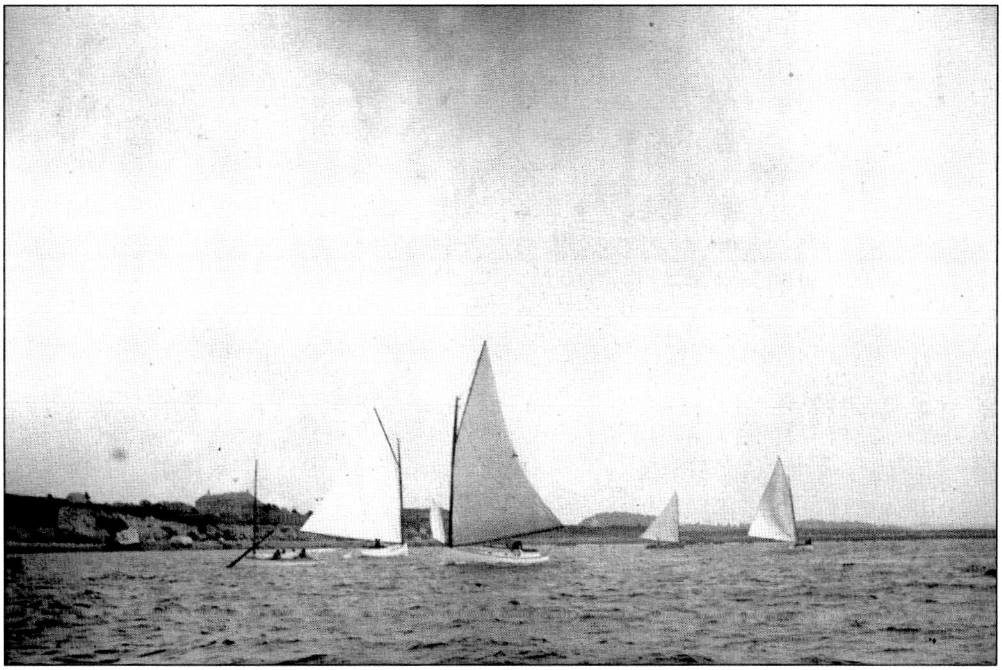

The *Mist* was a Feeney cat built in 1887 for George H. Lyman Jr. Its length was 23.3 feet, length on the waterline was 22.9 feet, and its beam was 11.6 feet. It won the Beverly Yacht Club Championship in 1888, 1889, and 1890.

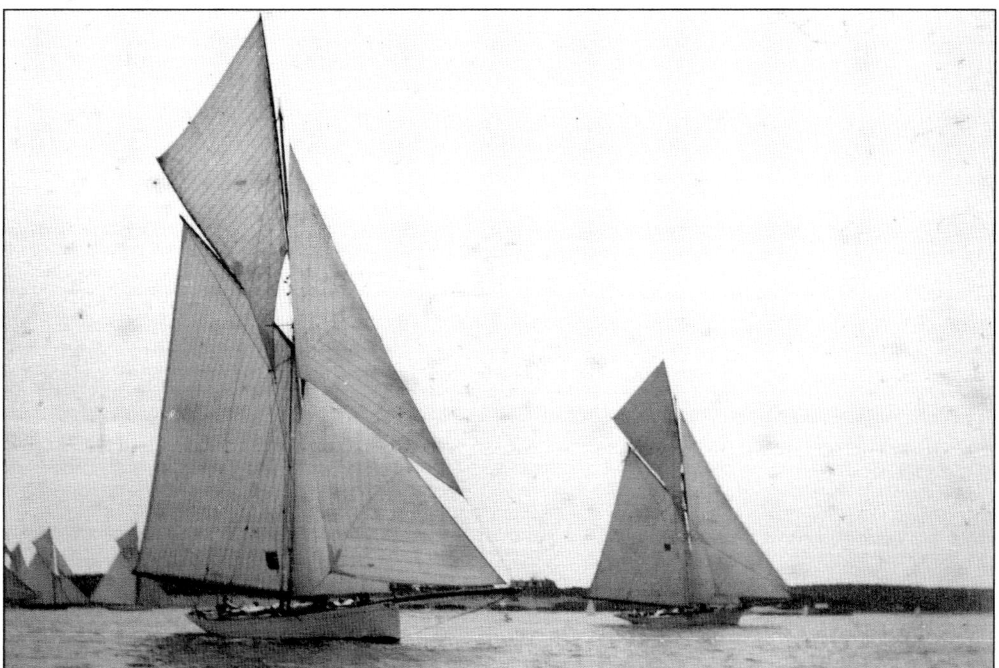

The *Pappoose*, on the left, was a keelboat owned by J. Simpkins from Yarmouthport. It was designed by Beverly Yacht Club founder and first commodore Edward Burgess and built by G. Lawley and Son in 1887. It was 36 feet on the waterline and 44 feet overall.

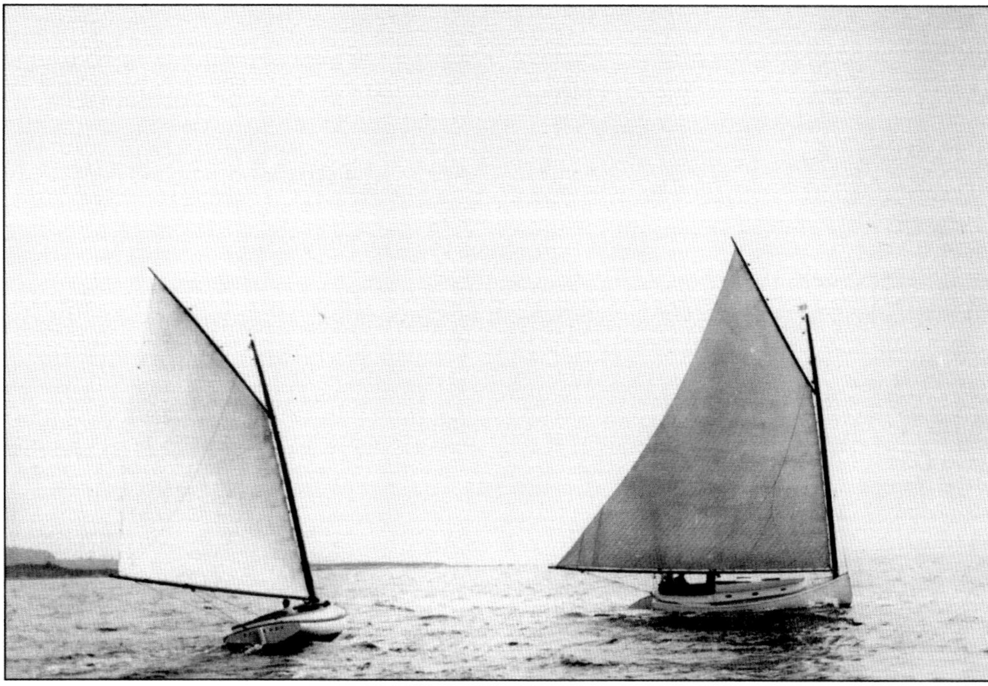

This photograph shows two Beverly Yacht Club catboats, the *Quissett* and the *Violet*, in 1886 racing at Monument Beach. The *Quissett* was owned by R. B. Hiller and was 29 feet 6 inches. The *Violet* was a Crosby cat owned by G. H. Richards. It was 27 feet 6 inches and won the Beverly Yacht Club Championship for its class in 1891, 1892, and 1894.

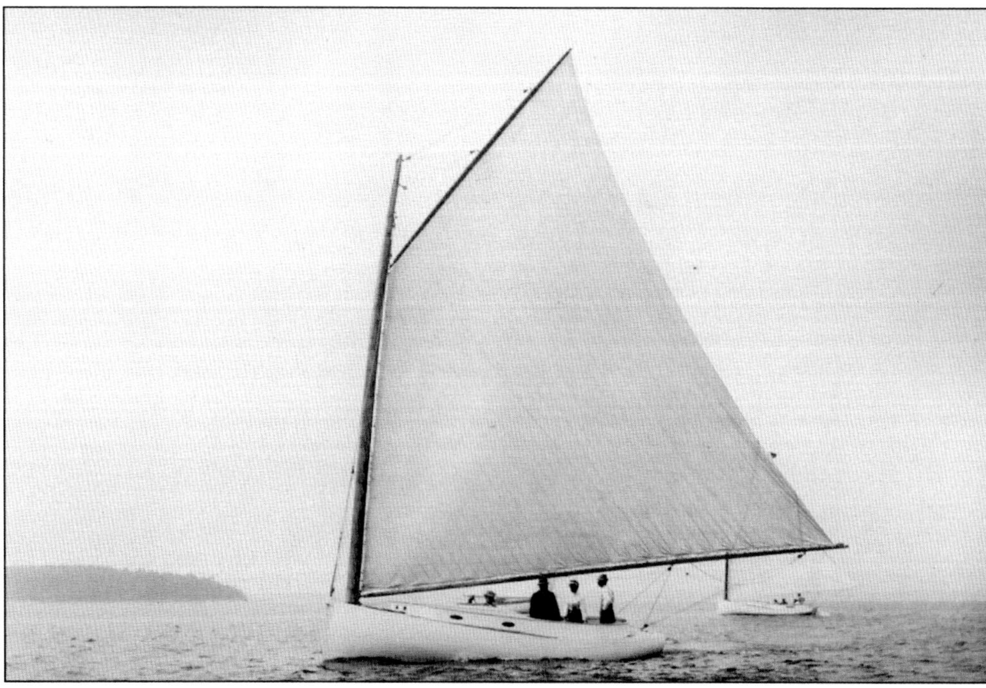

The *Surprise* was another Beverly Yacht Club catboat, owned by club member J. M. Codman. It was 24 feet 6 inches in length and was built in 1884 by C. C. Hanley of Monument Beach.

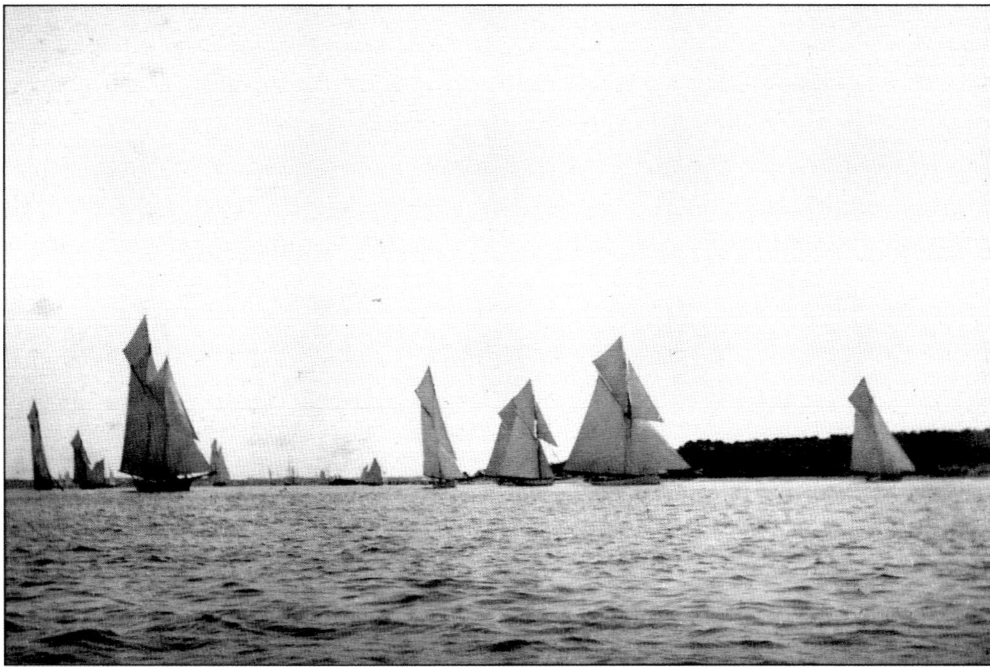

The *Tatania*, the second boat from the right, was owned by C. O. Iselin. It was designed by Beverly Yacht Club founder Edward Burgess and built by H. Piepgras in 1887. It was 69.9 feet on the waterline.

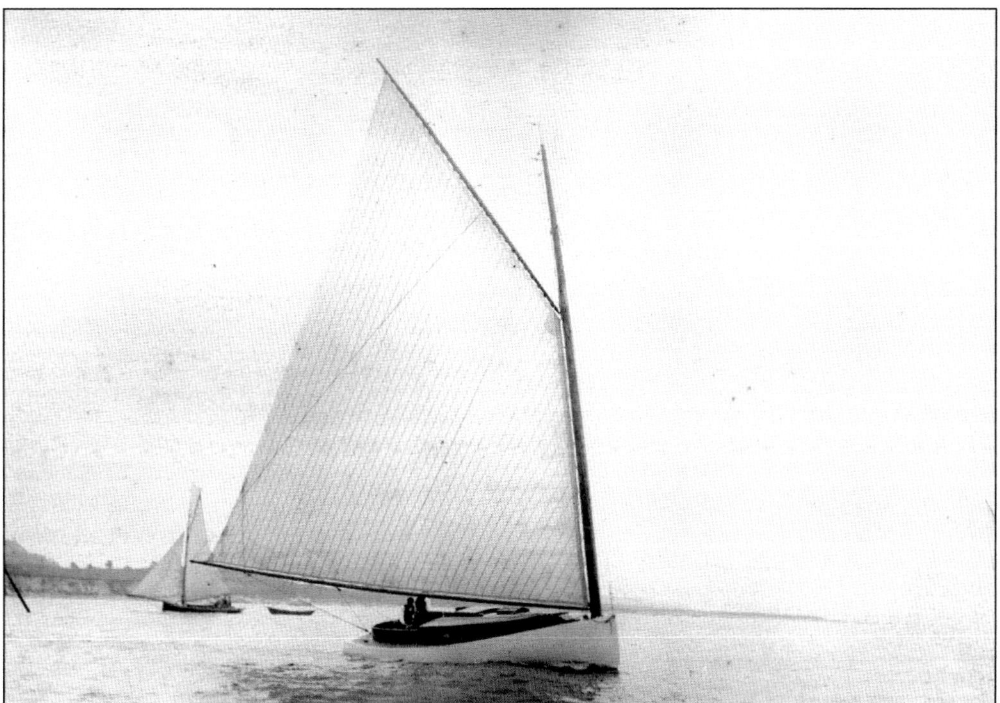

The *Squeak* was a New Bedford Yacht Club catboat that sailed in Beverly Yacht Club races in the 1880s.

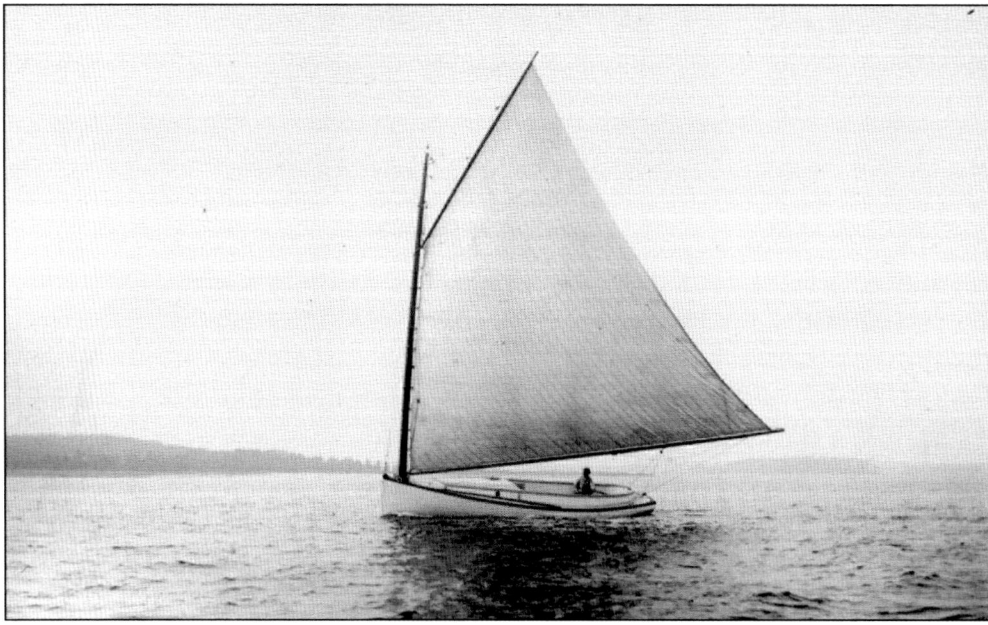

The *Violet* was a Crosby cat built in 1882. It was owned by G. H. Richards and was 27 feet 6 inches in length overall. The *Violet* won the Beverly Yacht Club Championship in its class in 1888, 1889, and 1890.

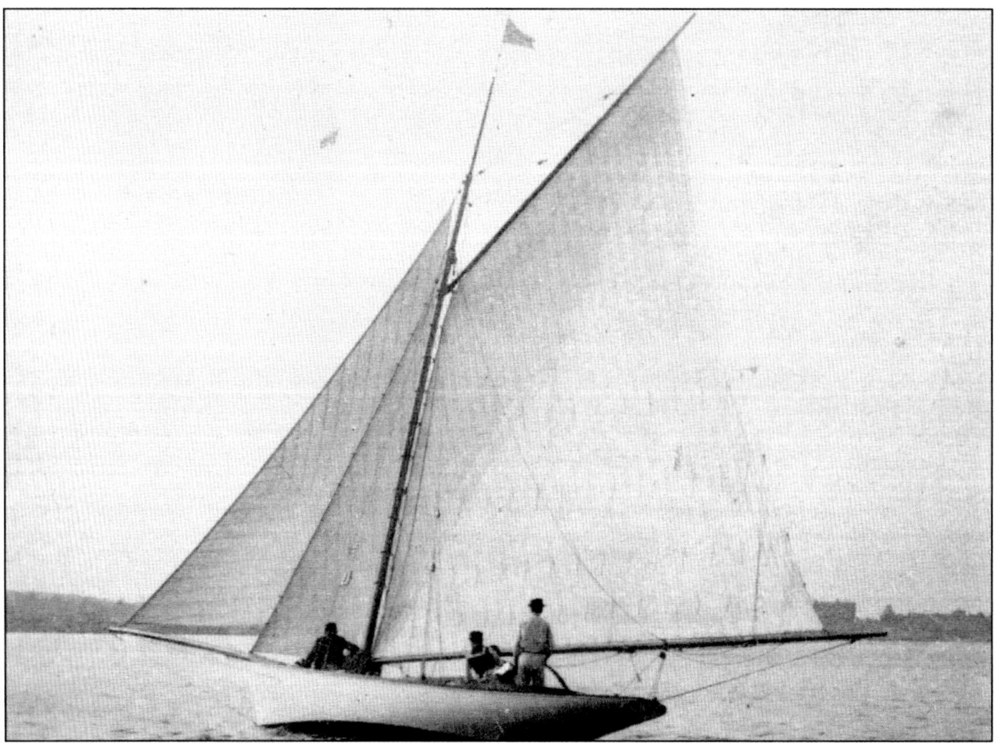

The *Xenia*, a sloop owned by Marshall T. Field, sailed out of Beverly. It was 26.4 feet overall and 19.7 feet on the waterline. It was designed by Beverly Yacht Club founder and first commodore Edward Burgess and built by John McPhail in 1888.

Three

NATHANAEL HERRESHOFF 1898–1914

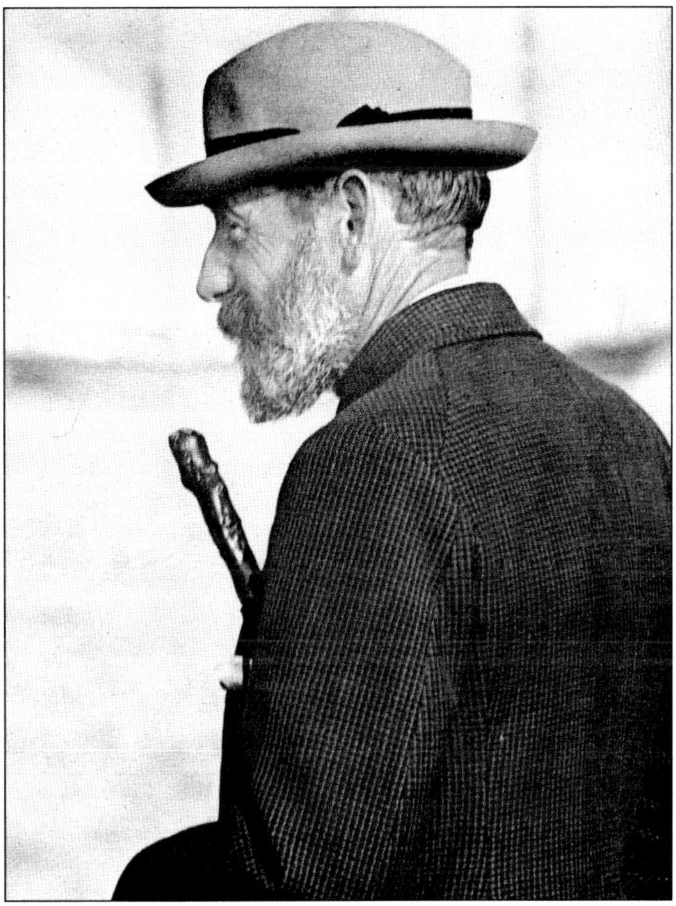

Nathanael Herreshoff was the famous yacht designer whose boats were important to the history of the Beverly Yacht Club's racing program. Herreshoff also designed America's Cup racing yachts in the late 19th century. Nathanael's older brother, John (who was blind), opened the Herreshoff boat building business in Bristol, Rhode Island, in 1863, and by the early 1900s, it became the leading yacht designer and builder of its day. Nathanael Herreshoff retired in 1924.

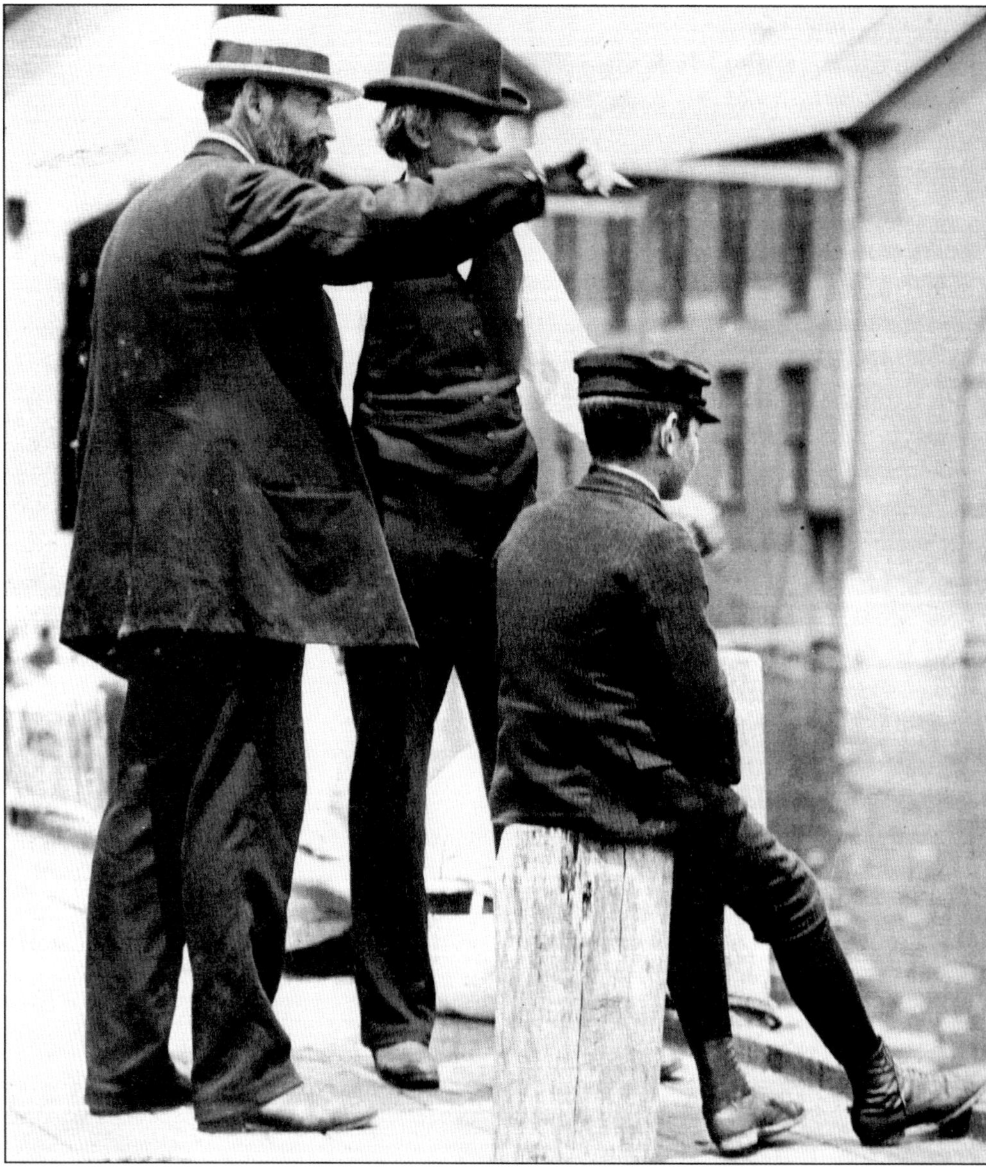

Nathanael Herreshoff (left) was a genius yacht designer who designed America's Cup defenders, including the *Vigilant* (1893), the *Constitution* (1901), the *Reliance* (1903), and the *Resolute* (1914). His one-design Herreshoff 15 was designed in 1898 and was popular at the Beverly Yacht Club from 1899 to 1938. He also designed, in 1912, the one-design Buzzards Bay 25. His 12.5 footer designed in 1914 (called the H12) was the most popular one-design class at the Beverly Yacht Club from 1914 until the present. He is shown here in front of the Herreshoff Manufacturing Company in Bristol, Rhode Island.

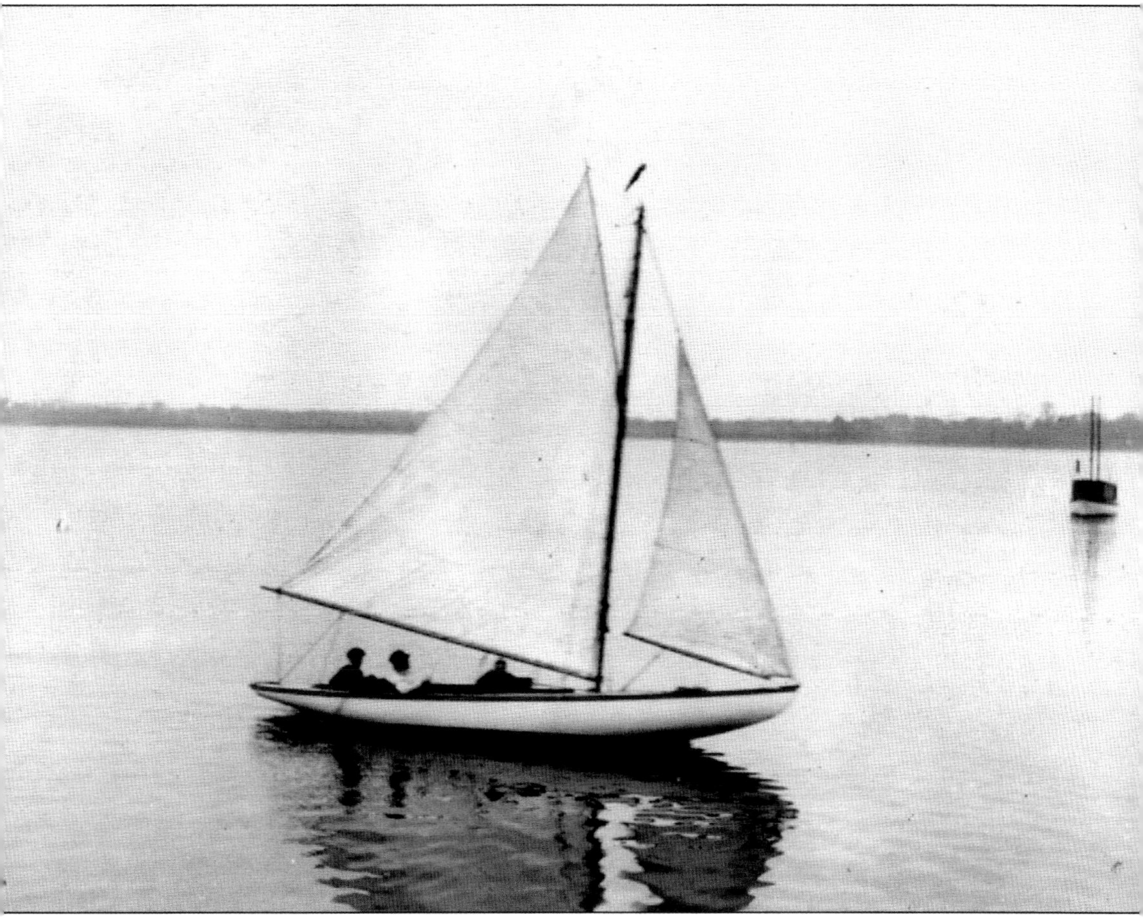

In 1899, Nathanael Herreshoff sailed up Buzzards Bay in his steam launch *Squib*, towing a line of 11 sloops that left a deep mark in Beverly Yacht Club's history, the one-design Herreshoff 15 footers. This design (also referred to as the E class or *E*s because it started in Beverly Yacht Cub's E class), with 24.5-foot overall length, was peculiarly adapted to Buzzards Bay. Some people insist it was modeled on the famous American's Cup defender *Columbia.* Lots were drawn for these first boats at the Beverly Yacht Club, and in the ensuing years, the class became very popular.

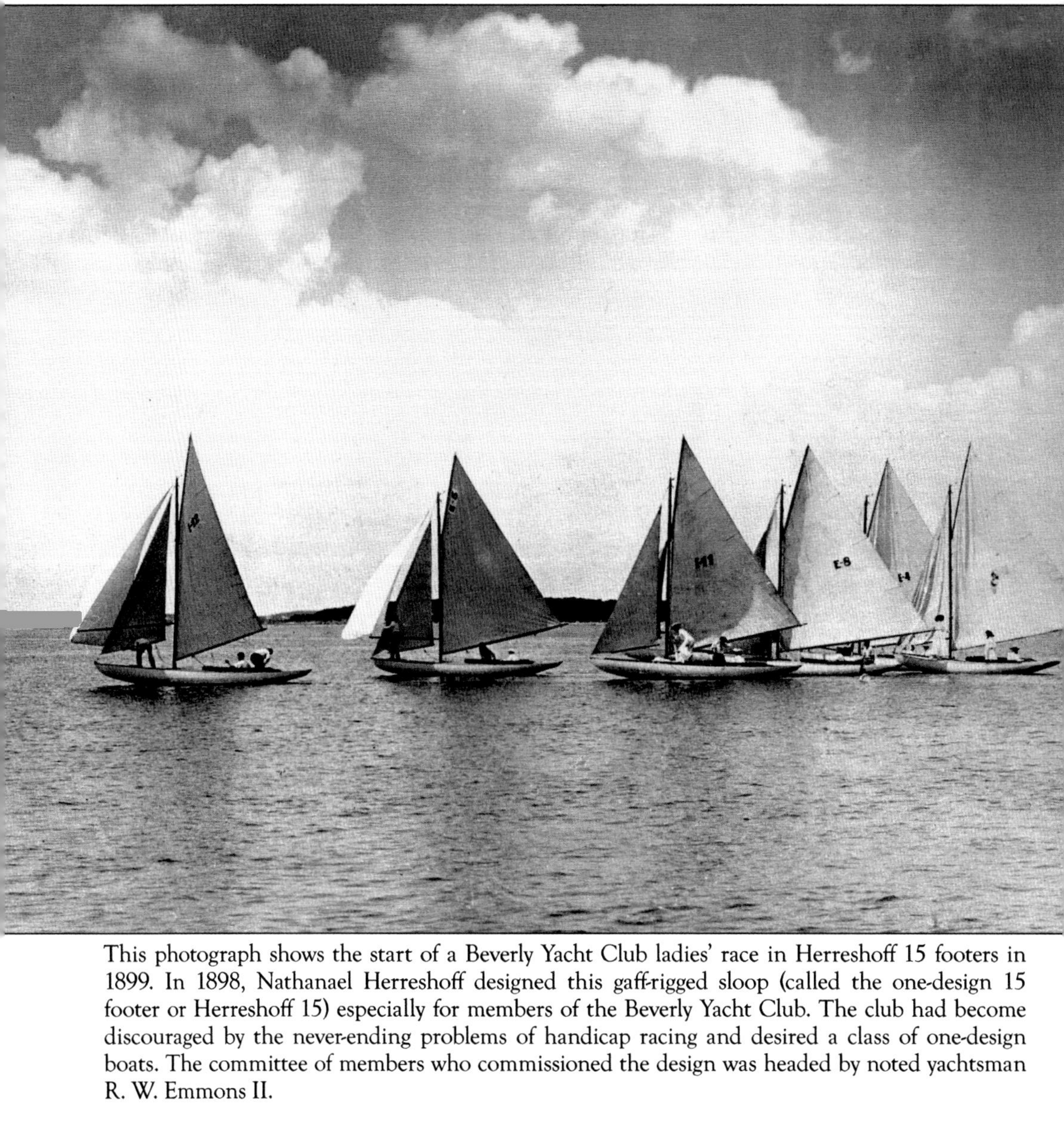

This photograph shows the start of a Beverly Yacht Club ladies' race in Herreshoff 15 footers in 1899. In 1898, Nathanael Herreshoff designed this gaff-rigged sloop (called the one-design 15 footer or Herreshoff 15) especially for members of the Beverly Yacht Club. The club had become discouraged by the never-ending problems of handicap racing and desired a class of one-design boats. The committee of members who commissioned the design was headed by noted yachtsman R. W. Emmons II.

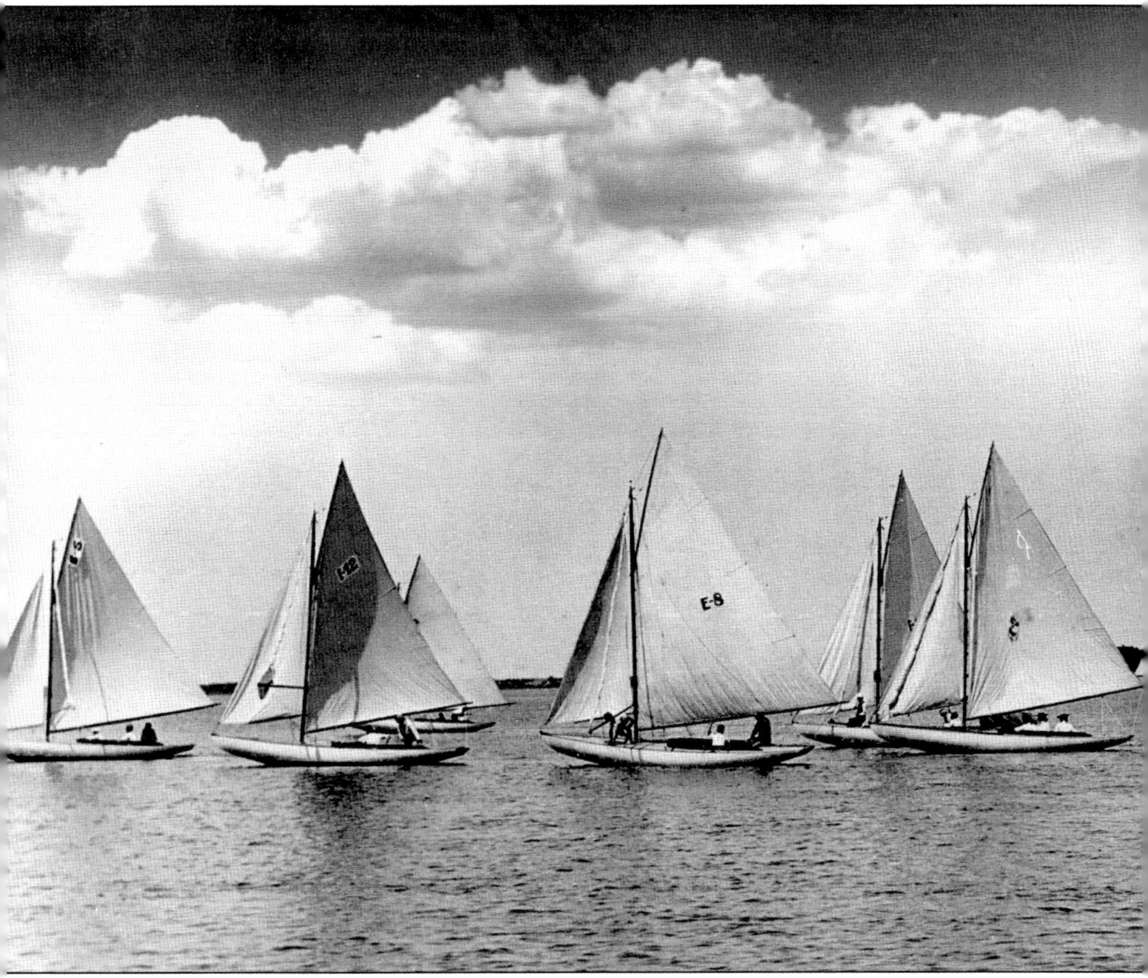

This image shows Herreshoff 15 footers racing in a Beverly Yacht Club race. The Herreshoff 15 measured 24 feet 6 inches overall and 15 feet on the waterline, with a beam of 6 feet 9 inches and a draft of 2 feet 6 inches with the board up. It was particularly well adapted to Buzzards Bay. Thirty-one of these boats had racing numbers at the Beverly Yacht Club as late as 1937, but the class died out after many of the boats were destroyed in the 1938 hurricane.

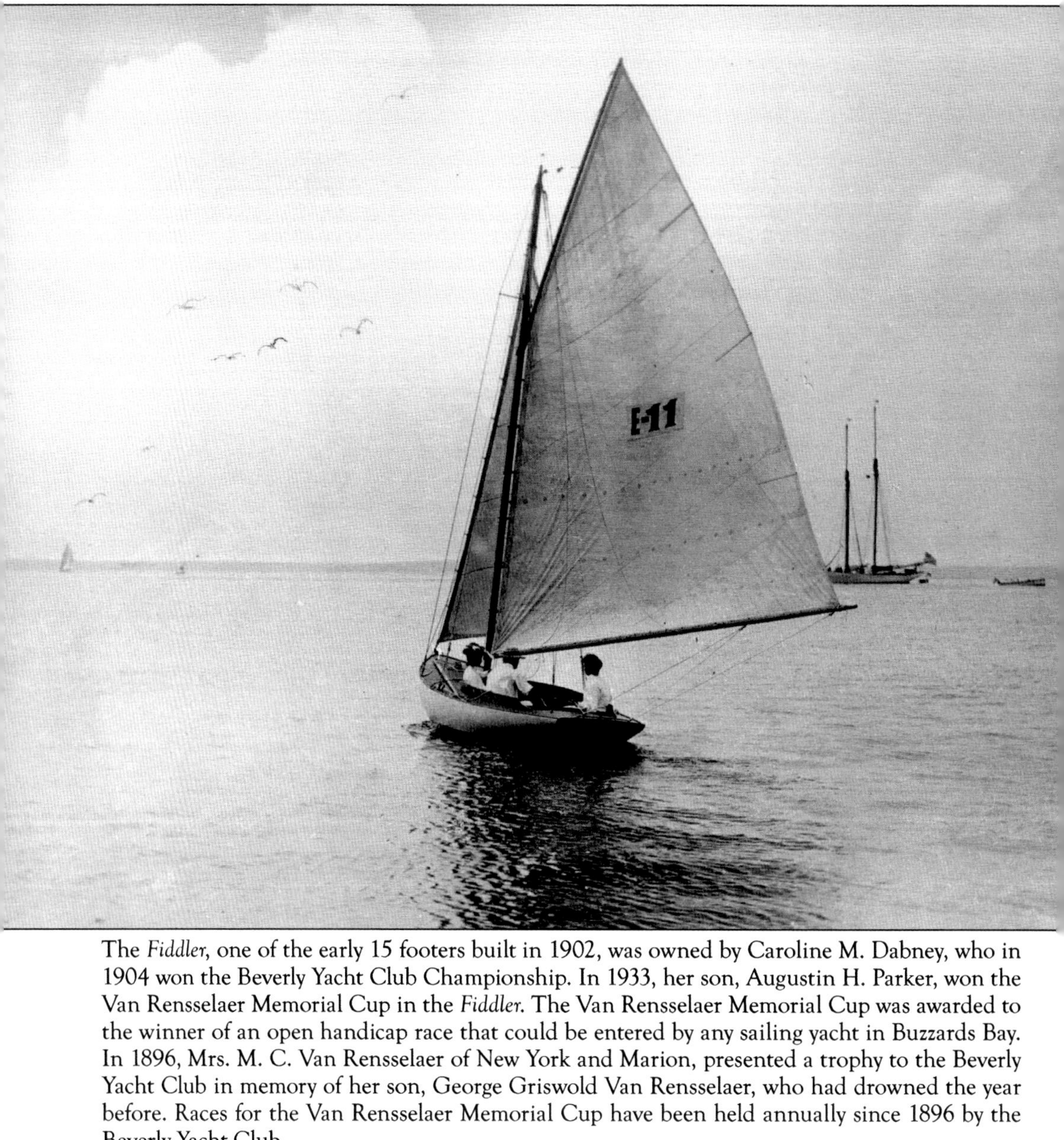

The *Fiddler*, one of the early 15 footers built in 1902, was owned by Caroline M. Dabney, who in 1904 won the Beverly Yacht Club Championship. In 1933, her son, Augustin H. Parker, won the Van Rensselaer Memorial Cup in the *Fiddler*. The Van Rensselaer Memorial Cup was awarded to the winner of an open handicap race that could be entered by any sailing yacht in Buzzards Bay. In 1896, Mrs. M. C. Van Rensselaer of New York and Marion, presented a trophy to the Beverly Yacht Club in memory of her son, George Griswold Van Rensselaer, who had drowned the year before. Races for the Van Rensselaer Memorial Cup have been held annually since 1896 by the Beverly Yacht Club.

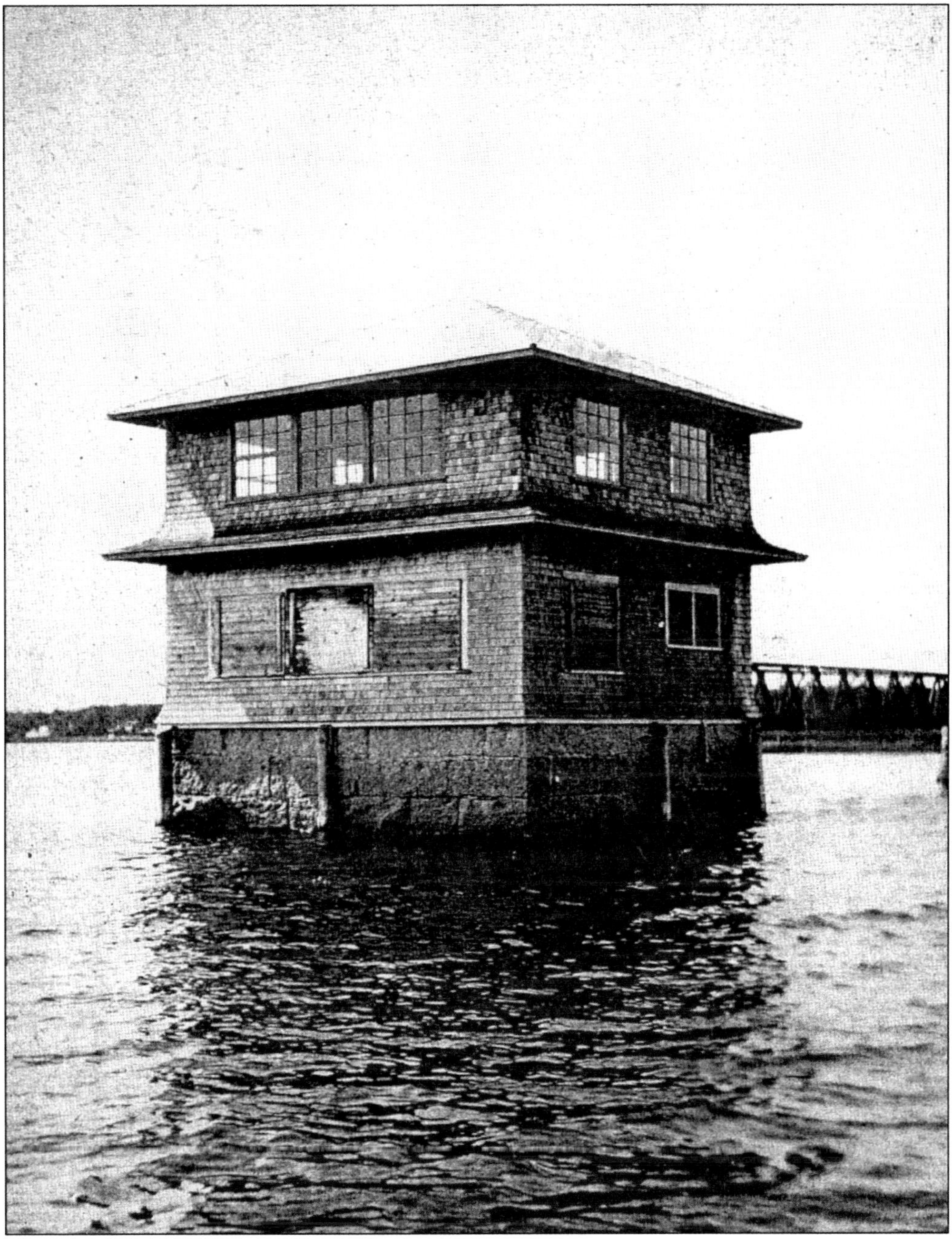

The Sippican Yacht Club was founded in 1877 and was incorporated in 1902. Its clubhouse was located on a substantial stone pier just south of Silvershell Beach in Marion. A two-story pavilion stood on the end of the pier, where race launches and teas were served by the wives of members, who brought the food down over the marsh. The Sippican Yacht Club merged into the Beverly Yacht Club in 1913 when the Beverly Yacht Club moved to Butler's Point in Marion. The pavilion stood forlornly until August 10, 1941, when it was burned down by local pranksters.

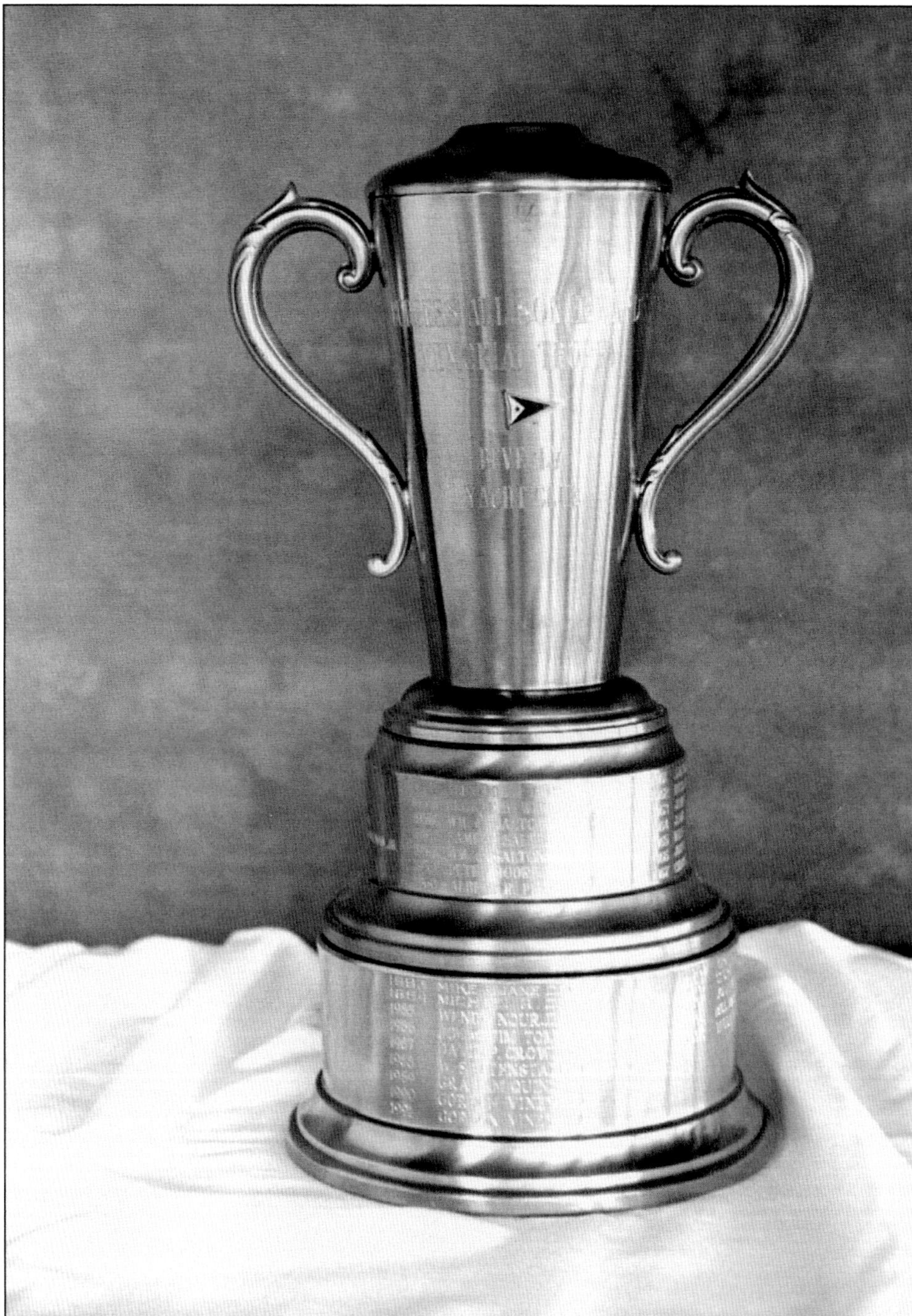

Allison Edwards was an enthusiastic racer in the Beverly Yacht Club for many years, especially in the Herreshoff 15-foot class. This trophy was originally awarded to the champion of the Herreshoff 15-foot class. When the class died out, the Beverly Yacht Club awarded this lovely trophy to the winner of the championship in a one-design class other than the H12 class. Over the years, this trophy has also been awarded to champions in the 30-square-meter, Yankee, and 110 classes. The first winner of this trophy was the *Rascal*, sailed by H. Nelson Emmons in 1928.

The Buzzards Bay 25 one-design class was designed in 1912 by Nathanael Herreshoff and built by the Herreshoff Manufacturing Company in Bristol, Rhode Island. Shown here is the Buzzards Bay 25 *Bagatelle*.

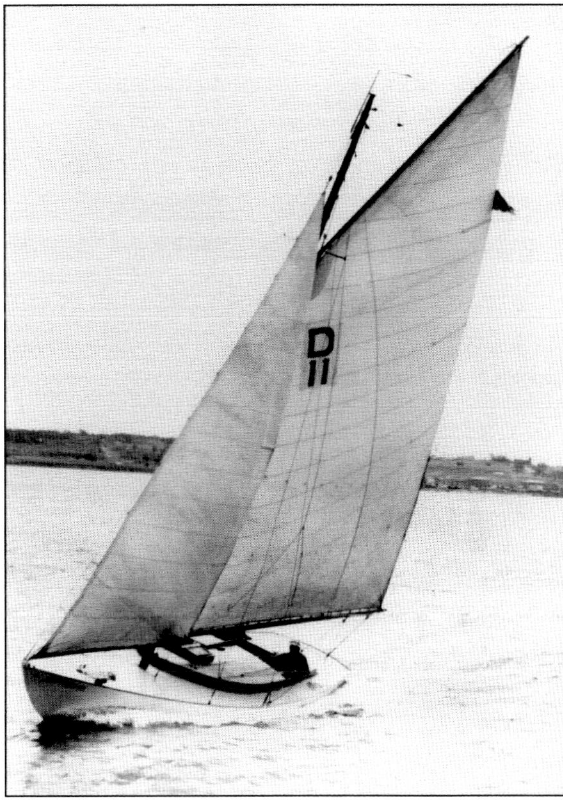

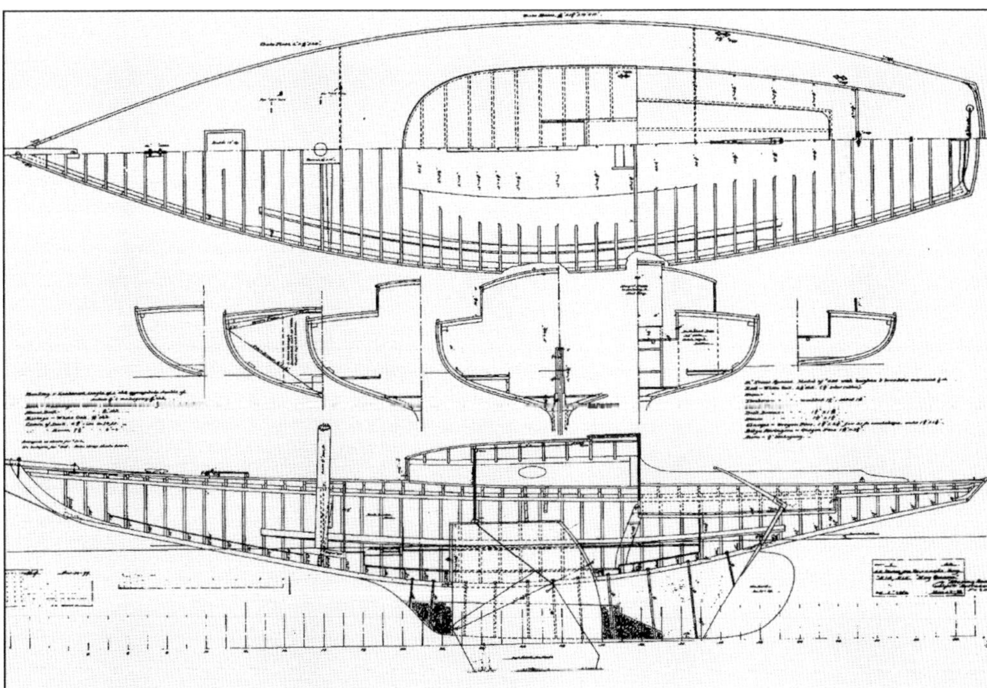

Construction plan 25-foot class for Buzzards Bay, HMC # 514, plan # 1-20, Series V.

The Buzzards Bay 25 plans are shown here.

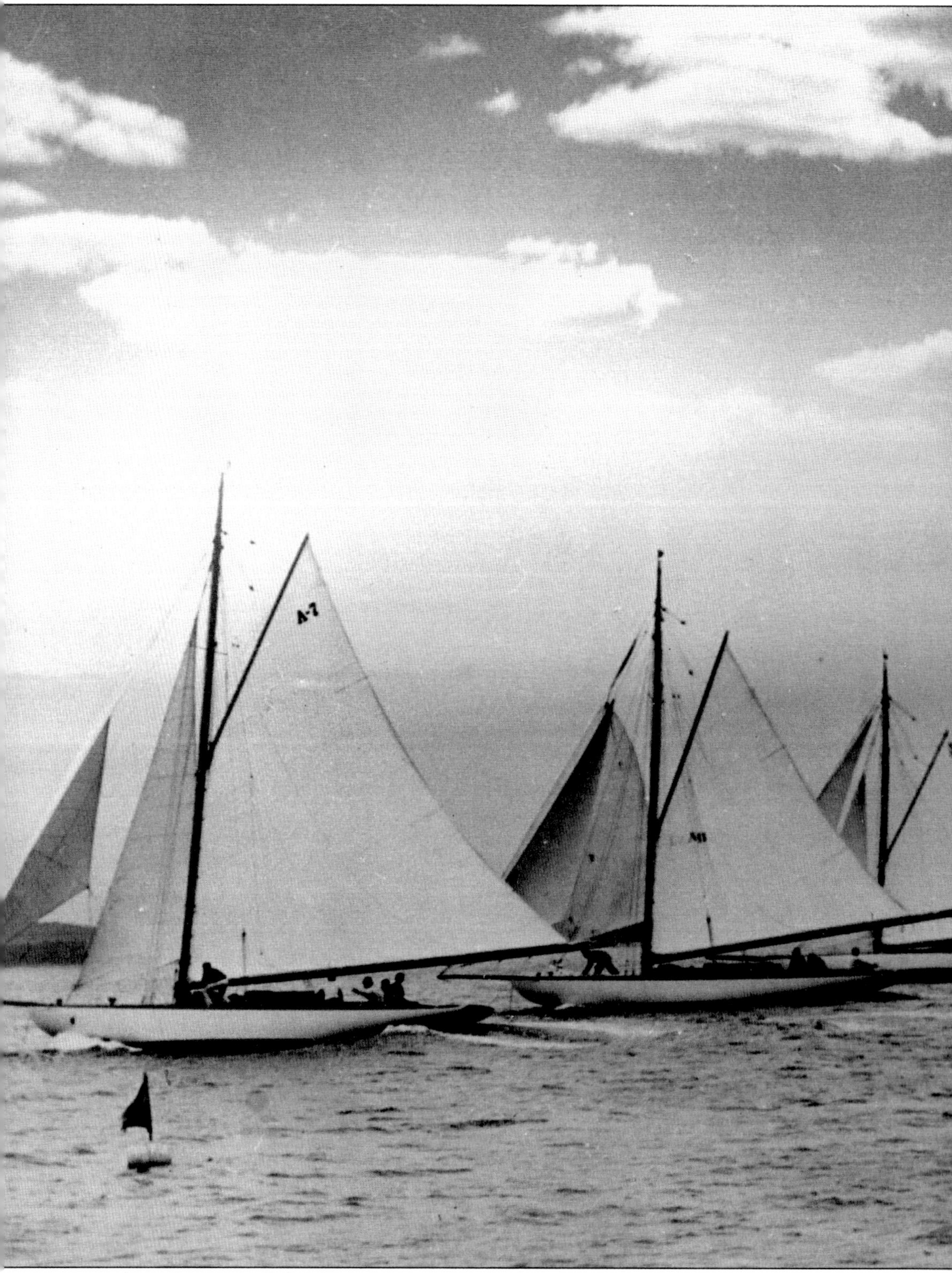

Nathanael Herreshoff also designed the Buzzards Bay 30 one-design class in 1902. This photograph

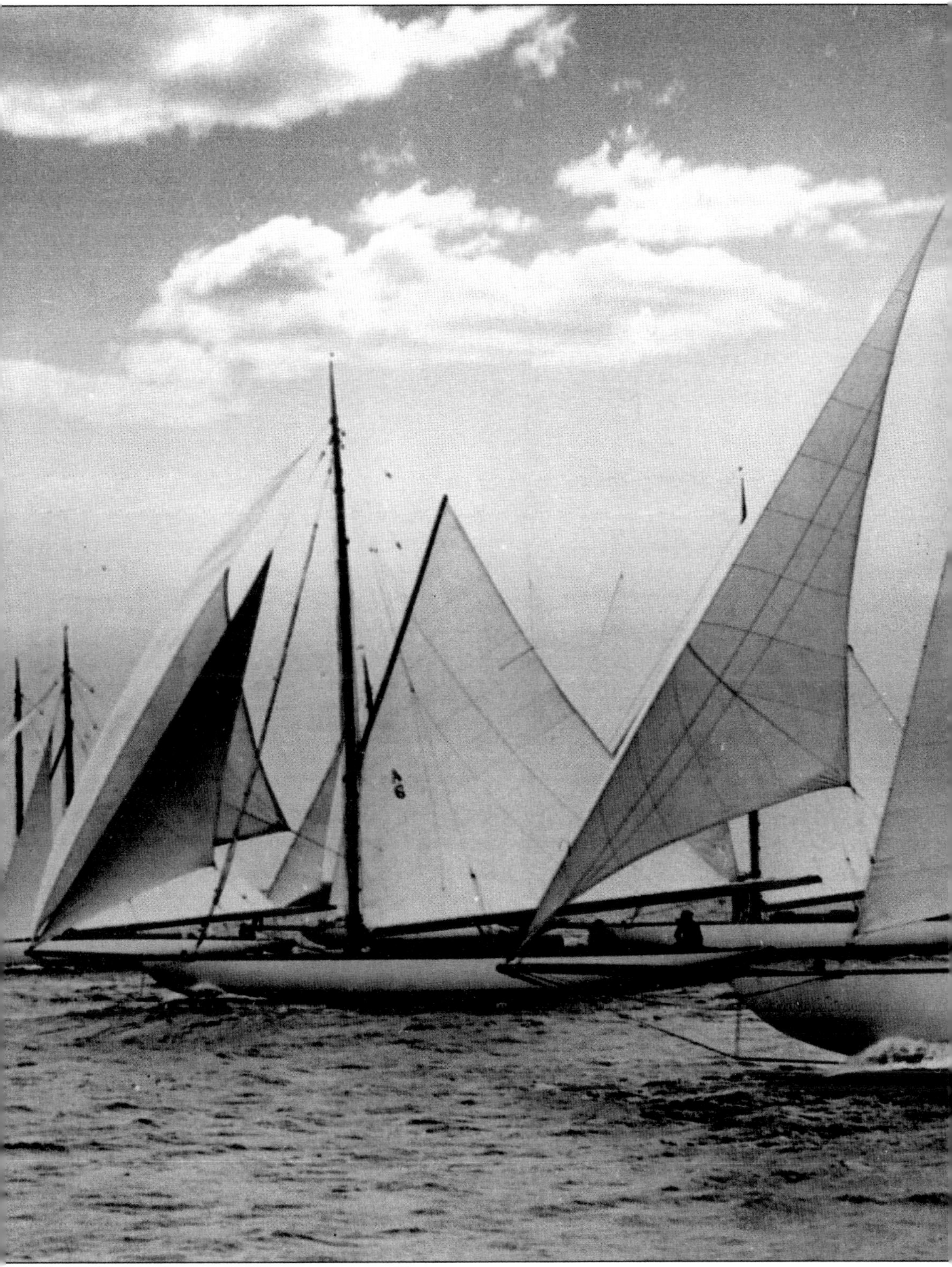

shows Buzzards Bay 30s racing in a Beverly Yacht Club race off Wing's Neck in 1902.

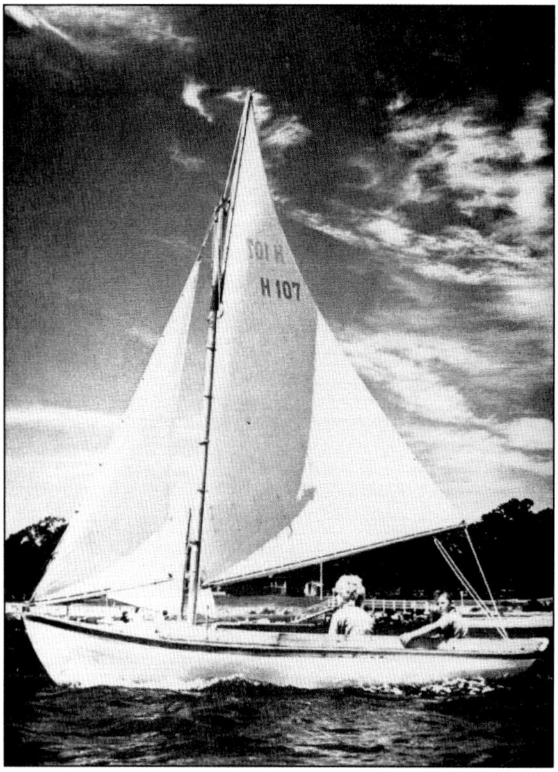

The most popular of all the classes ever raced at the Beverly Yacht Club was the H12 designed by Nathanael Herreshoff in 1914. As with all his designs, Herreshoff used a carved hull model instead of line drawings in designing the boat. Offsets were taken from the model, and from these, molds were constructed to shape the hull. The boat was originally framed in oak and planked in cedar, although the familiar oak trim was changed to mahogany in 1936. The first boats sold for between $400 and $500, sails included, a figure that was considered high in those days. This photograph shows Beverly Yacht Club member Earl W. De Walt sailing his H12 *Cloud Nine* in Sippican Harbor.

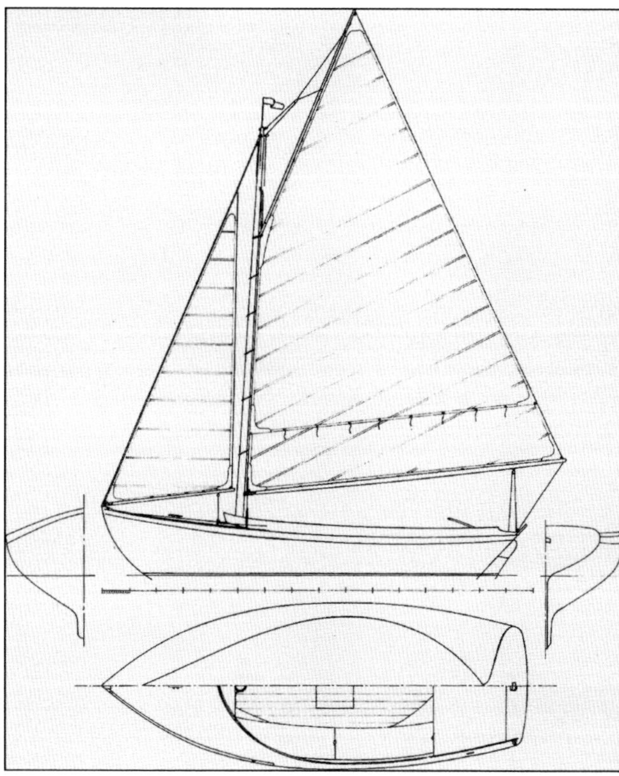

This image is a drawing of the H12 sail plan.

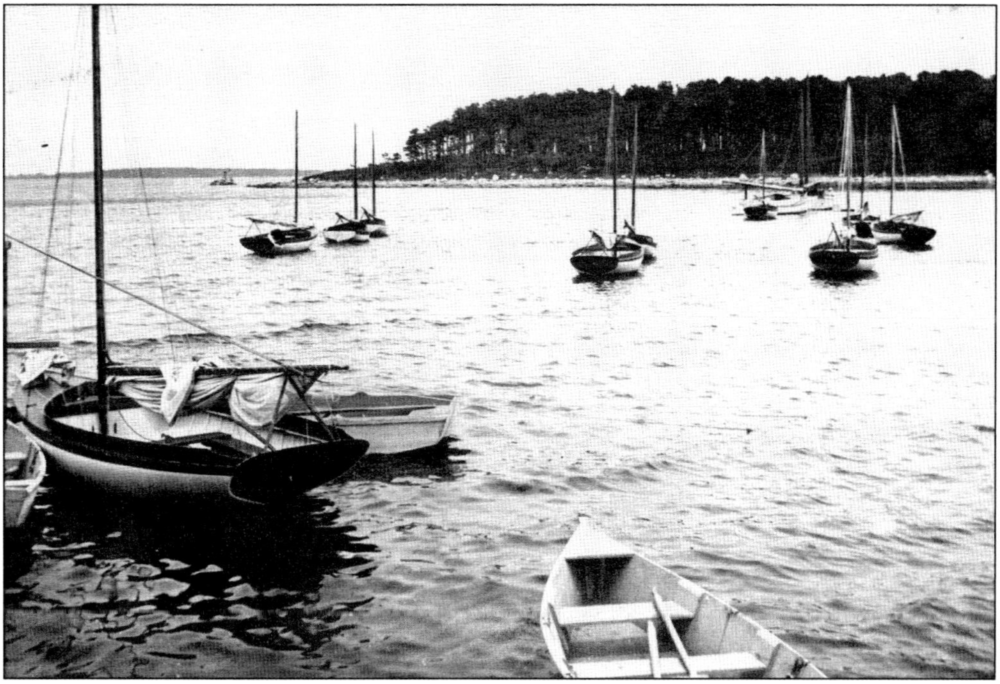
This photograph shows the Beverly Yacht Club's H12 fleet moored at Wing's Neck in 1914.

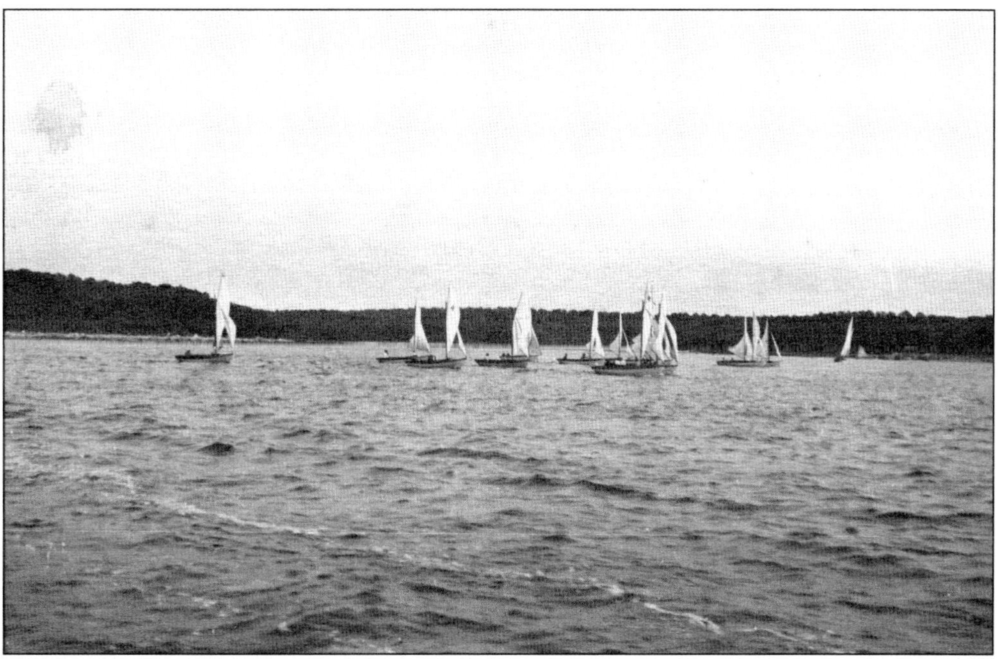
Here the H12s race off Wing's Neck in 1914.

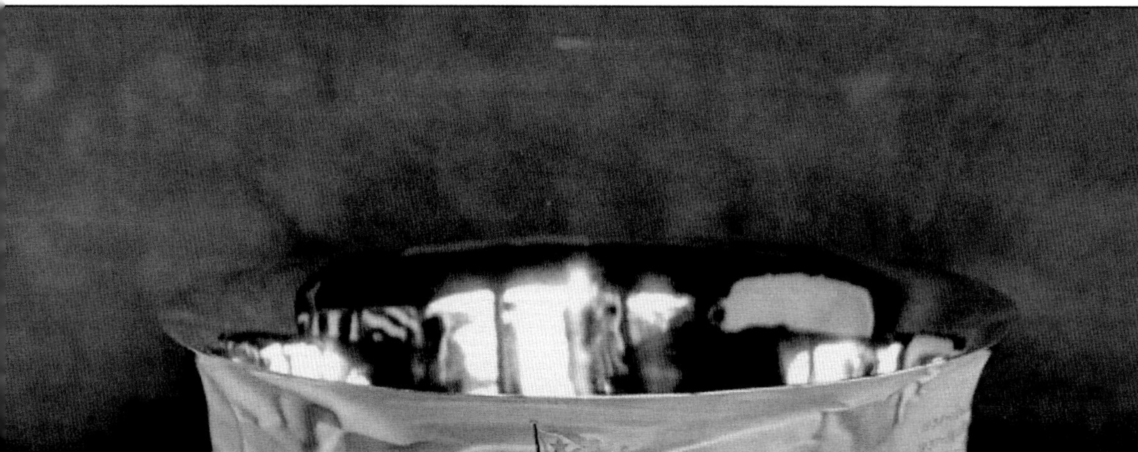

The Cudahy family from Chicago summered in Marion and was well known among the racing and sailing enthusiasts in the Beverly Yacht Club for many years. This trophy, given in 1936 in memory of Norah Cudahy, was originally to be awarded to the owner of an H12 first winning the championship three times, not necessarily in succession. The first trophy was retired in 1954 after Albert R. Pierce Jr., owner of the *Skip II*, won the H12 championship in 1952, 1953, and 1954. He went on to win the championship in 1957, 1959, 1960, 1961, 1962, 1963, 1965, 1966, 1968, and 1969. This second trophy is now a perpetual award trophy.

Four

Wing's Neck 1895–1913

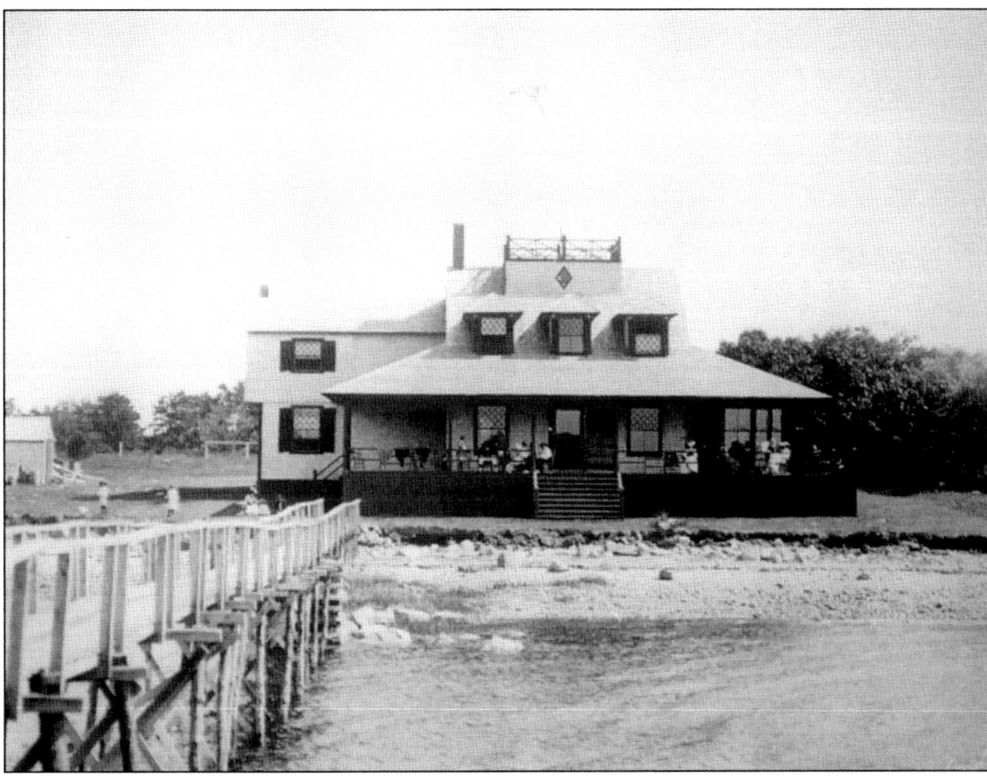

After floating about as a yacht-racing association for its first 23 years, the Beverly Yacht Club finally settled down at its first station in 1895 with the leasing of a house at Wing's Neck, which it purchased four years later in 1899. This is an early photograph of the Wing's Neck clubhouse.

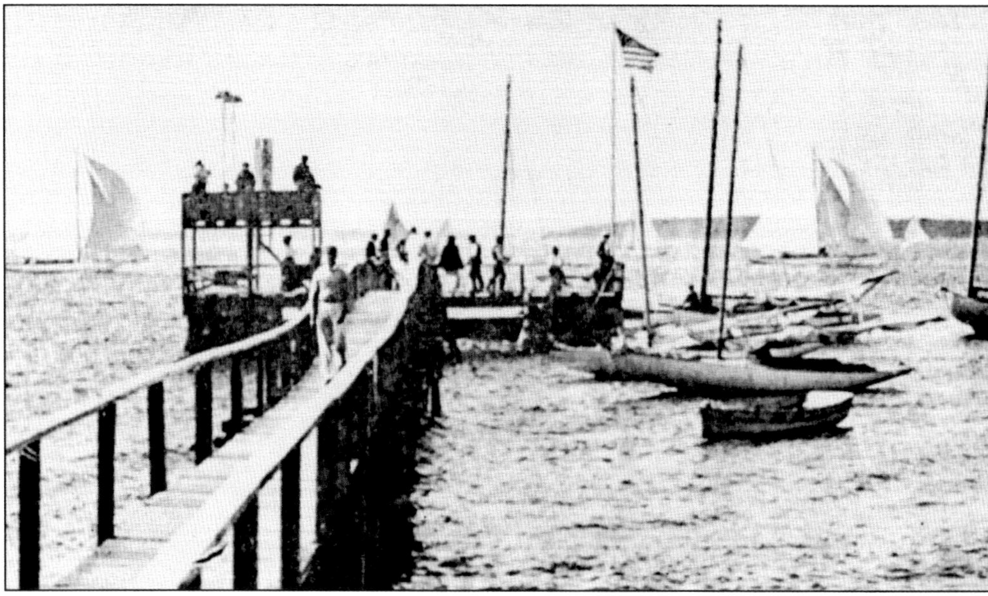

This photograph shows the finish of a race at the Wing's Neck pier. The first regatta at Monument Beach was held on August 28, 1880. By the mid-1880s, regattas were pretty evenly divided between Monument Beach and Marblehead, but as the Buzzards Bay membership increased while that at Marblehead steadily declined, the shift to Buzzards Bay became more and more pronounced. The Beverly Yacht Club wound up its Massachusetts Bay activities finally in 1897.

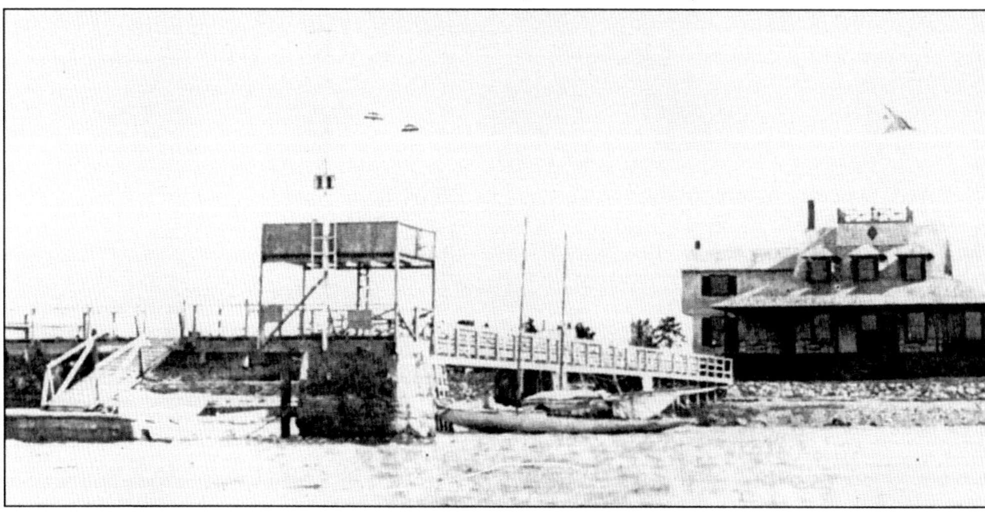

The Wing's Neck clubhouse was a building about 50 feet square, with enclosed verandas and a modest second story. A long wooden pier extended out to two large stone piers, which supported a platform and a second higher platform at the west end for signals and judging. The end of the pier constituted the end of the starting line. Rooms could be engaged in the Wing's Neck clubhouse for $1.00 a day. For the benefit of members stopping there, the club agreed to supply tea or coffee, milk, butter, bread, oatmeal, potatoes, sugar, salt, and so on at a cost of an additional $1 per day. All vegetables, meat, fish, and eggs were extra and could be obtained by the steward from local dealers. Members were asked to see that their bills were submitted to them by the steward and settled by them before departure. When the Cape Cod Canal was built, the traffic in the canal interfered with the Wing's Neck starting line.

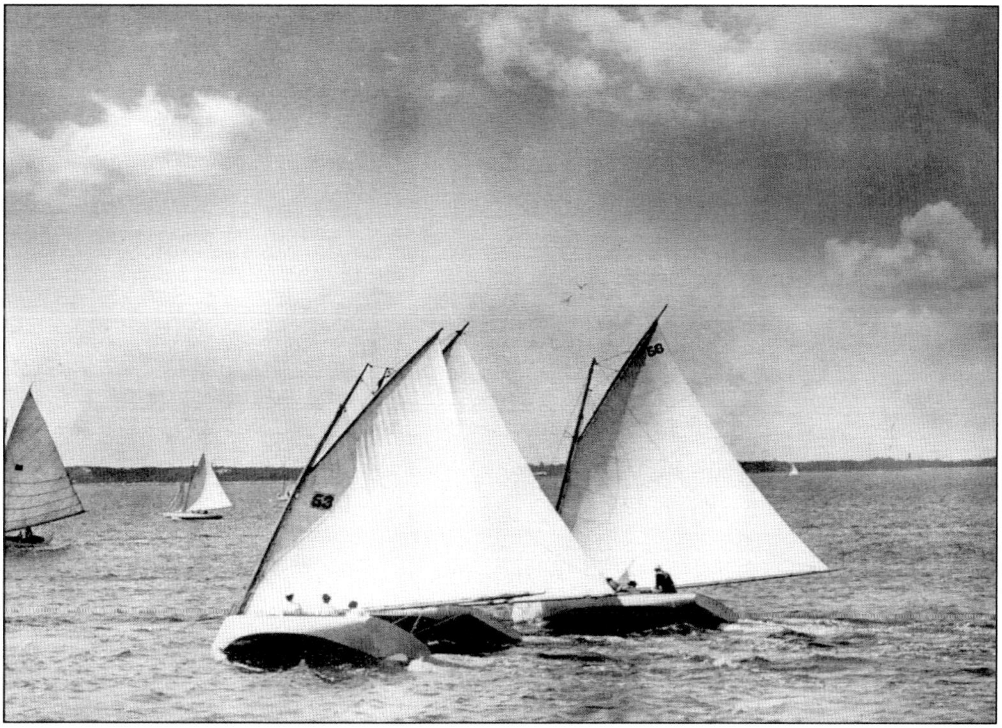

This is an early photograph of catboats racing off the Beverly Yacht Club's Wing's Neck station in 1904.

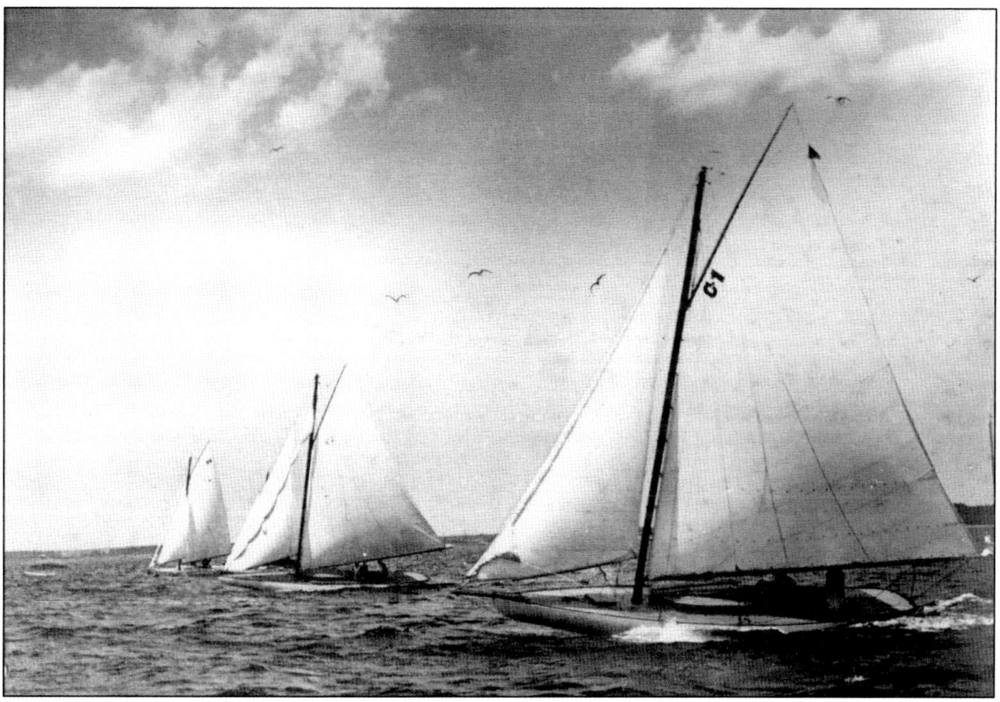

Longtime member Kathy Saltonstall provided this photograph of Beverly Yacht Club races at the Wing's Neck station in 1904.

Races in Buzzards Bay were first started in the area between the Tobey Club, a club having no yachting interest, and Mashness Island, off Monument Beach. Tobey Island was located north of Wing's Neck. Its clubhouse provided lovely views of Buzzards Bay.

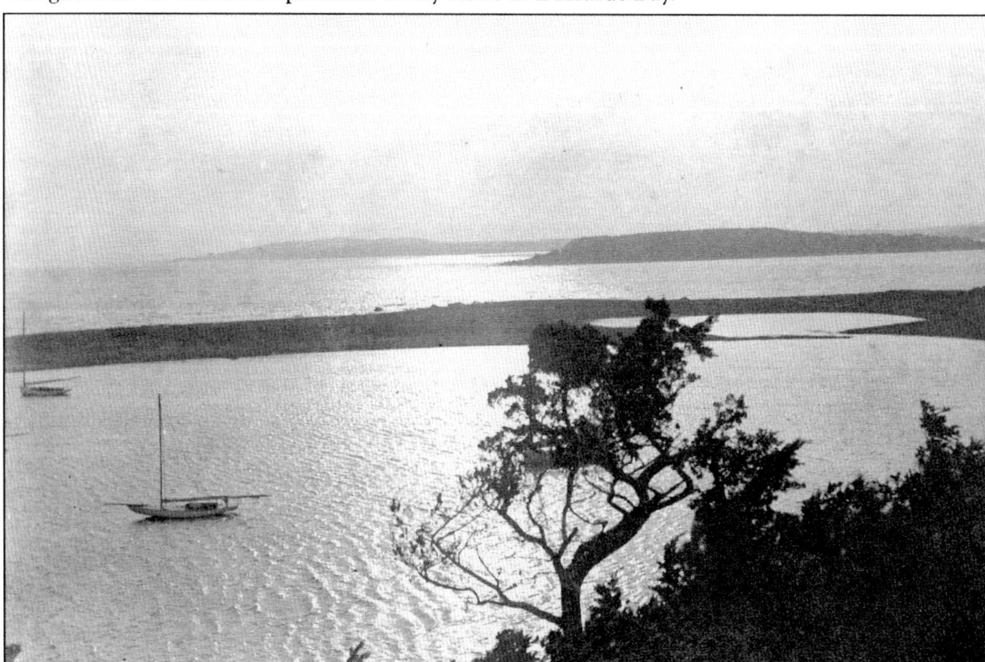

This photograph shows Tobey Island Lagoon from its clubhouse.

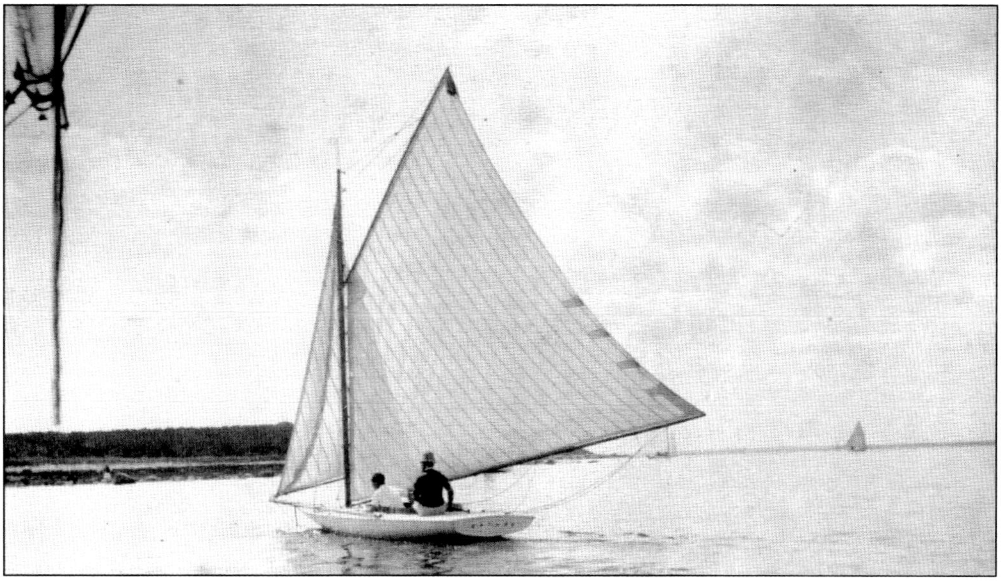

The racing off Monument Beach was enjoyable until the Cape Cod Canal was built. The canal's lower channel crossed the starting line off the Wing's Neck station, causing disruptions in the Beverly Yacht Club's races held there.

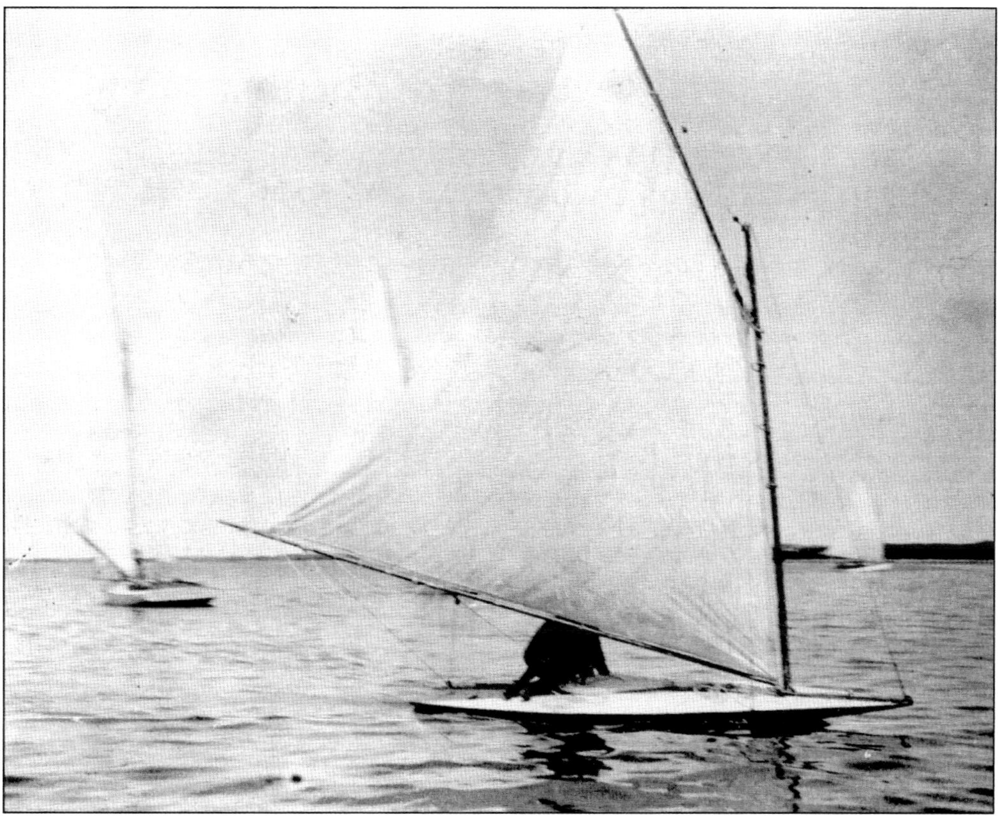

The Beverly Yacht Club's archives contain this old photograph of a catboat racing at Monument Beach.

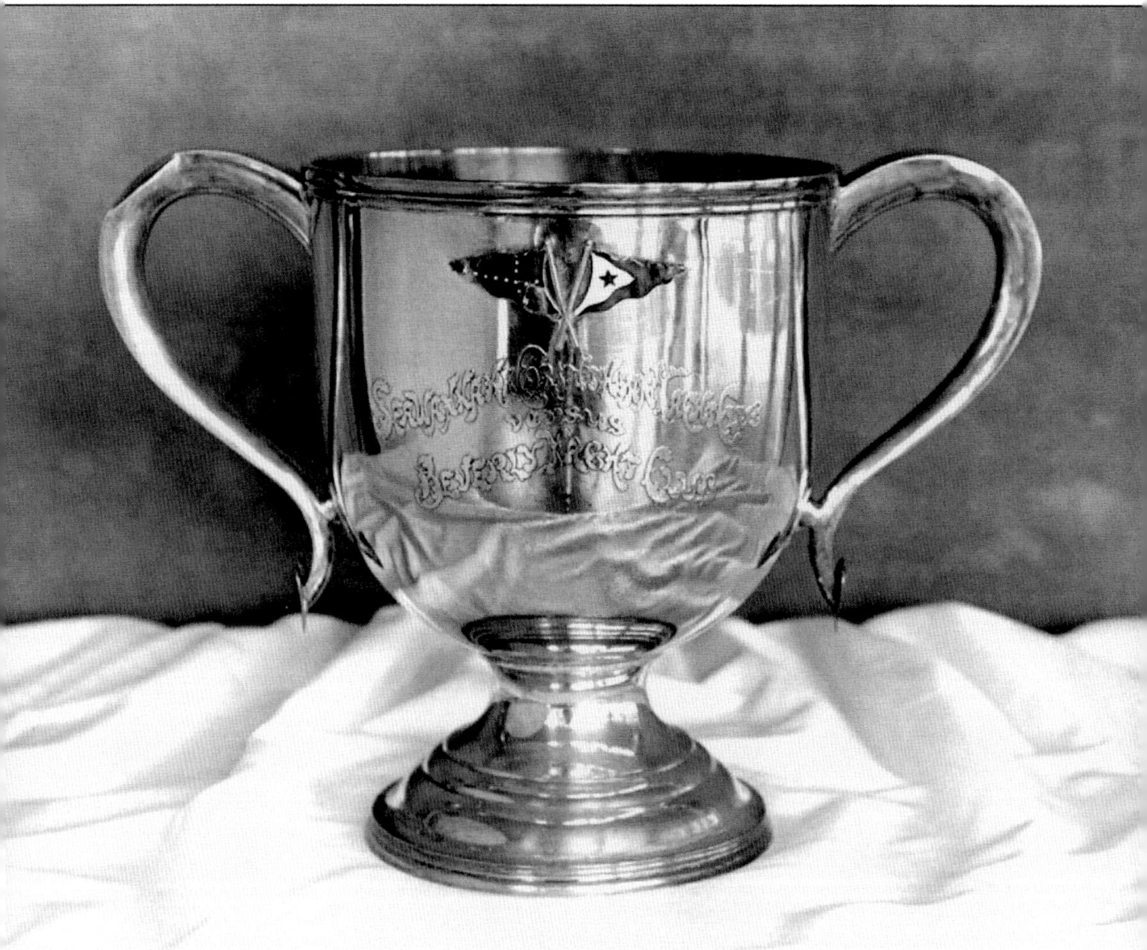

In 1875, most American yachts were wide, shallow draft boats with inside ballast. The boats racing in Beverly Yacht Club races in the 1870s were mainly a variety of catboats under 30 feet waterline length, as limited by the club's rules. By 1880, the spoon bow made its appearance and changed the whole aspect of yachting design. By this time, the Beverly Yacht Club was using different classifications in its Massachusetts Bay and Buzzards Bay racing due to the shallower draft designs in the Buzzards Bay entries. In 1895, practically all of the Beverly Yacht Club's racing was carried on in Buzzards Bay, and the club had become more local in its activities. The restricted classes were beginning to appear. Of these, the most durable, in terms of popularity, were the restricted 21 footers. This class was restricted as to waterline, length, beam, freeboard, cabin house, ballast and draft, scantling, planking and construction, sails, and equipment. Beverly Yacht Club members Lewis Stackpole, Dick Hoyt, and the Eustices, competed vigorously in restricted 21 footers. These boats were raced up to 1920. In August 1902, team races were held between Seawanhaka of Long Island and the Beverly Yacht Club of Wing's Neck at Newport in the restricted 21s. Beverly Yacht Club won this beautiful team race trophy in 1902. Return matches were held at Wing's Neck in 1903, and again the Beverly Yacht Club won.

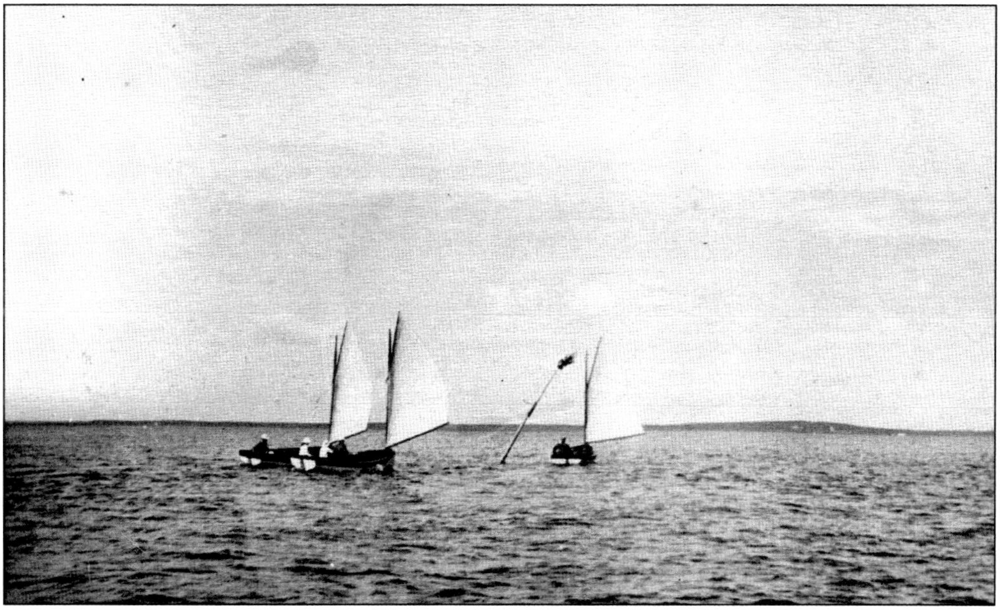

The archives of the Beverly Yacht Club contain many early photographs of catboats racing off Wing's Neck. This image shows a Beverly Yacht Club race around 1904.

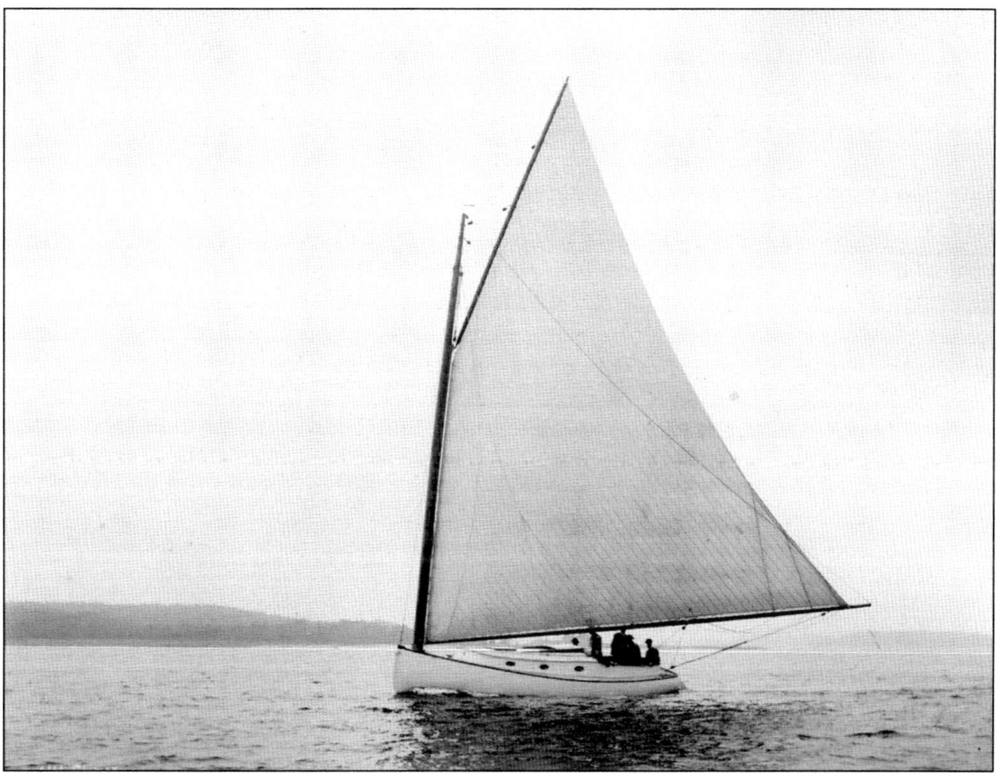

This catboat, the *Climax*, is shown racing in a Beverly Yacht Club race off Wing's Neck.

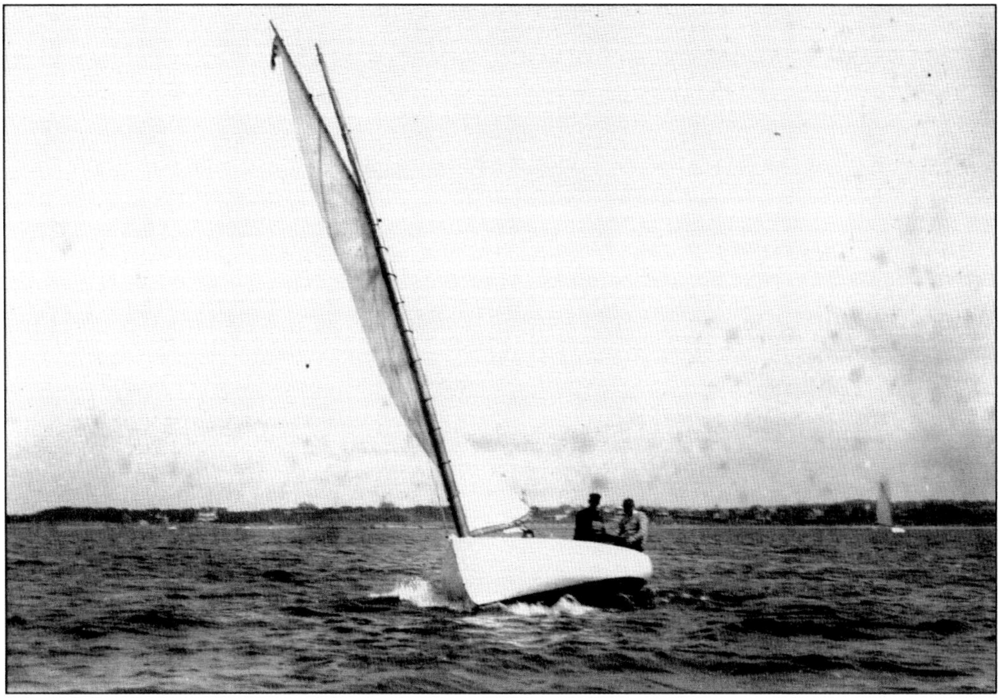

This old photograph contained in the historical records of the Beverly Yacht Club shows an early catboat racing in a Beverly Yacht Club race held off its Wing's Neck station.

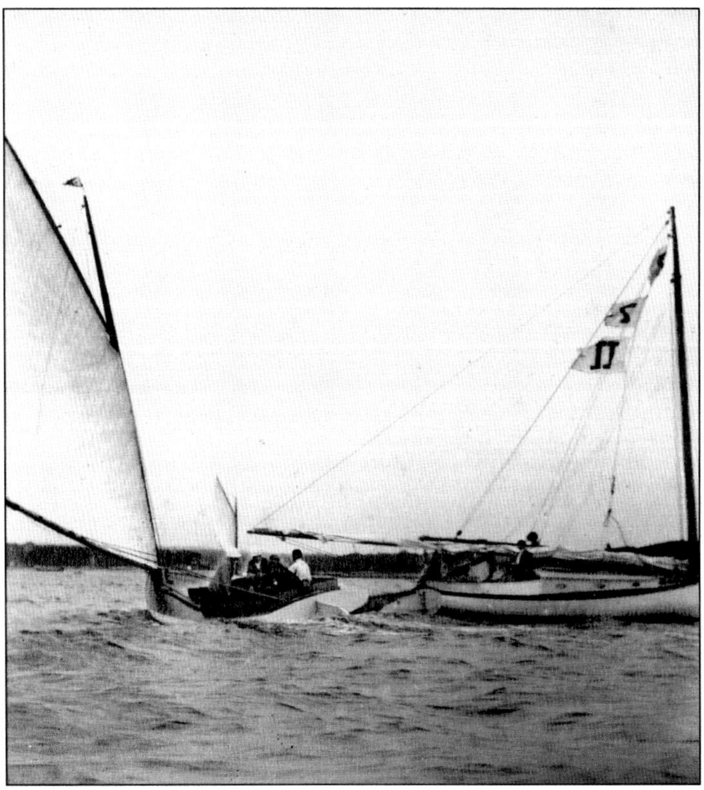

Here Beverly Yacht Club boats finish the race at the committee boat off Wing's Neck.

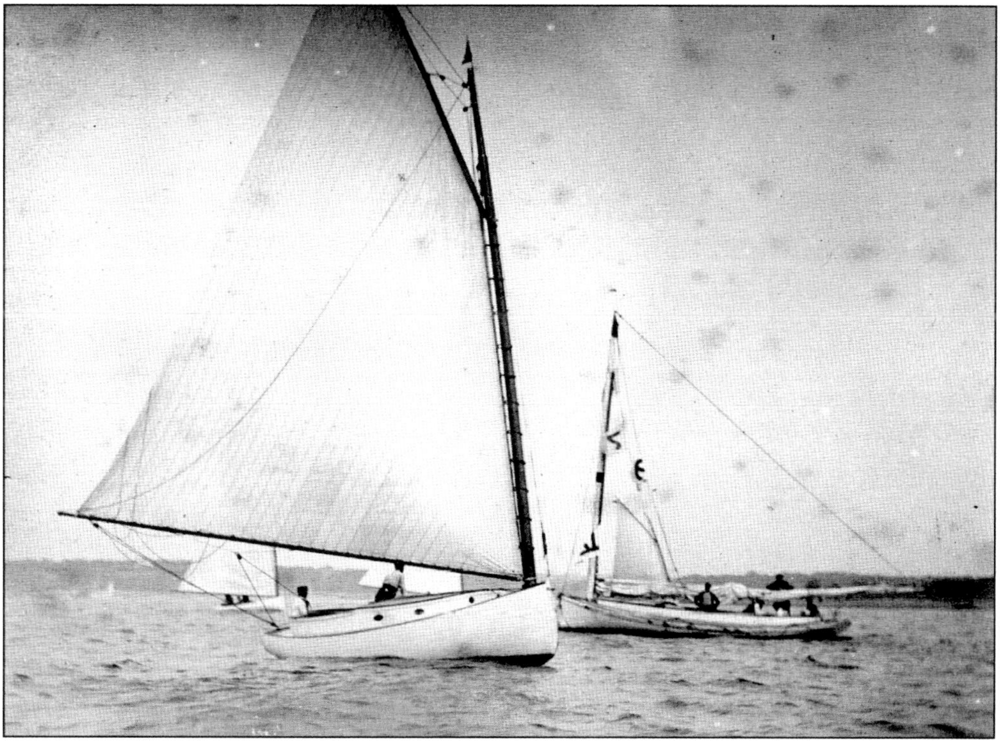

Another catboat is shown finishing a Beverly Yacht Club race off Wing's Neck.

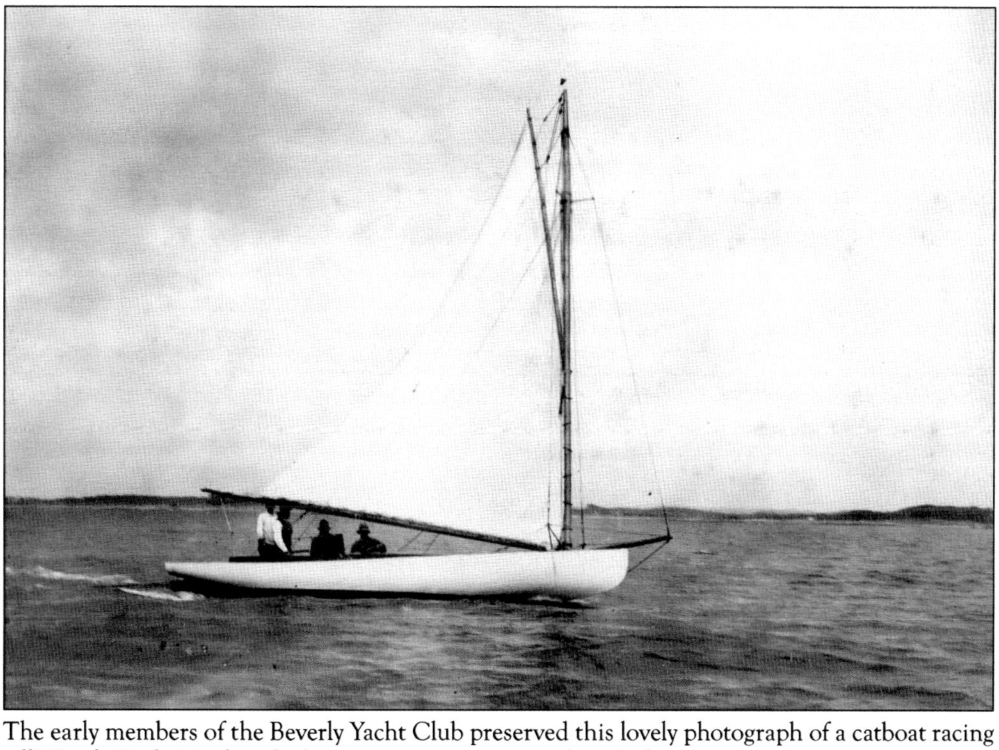

The early members of the Beverly Yacht Club preserved this lovely photograph of a catboat racing off Wing's Neck. Neither the boat nor its owner were identified.

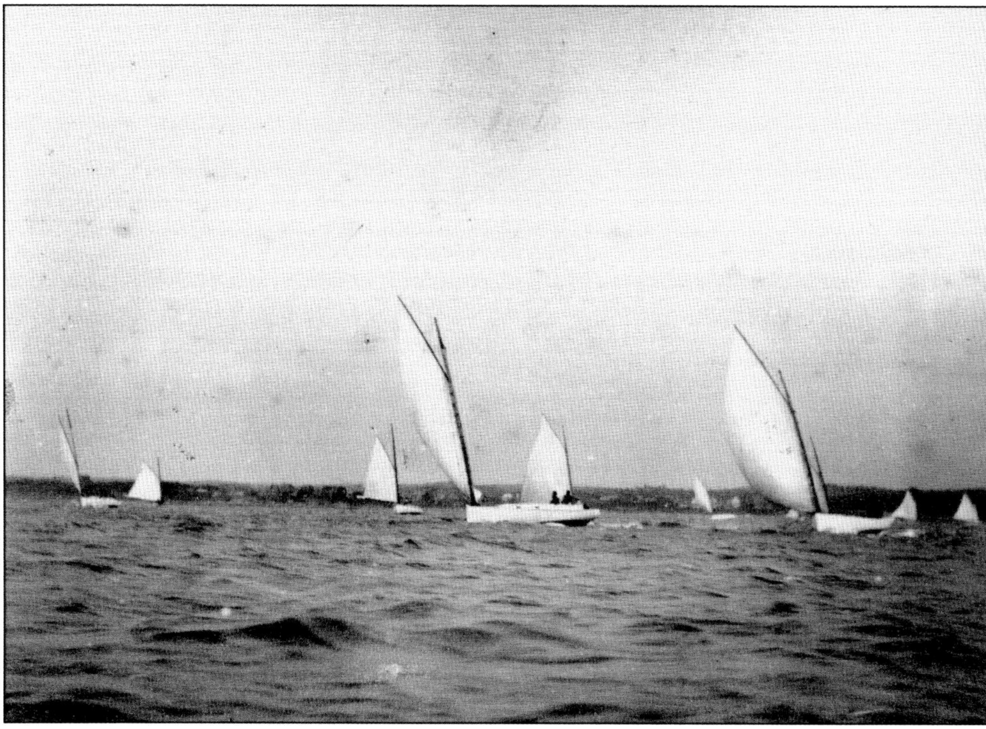

The early days of racing small boats are captured in these two photographs of Beverly Yacht Club races off Wing's Neck.

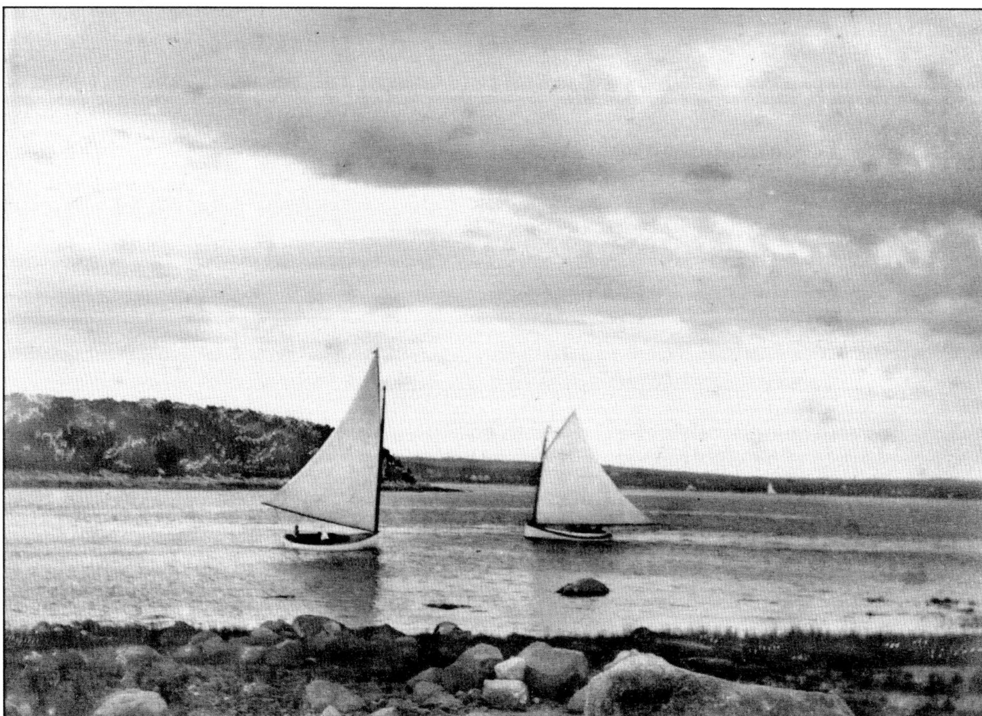

Five

SONDERKLASSE 1909–1918

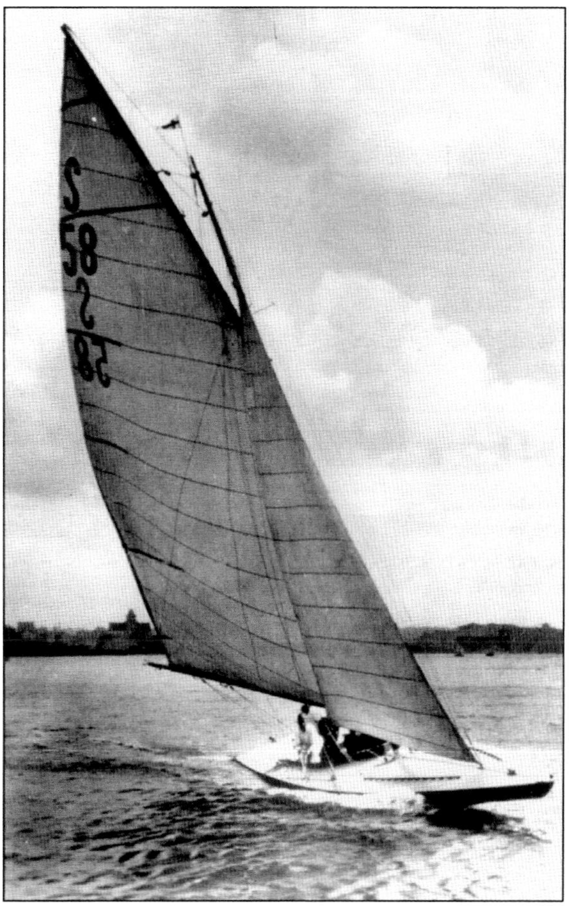

The Sonderklasse (special class), which originated in Germany, was raced in large numbers in America from 1909 to 1918. The Germans came over to race these boats in Marblehead, and the Americans went over to Germany to race Sonderklasse boats there. The Americans were not very successful in the Sonderklasse races until Buzzards Bay, where the wind and water were similar to those in Kiel, Germany, was chosen as a place for trials. In September 1910, trials were held off No. 13 buoy in Buzzards Bay and were dominated by Beverly Yacht Club skippers and boats, who placed two out of three chosen from the 16 entries. The historical archives of the Beverly Yacht Club contain an entire photo album of images of Sonderklasse boats owned by Beverly Yacht Club members.

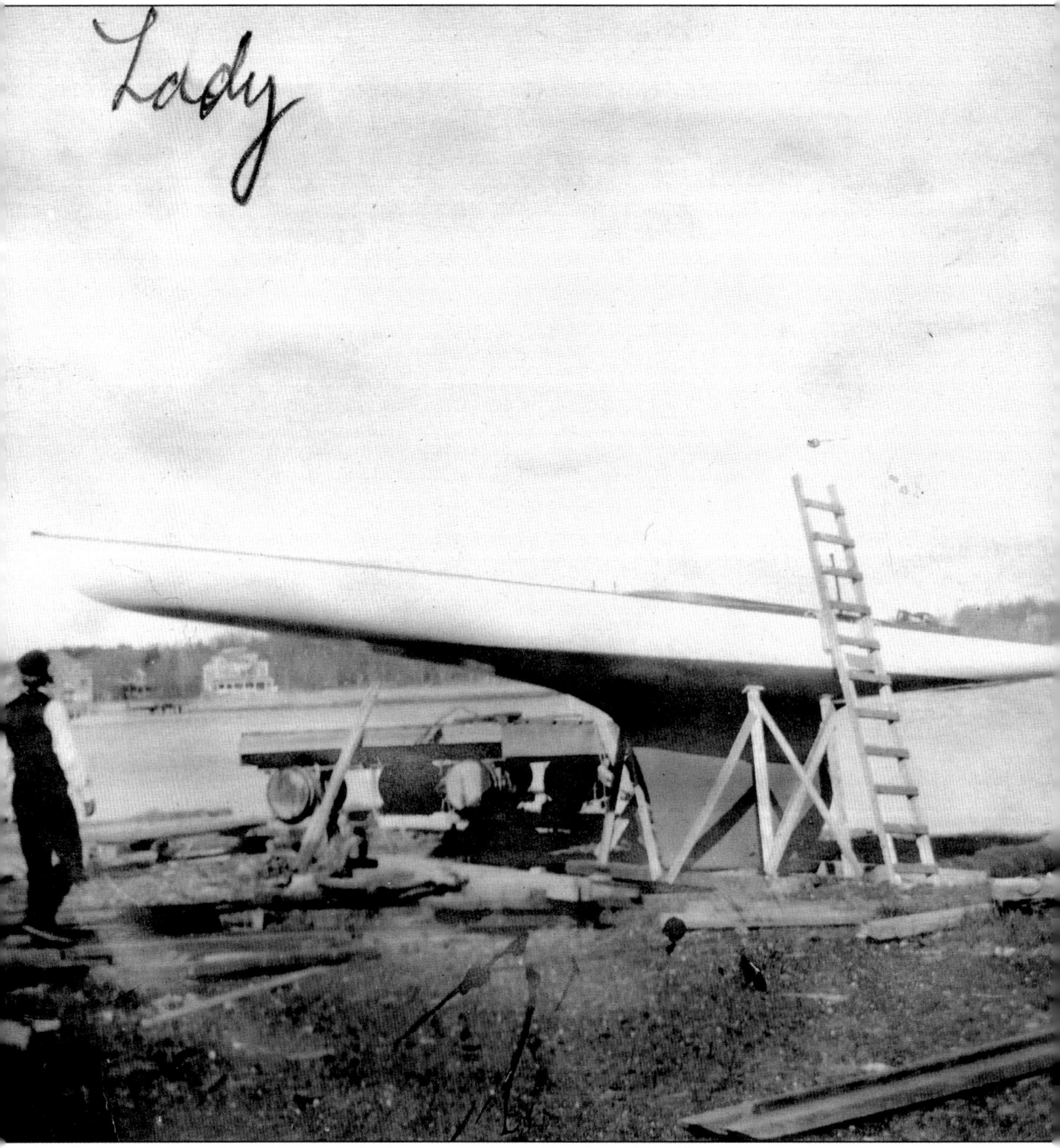

On May 12, 1909, the Sonderklasse *Lady* was christened and launched in Manchester. Its owner was R. D. Boardman, and its designer was Edwin A. Boardman.

DEMON PERFORMED WELL.

Francis F. Boardman's New Sonder Boat Had Trial Sail.

The first of the six sonder boats designed by Edwin A. Boardman for this year's German-American match was given a trial in Manchester harbor last Monday afternoon. This was the boat built for Francis F. Boardman by the David Fenton company, which has been named Demon. She proved to be an easily handled boat in the short sail in the stiff northwester, and seemed quite fast. Frank Crowninshield, her owner, was at the helm and was much pleased with the boat. The Demon will be sailed over to Marblehead some day this week and will be moored off her owner's summer home at Peaches point.

This May 1909 article reports on Frank Crowninshield's Sonderklasse boat *Demon*, which was designed by Edwin A. Boardman. The reporter wrote that the boat "proved to be an easily handled boat in the short sail in the stiff northwester and seemed quite fast. Frank Crowninshield, her owner, was at the helm and was much pleased with the boat."

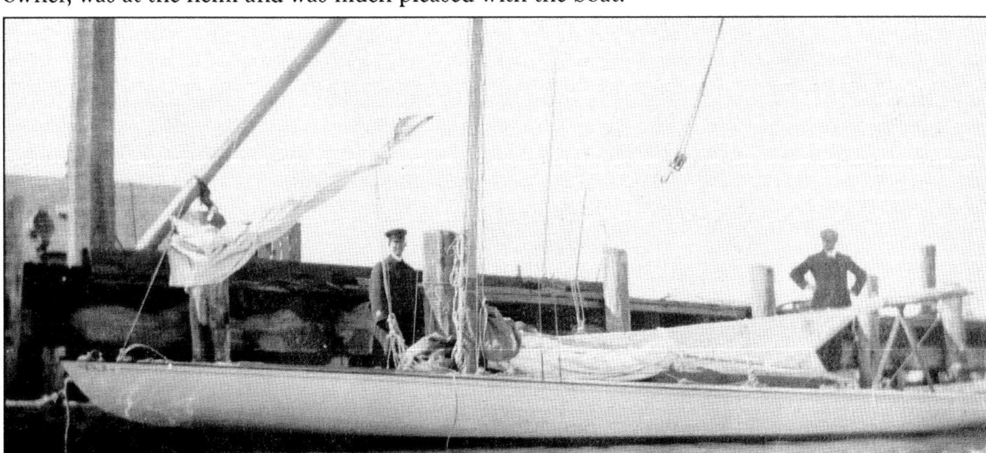

Here Crowninshield's Sonderklasse *Demon* is shown at the dock.

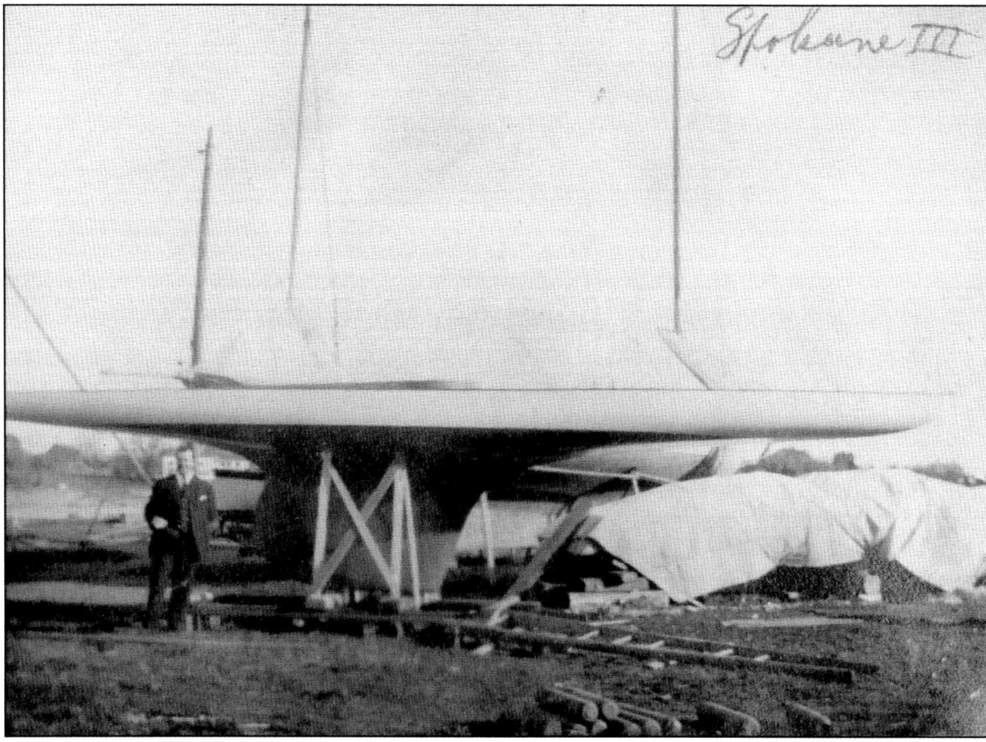

Another photograph in the Beverly Yacht Club archives shows the Sonderklasse *Spokane III* in the boatyard. It was owned by F. Lewis Clark.

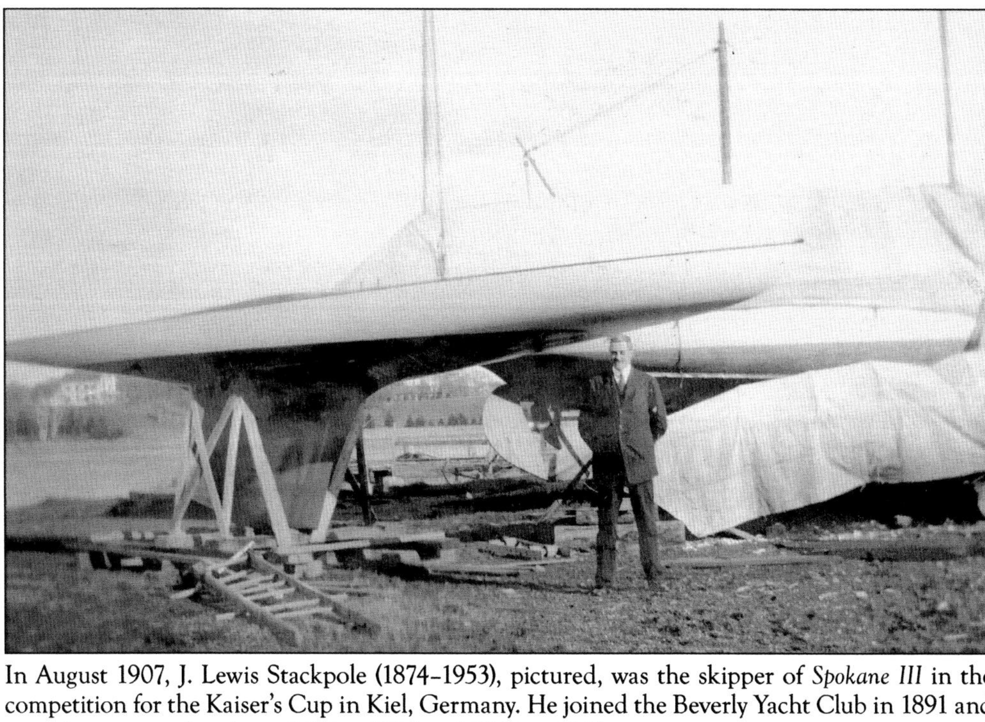

In August 1907, J. Lewis Stackpole (1874–1953), pictured, was the skipper of *Spokane III* in the competition for the Kaiser's Cup in Kiel, Germany. He joined the Beverly Yacht Club in 1891 and served as commodore from 1919 to 1925 and 1942 to 1945.

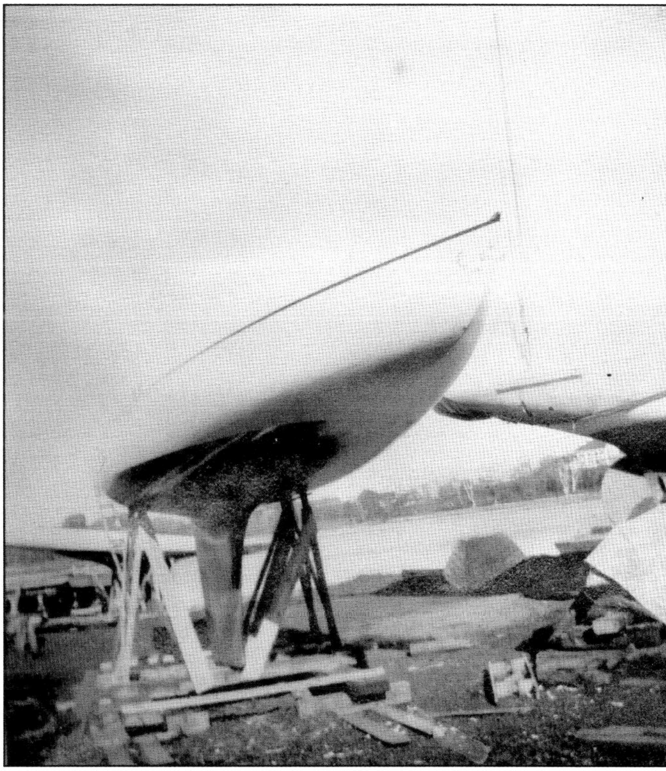

The photographer shows several views of the Sonderklasse *Spokane III* in the boatyard.

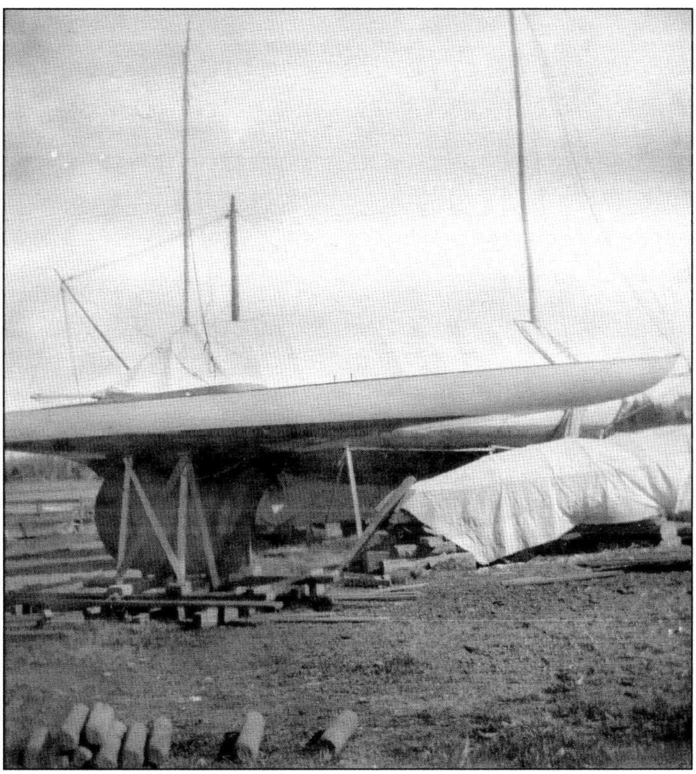

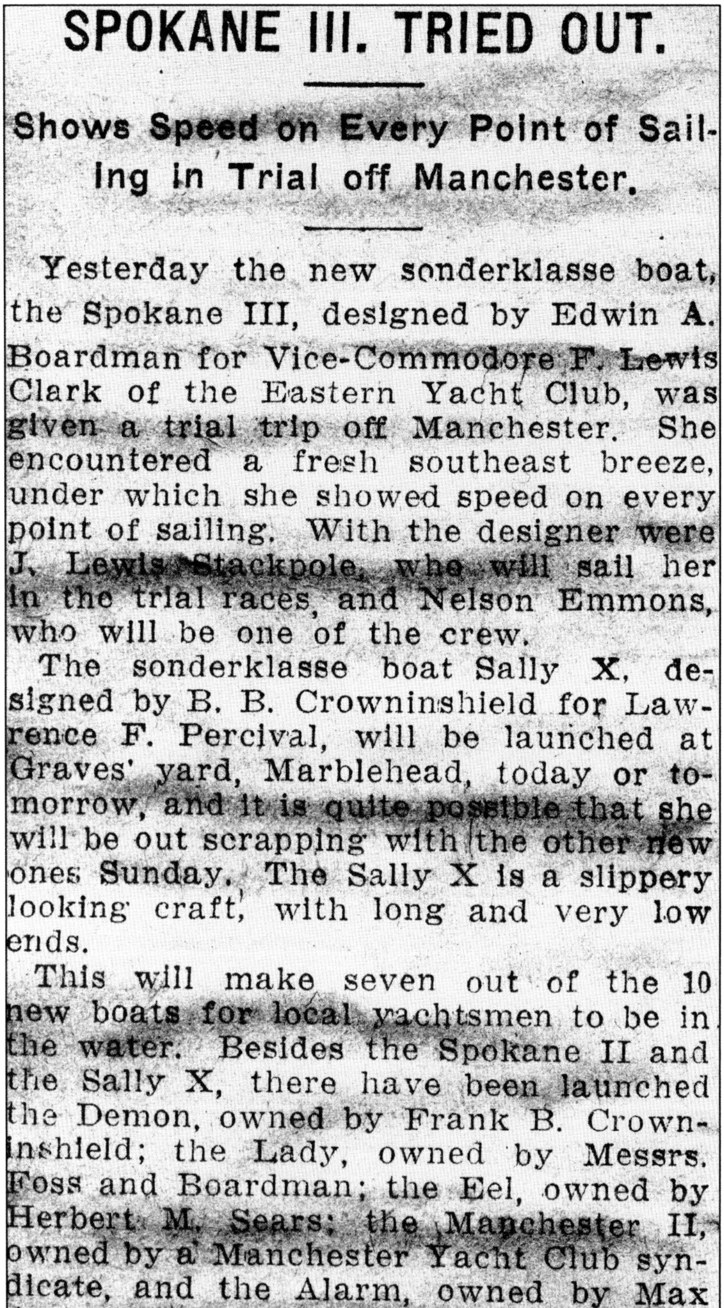

SPOKANE III. TRIED OUT.

Shows Speed on Every Point of Sailing in Trial off Manchester.

Yesterday the new sonderklasse boat, the Spokane III, designed by Edwin A. Boardman for Vice-Commodore F. Lewis Clark of the Eastern Yacht Club, was given a trial trip off Manchester. She encountered a fresh southeast breeze, under which she showed speed on every point of sailing. With the designer were J. Lewis Stackpole, who will sail her in the trial races, and Nelson Emmons, who will be one of the crew.

The sonderklasse boat Sally X, designed by B. B. Crowninshield for Lawrence F. Percival, will be launched at Graves' yard, Marblehead, today or tomorrow, and it is quite possible that she will be out scrapping with the other new ones Sunday. The Sally X is a slippery looking craft, with long and very low ends.

This will make seven out of the 10 new boats for local yachtsmen to be in the water. Besides the Spokane II and the Sally X, there have been launched the Demon, owned by Frank B. Crowninshield; the Lady, owned by Messrs. Foss and Boardman; the Eel, owned by Herbert M. Sears; the Manchester II, owned by a Manchester Yacht Club syndicate, and the Alarm, owned by Max Agassiz.

This article, published on May 21, 1909, reported that the new Sonderklasse *Spokane III* was given a trial sail off of Manchester and that it "showed speed on every point of sailing." It was designed by Edwin A. Boardman for F. Lewis Clark, vice commodore of the Eastern Yacht Club. J. Lewis Stackpole was chosen to skipper *Spokane III* in its trials, and H. Nelson Emmons was chosen to be one of the crew. J. Lewis Stackpole was vice commodore of the Beverly Yacht Club from 1915 to 1919 and its commodore from 1919 to 1926. H. Nelson Emmons was vice commodore of the Beverly Yacht Club from 1928 to 1934.

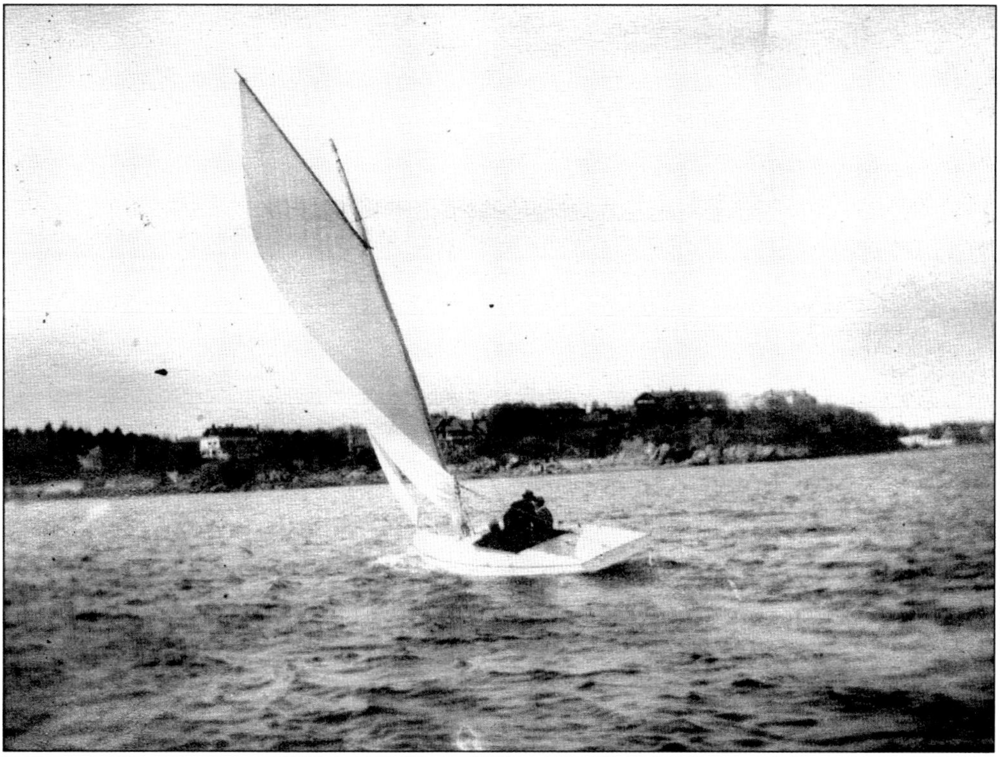

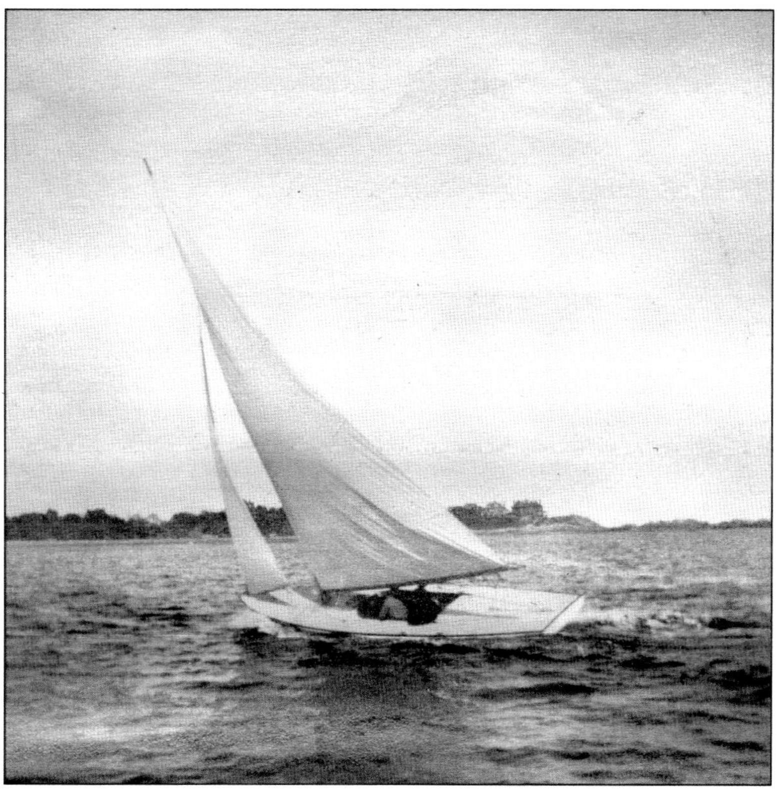

These photographs of the early sailing trials of the Sonderklasse *Spokane III* were probably preserved in the historical records of the Beverly Yacht Club by J. Lewis Stackpole and H. Nelson Emmons.

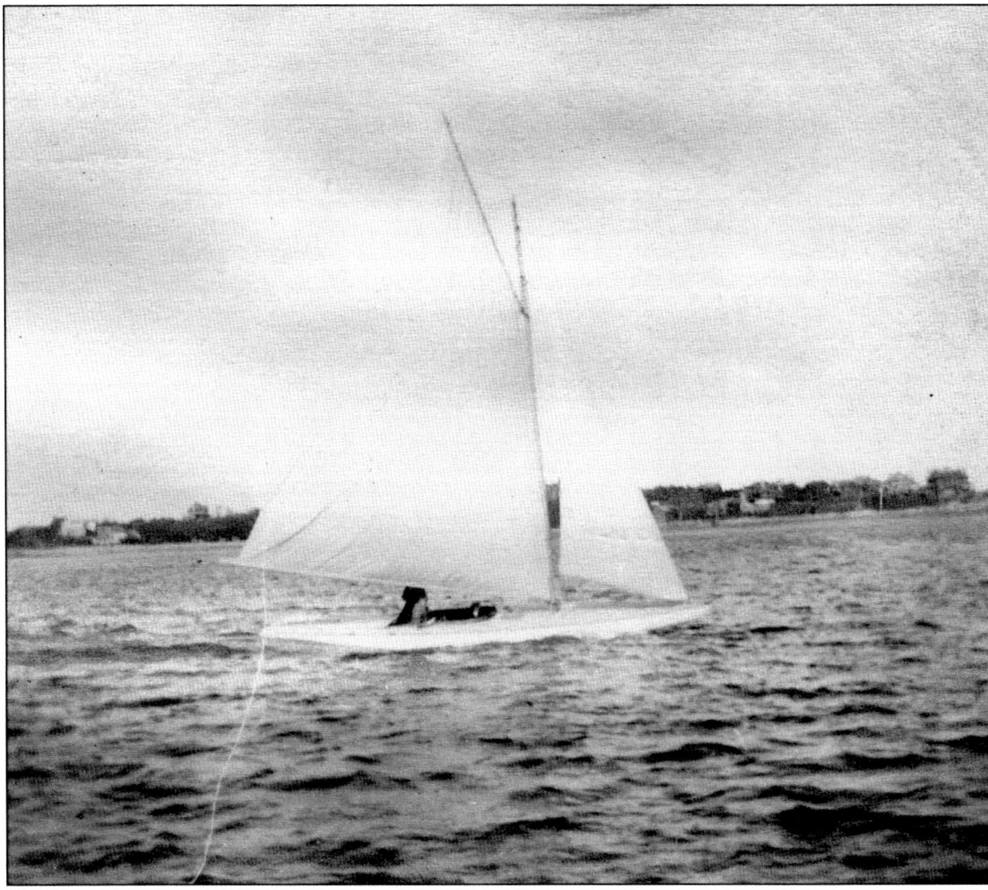

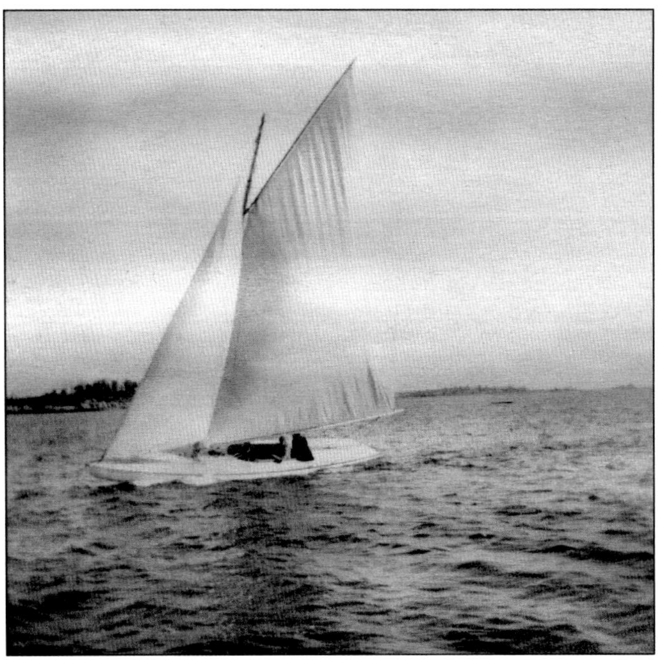

Shown here are two more photographs of the sea trial of the Sonderklasse *Spokane III*.

On July 14, 1909, the Sonderklasse *Peg*, owned by Marion summer resident Galen L. Stone, took first place in the open Sonderklasse regatta held by the nine boats owned by Beverly Yacht Club members. The boats were sent over course No. 11—to Bird Island buoys Nos. 13 and 2, leaving them to starboard; Bow Bells buoy and Bird Island buoys Nos. 2 and 13 to port; and Beverly Yacht Club buoys Nos. 1, 2, and 3 to starboard and return, a distance of 11.75 miles.

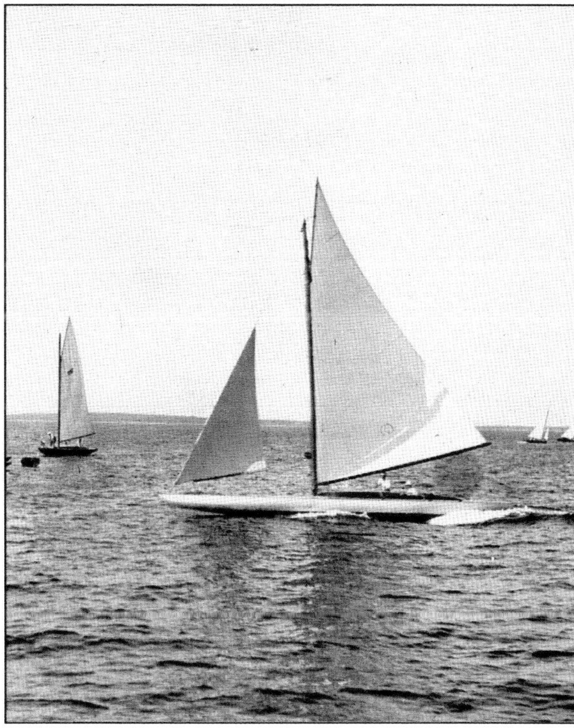

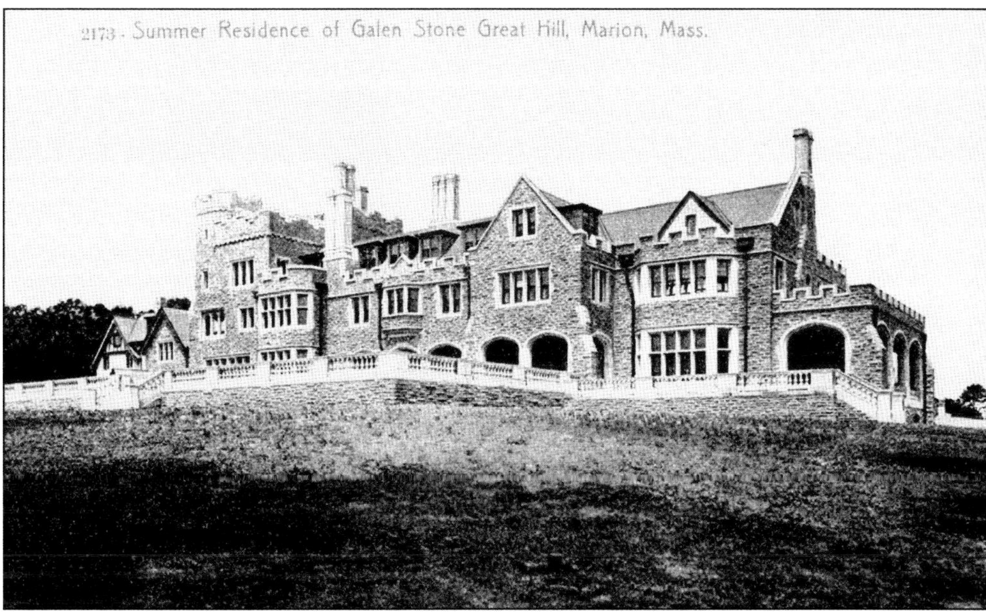

Galen L. Stone built a large summer home in Marion called Great Hill because it was built on a glacial hill 127 feet above sea level on a large peninsula consisting of 313 acres that jut out into Buzzards Bay. In 1907, Stone, a Boston investment banker, purchased the property and hired architect Horace S. Fraser to design a rambling mansion built out of Hayden stone taken from the Philadelphia area. The family firm was called Hayden Stone, and thus the use of that type of stone. The Tudor main house was based on an estate north of London called Compton Wyngates. Many descendants of Galen L. Stone are active members of the Beverly Yacht Club today.

FINE BREEZE AT MARION.

Beverly Yacht Club Fleet Provides a Lively Card in Its Third Regatta.

MARION, June 28—There was a large gathering at the third race of the Beverly Yacht Club today, the new clubhouse be ng packed. There was a decided increase in the 21-footers and 15-footer classes, and the indications point to their being popular.

The boats started in a light easterly breeze for Centre Board Ledge. The Crane design class went to Abiels Ledge while the Herreshoffs were given the course to Angelica buoy and Bird Island.

The wind soon shifted to a fresh wholesail southwest breeze which was pleasing to yachtsmen and spectators, and the boats were seen at their best. The Kacoona, with designer Stackpole at the helm, proved a good all-around boat and clearly demonstrated that she is in line for blue flags. The Saracen sailed by the Bradley brothers, d d well while the Kim lost a point but held to her flag-w nning record for the season. The sonder Peg added one more to an unbroken record, closely pressed by the Fin. The Waterwitch again brought joy to her owner and behaved handsomely in skillful hands. The 15-footers were well bunched at the close. The finish was full of interest.

Rarely are so many boats so close together and there were many thrills among the friends of sailors as only seconds separated several of the boats. Judges Whitimore and Rice were kept on the alert and kept the record clear. The Anita opened the season with old-time vigor and will have to be counted in her class. The summary:

TWENTY-FOOTERS

Name and owner	El time
Kacoona; J L Stackpole	1:49:5
Saracena, Robert Winsor	1:50:3
Kim, Charles E Hellier	1:52:4
Mirpeh, R W Cummings	1:50:3
Skat, W E C Eustis	1:57:1

SONDER CLASS

Name and owner	El time
Peg, G L Stone	2:06:2
Fin, H Stockton Jr	2:06:4
Marla, Ralph White	2:13:2

CRANE ONE DESIGN

Name and owner	El time
Waterwitch, Miss Isabel Coolidge	1:40:4
Niobe, Mosely Taylor	1:42:0
Gifted, George U Parker	1:42:1
Pioneer, F B Austin	1:42:1
Charmion, W Crane Jr	1:42:2
Nabob, C H Bright	1:43:0
Pam, Miss Manning Lionbeger	1:43:2

HERRESHOFF ONE DESIGN

Name and owner	El time
Anita, E A Clark	1:36:4
Vim, Miss Eunice Taylor	1:37:1
No Name, E G Webster	1:38:2
Endeavor, G H Fiske	1:39:1
Snail, A H Newman	1:41:4
Fly, Miss Constance Morss	1:41:5

This June 28, 1913, newspaper article reported that the *Peg*, owned by Galen L. Stone, won first place in the Sonderklasse. The new clubhouse of the Beverly Yacht Club, built in 1913 on Butler's Point in Marion, was "packed," according to the article. Three Sonderklasse boats raced that day with the *Peg* taking first place. Second place went to the *Fin*, owned by H. Stockton Jr., and third place went to the *Marla*, owned by Ralph White.

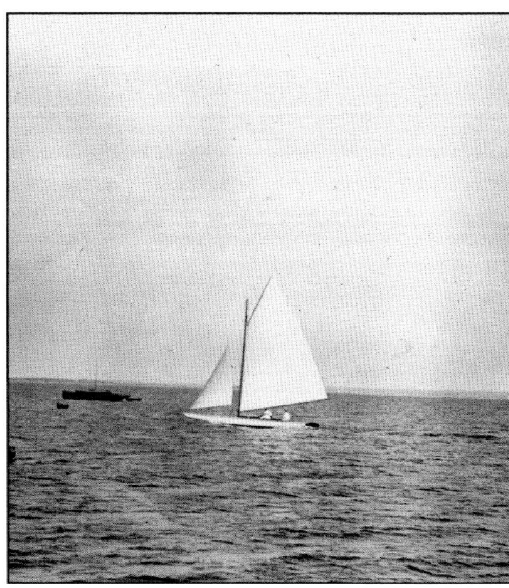

On June 28, 1913, the Sonderklasse *Peg*, owned by Galen L. Stone, added one more win to an unbroken record at a Beverly Yacht Club race at Marion.

NIOBE WINS JEFFERIES CUP.

Beverly Yacht Club Favored With a 20-Knot Breeze for the Regatta at Marion.

MARION, Aug 30—In a 20-knot southwest breeze the racing fleet of the Beverly Yacht Club held one of the prettiest races of the season today. The contest was for the Jefferies Cup, and owing to the excellent handicap, proved to be one of the most closely fought races of the series. The course was 10 knots around the Angelica and Abiels Ledge buoys.

A large number of spectators crowded to the pier to see the Niobe carry off the splendid trophy offered by J. T. L. Jefferies, as she had already won the handsome Van Rensselaer Cup. There was keen disappointment when the Kacoona was obliged to withdraw, having fouled the Kim soon after starting. The Uarda got hopelessl entangled in the buoy off Angelica Point and could not finish.

The sonder Peg added to her creditable record by securing the second prize, a cup, while the winners in the respective classes were given pennants. The summary:

Name and owner	El time
Niobe, Moseley	3:16:29
Peg, D L Stone	3:16:40
Awahned, Miss Frances Webster	3:17:02
Peacock, Fred L Winsor	3:17:25
Vim, Miss Eunice Taylor	3:17:41
Mupeh, R W Cummings	3:17:51
Pioneer, T Danstin	3:18:25
Kim, C E Hellier	3:18:27
Saracen, Robert Winsor Jr	3:19:09
Anita, E A Clark Jr	3:19:29
Endeavor, G H Fiske	3:19:40
Charmion, Joshua Crane Jr	3:19:40
Nabob, E H Bright	3:19:56
Tinker, R W Emmons 3d	3:20:27
Skate, W E C Eustis	3:20:41
Pheasant, Alex Winsor	3:21:27
Sea Coon, A F Goodwin	3:22:25
Gifted, G U Crocker	3:22:50
Sally, C E Hellier	3:23:10
Fin, Howard Stockton Jr	3:24:15
Fly, Miss Constance Morss	3:24:38
Snail, A H Newman	3:26:10
Uarda, J Hawkinson	Withdrew
Kacoona, J L Stackpole	Withdrew

On August 30, 1913, a handicap race sponsored by the Beverly Yacht Club was held to award the Jeffries Cup. Walter Lloyd Jeffries and William A. Jeffries were both founding members of the Beverly Yacht Club and active racers in the club's early years. Walter Lloyd Jeffries was responsible for diligently recording the history of the club in its early years. The Jeffries Cup was won by the *Niobe*, a Crane 15-footer owned by Moseley Taylor. The *Niobe* also won the coveted Van Rensselaer Memorial Cup in a prior race. The *Peg*, a Sonderklasse owned by Galen L. Stone, finished second, just 11 seconds behind in what the article described as "one of the most closely fought races of the series."

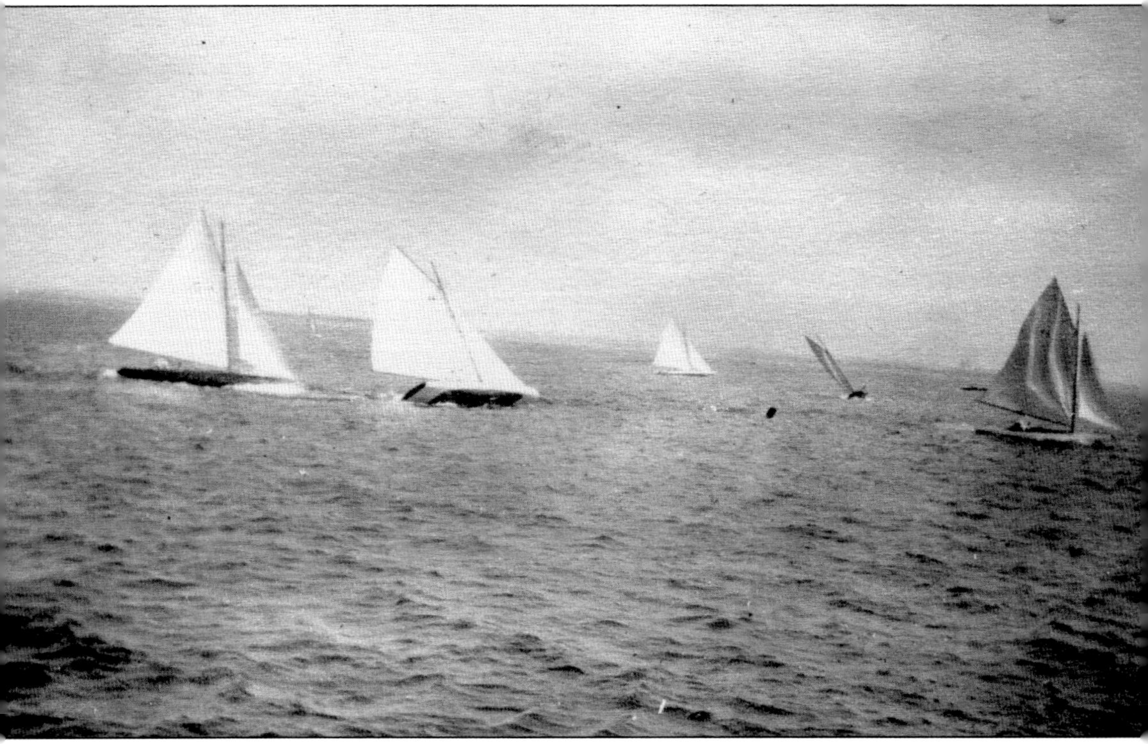

This photograph was taken on August 30, 1913, during the Jeffries Cup handicap race.

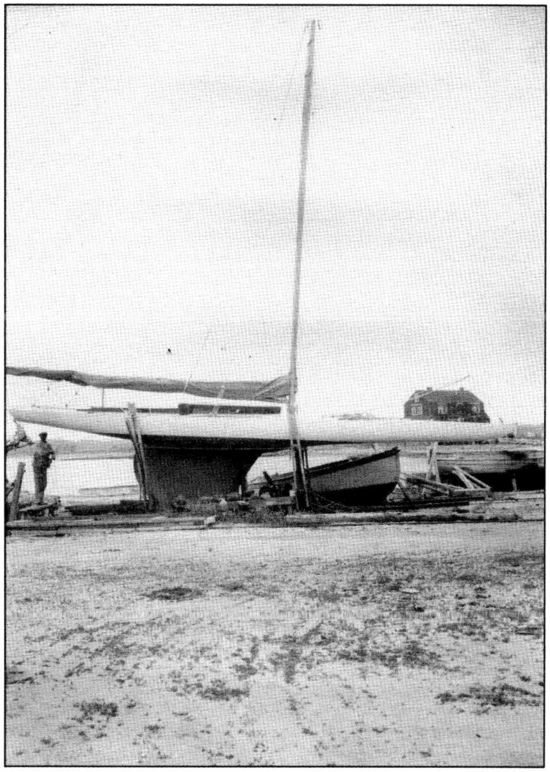

These two photographs, from the archives of the Beverly Yacht Club, show the Sonderklasse boat *Kacoona*, owned by J. Lewis Stackpole, hauled out at the Mattapoisett Town Docks in September 1913. The Stackpole home, "The Sands," is shown at the right rear of the top photograph.

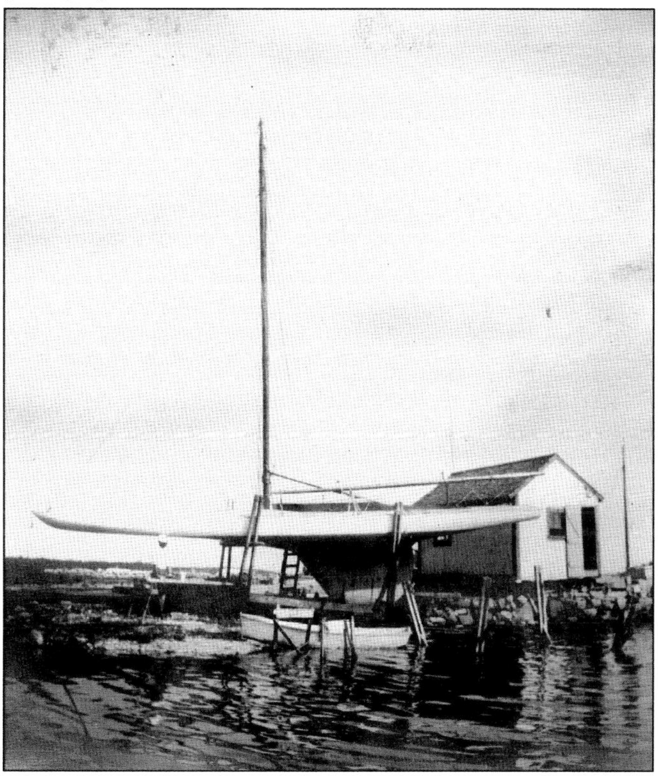

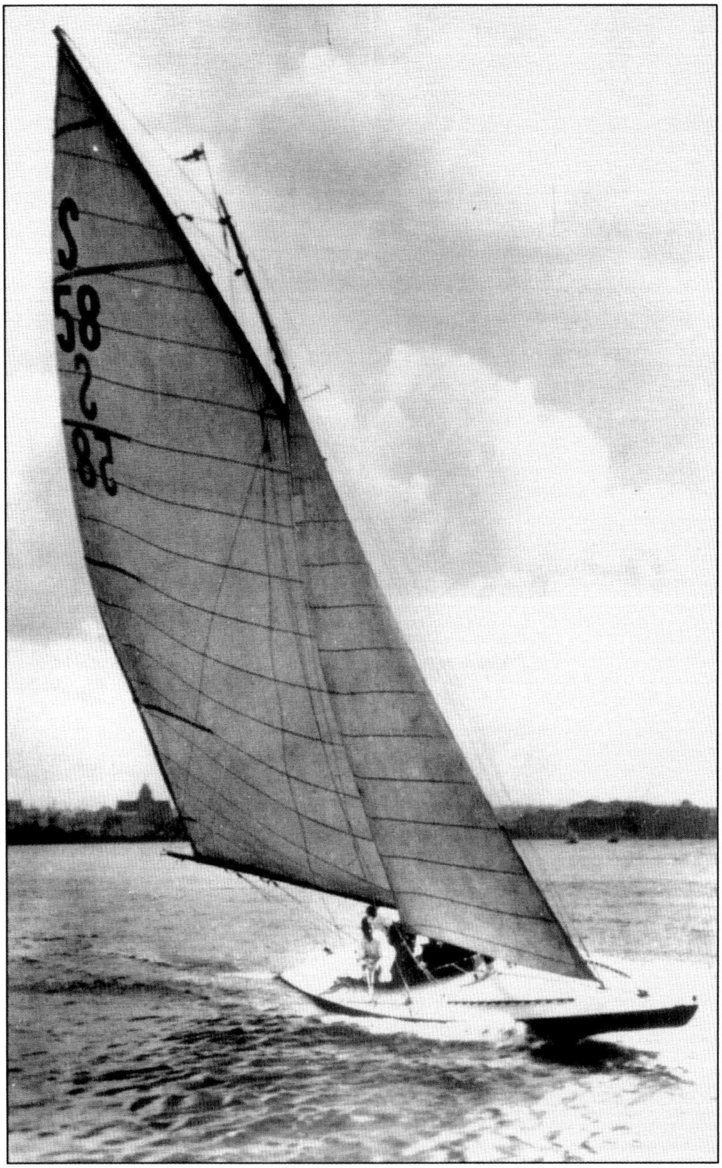

In the three international team races in Kiel, Germany, in June 1911, the American boats finished first, second, and third in the first race; first, second, and third in the second race; and first, second, and fourth in the third race. The two Beverly Yacht Club boats then raced against each other for the Kaiser Cup as the two highest scorers in the series. J. Lewis Stackpole, future Beverly Yacht Club commodore, won the competition. The Sonderklasse was restricted to 32 feet for the combined total of waterline length, extreme beam, and extreme depth. They were restricted as to displacement, a cost of $2,400 including two sets of sails, construction of hulls, and so on. The sail area was limited to 559 square feet. In the Buzzards Bay trials, the average waterline length was about 19.5 feet, the average overall length about 35 feet, the average beam 7.5 feet, and the average depth 5.25 feet. For the most part, the boats had deep keels, sharp bows, long overhangs, and gaff rigs. They had a small cockpit and were very fast under the right conditions. Races for this class were held regularly in Marion as part of the Beverly Yacht Club's racing program.

Six

BUTLER'S POINT AND KITTANSETT CLUB 1913–1950

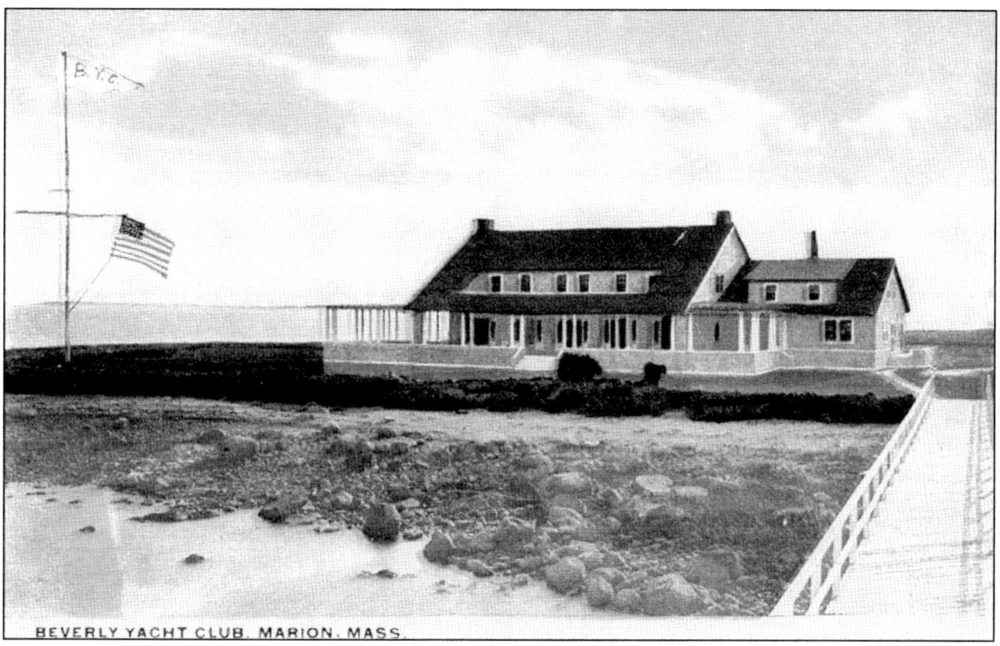

In January 1912, the Beverly Yacht Club purchased a point of land near Bird Island, known as Butler's (or Ruggle's) Point in Marion. The Beverly Yacht Club was incorporated on January 2, 1913, and a clubhouse and wharf were built at Butler's Point in Marion during the spring of that year. The Beverly Yacht Club left its Wing's Neck station because of its proximity to the Cape Cod Canal, whose lower channel crossed the starting line off the Wing's Neck Station.

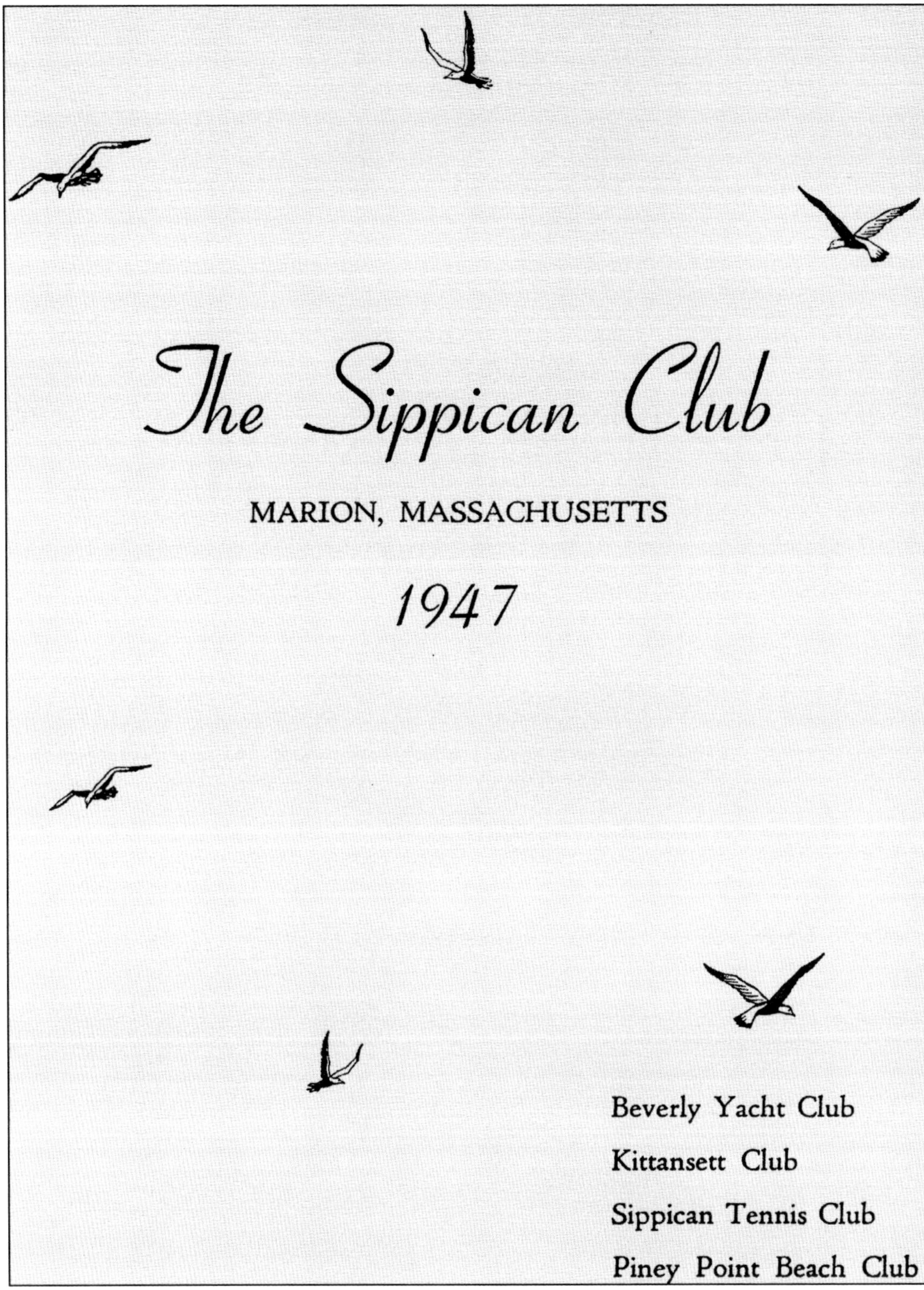

The Sippican Club

MARION, MASSACHUSETTS

1947

Beverly Yacht Club

Kittansett Club

Sippican Tennis Club

Piney Point Beach Club

After the 1938 hurricane destroyed the Beverly Yacht Club's Butler's Point location, the club moved to the winter house of the Kittansett Club. In 1946, after World War II, the Sippican Club of Marion was formed, and an agreement was made whereby the administration and finances of four Marion clubs—yachting, golf, tennis, and beach—were centralized. In 1949, the agreement was terminated, and the Beverly Yacht Club sent out its own dues bills for membership and handled its own financial affairs once again.

Appearing in the late 1930s, the Yankee one-design class was the product of a designing competition and resulted in a collaboration between the two winning designs. The committee of yachtsmen headed by Waldo H. Brown of Boston wanted a "high, dry, and able" boat that would "stand up and take it" (be able to sail in rough conditions) in the frequently choppy and breezy waters of Buzzards Bay. At the same time, the boat had to have the speed and handling qualities that would appeal to first-rate racing skippers and be economical to build and maintain. The first sloop was built in 1937 by Britt Brothers of Saugus. It was 30 feet 6 inches long overall, 24 feet at the waterline, and had a beam of 6 feet 6 inches and a draft of 4 feet 6 inches. This photograph shows Yankees racing in Buzzards Bay in 1937.

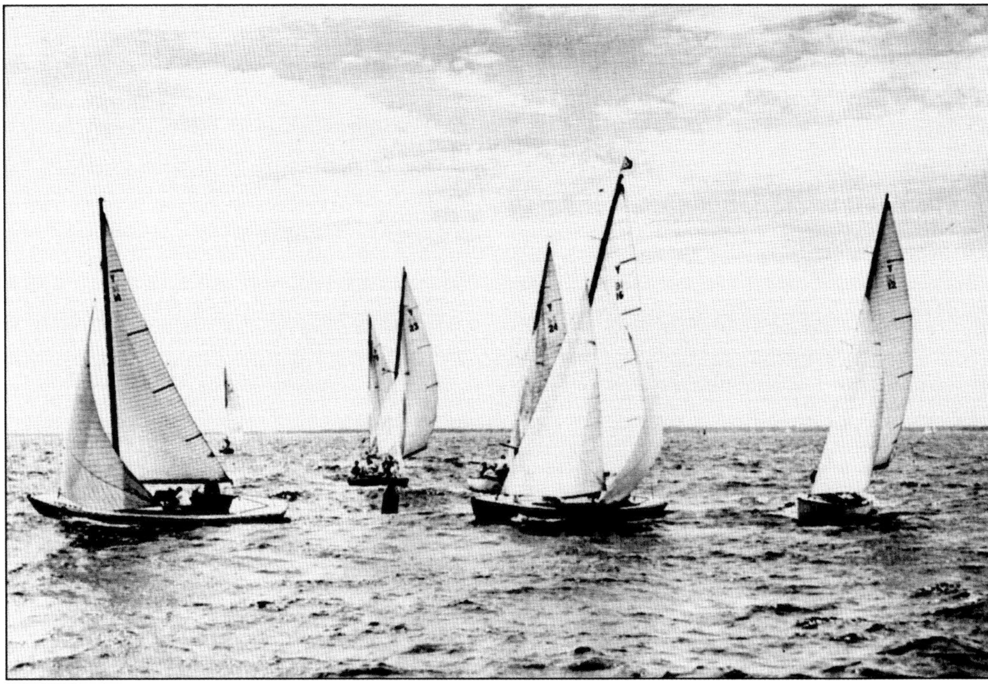

This photograph by noted marine photographer Norman Fortier shows Yankee one-designs rounding the leeward mark in a hotly contested race run by the Beverly Yacht Club in Buzzards Bay.

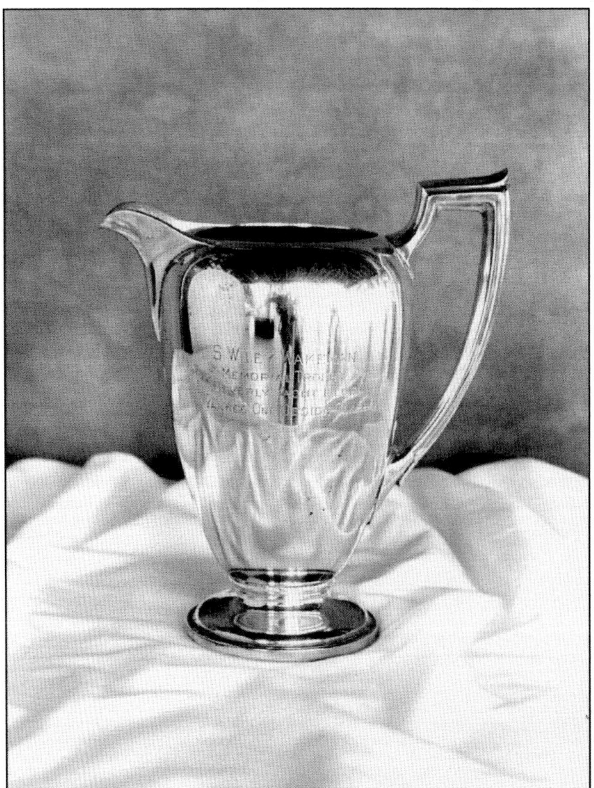

The S. Wiley Wakeman Memorial Trophy was given in 1946 to the Beverly Yacht Club by the family of S. Wiley Wakeman in his memory. The trophy was originally given to the winner of the Yankee one-design class. In 1946, the trophy was won by the *Monsoon*, owned by Richard V. Wakeman. In 1947, 1948, and 1949, it was won by W. Davis Taylor, who also won the trophy again in 1952 with John H. Cunningham Jr. When the Yankee one-design class died out, the trophy was awarded to the International 110 class from 1955 to 1966. When that class died out, the trophy was awarded to the Tempest class from 1967 to 1970. Today the trophy is awarded to the owner of the boat with the best score in the Beverly Yacht Club regatta as calculated by the point-scoring system.

Seven

Barden's Boatyard 1950–1954

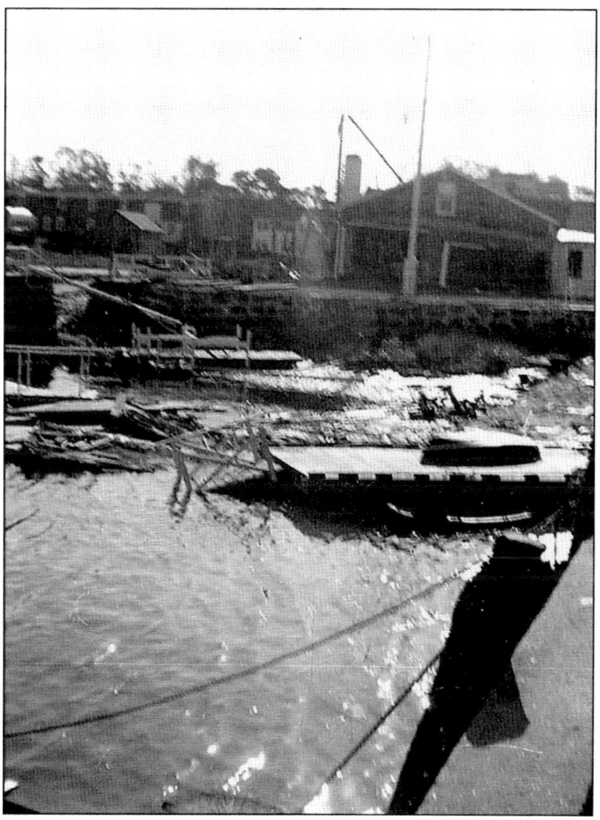

In 1950, the Beverly Yacht Club arranged to lease a new clubhouse at Barden's Boatyard, near the club's present location on Water Street in Marion Village. This photograph shows the Beverly Yacht Club clubhouse at Barden's Boatyard. The clubhouse had a large room with a fireplace and porch, a soda fountain bar, a small kitchen, and men's and women's bathrooms with showers in each. No hard liquor was served in the building because of the widespread use of the clubhouse by the junior program. The clubhouse was fully insulated so that it could be used during the winter by Beverly Yacht Club members. The facilities also included the exclusive use of Barden's pier and floats, with the exception of one for Barden's personal use. Races were started between Converse Point and Butler's Point. Beverly Yacht Club members also had courtesy moorings in Marion Harbor.

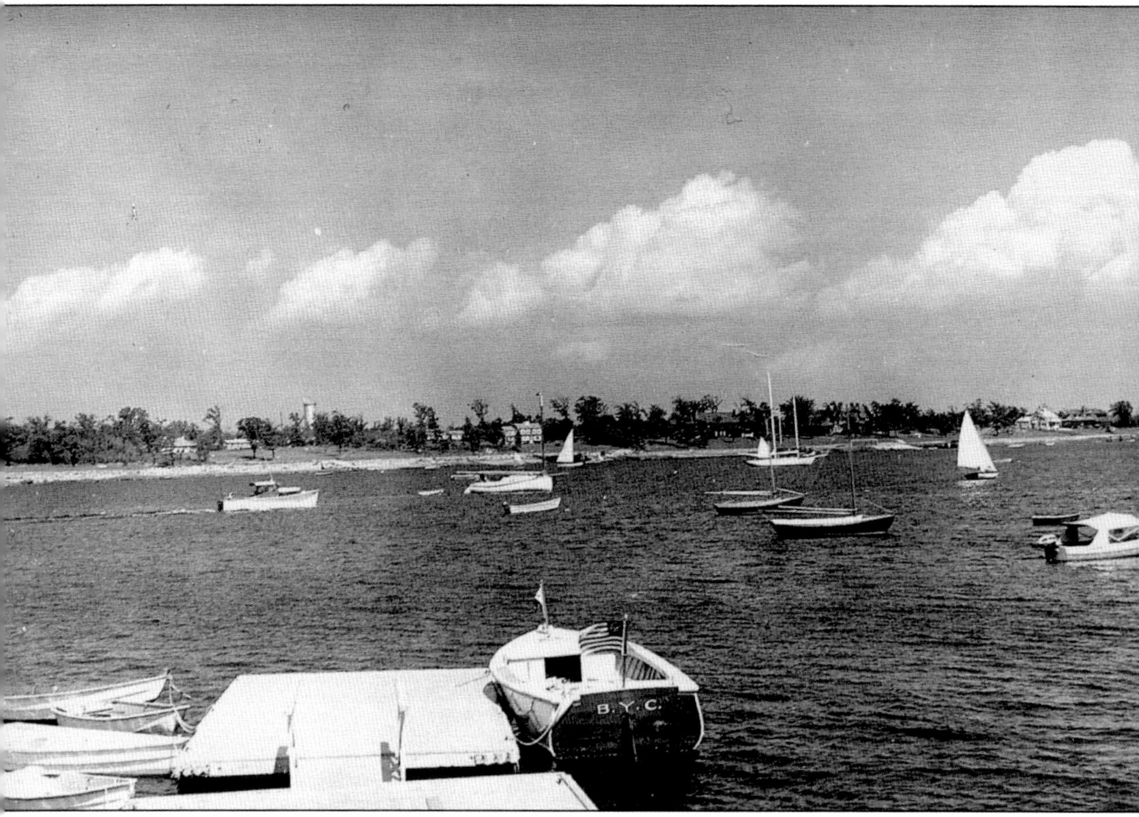

This photograph is a view of Sippican Harbor taken from the Beverly Yacht Club's pier at Barden's Boatyard in the early 1950s.

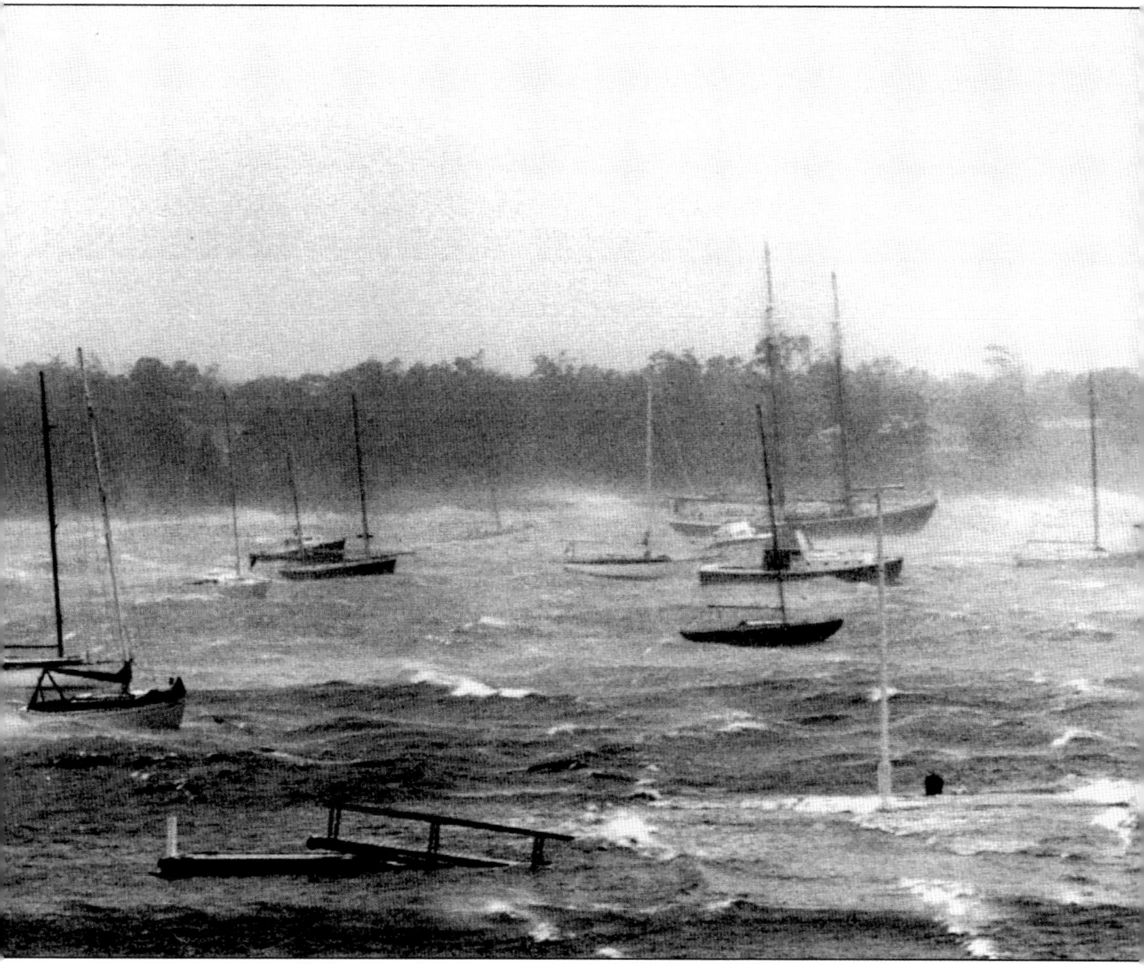

On August 31, 1954, Hurricane Carol struck, causing damage to many boats still in the water in Sippican Harbor.

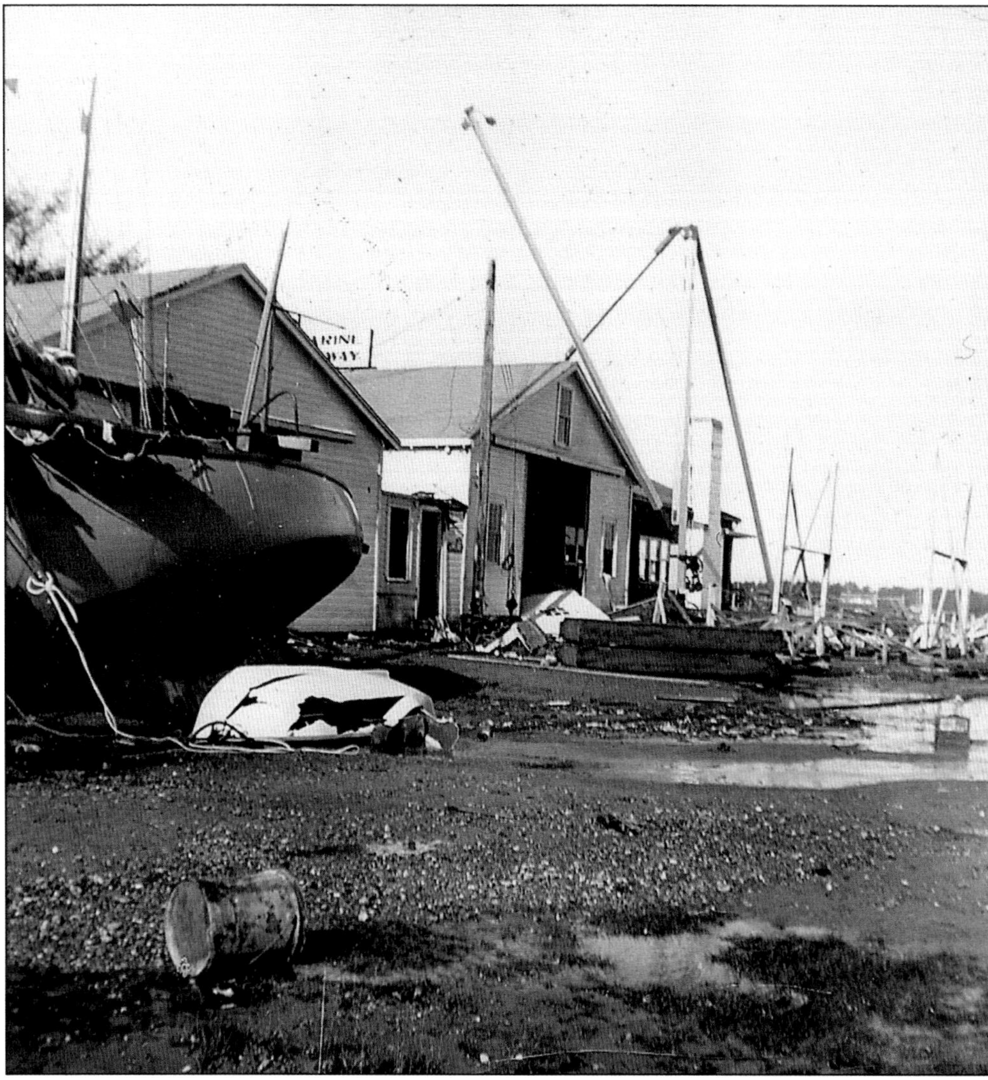

Hurricane Carol severely damaged the buildings in Barden's Boatyard, including the new location of the Beverly Yacht Club. Thus ended another era of the Beverly Yacht Club when its new quarters at Barden's were completely demolished by Hurricane Carol in 1954.

Eight

WATER STREET 1955–2006

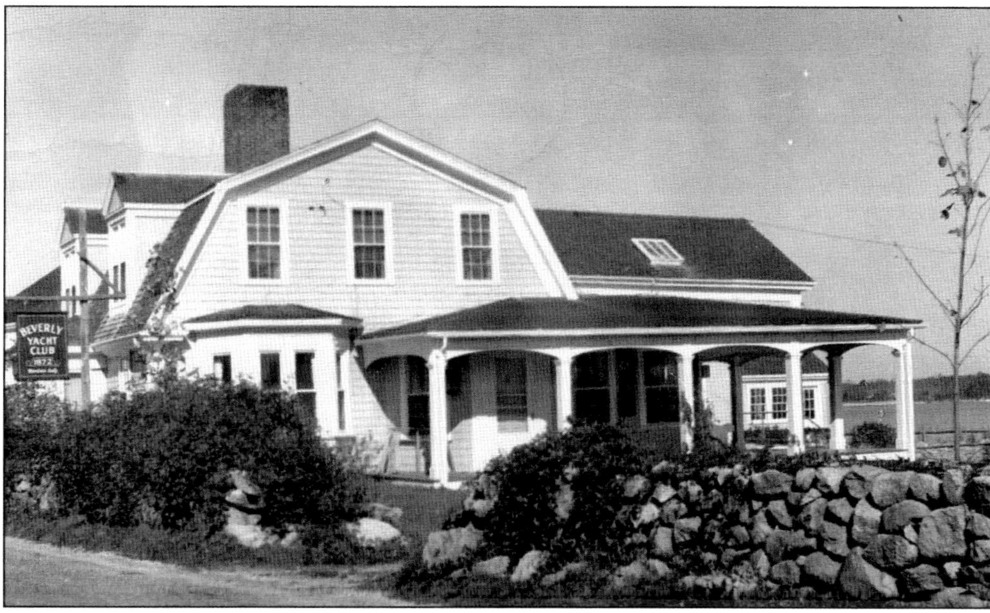

In 1955, the members of the Beverly Yacht Club purchased its present location at the end of Main and Water Streets in Marion. The historical house was built in 1806 as a ship chandler's store because of its location near Sherman's (or Central) Wharf (later called Long Wharf). Long Wharf was frequented often by whalers and was the home of Marion's last whaler, the *Admiral Blake*. This structure later became Sherman's Inn, a stagecoach stop on the Wareham-to-New Bedford route. In the 1870s, this building became the summer residence of Adm. Andrew A. Harwood, a great-grandson of Benjamin Franklin. Owned by Harwood's heirs in the early 1900s, it became the summer residence of Dr. William McDonald during the 1920s. Franklin D. Roosevelt sought Dr. McDonald's medical expertise after contracting polio in 1921 and visited him often. Certain Beverly Yacht Club members raised the necessary funds to purchase the home, which has been the Beverly Yacht Club clubhouse for over 50 years.

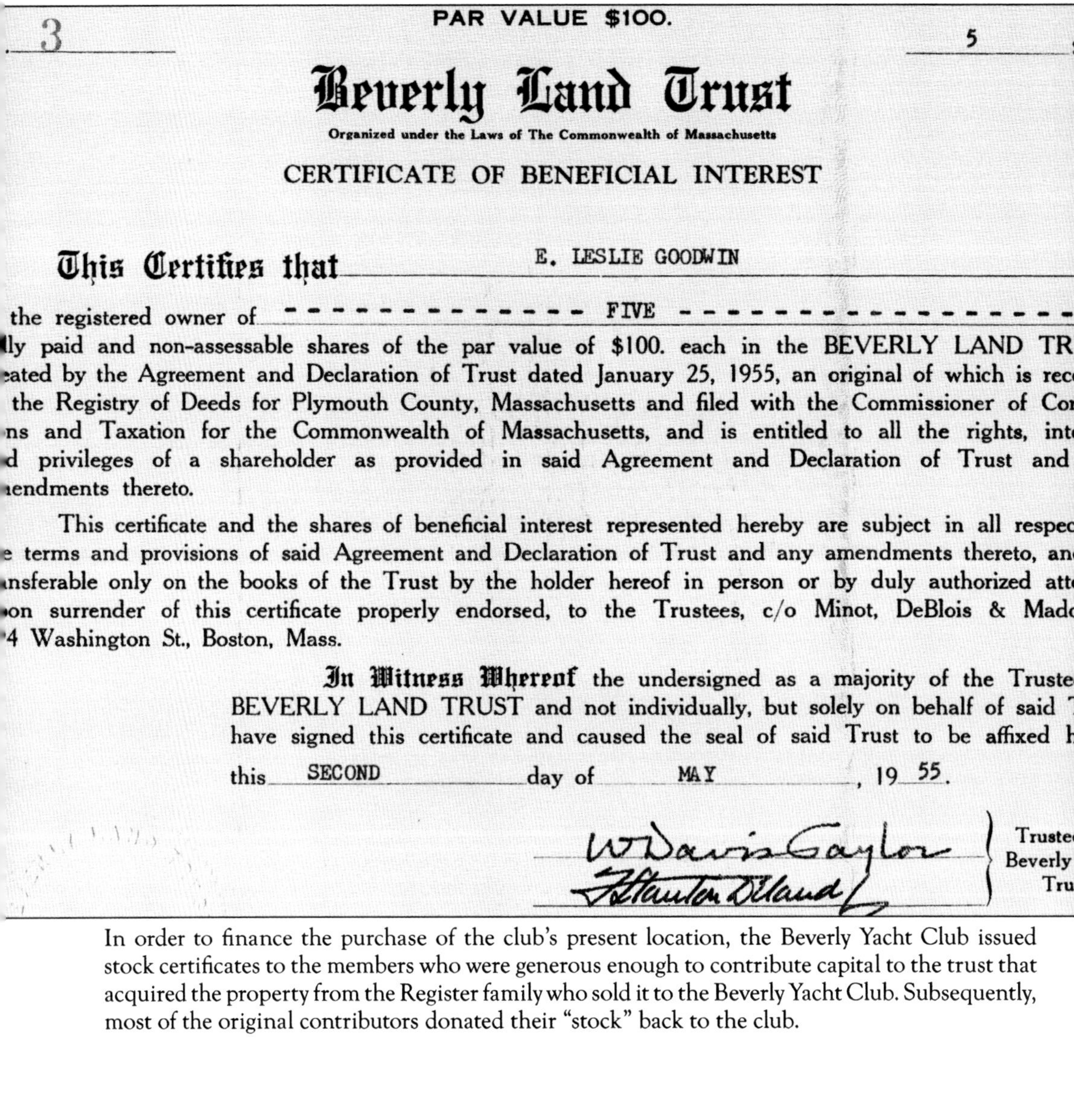

3 PAR VALUE $100. 5

Beverly Land Trust

Organized under the Laws of The Commonwealth of Massachusetts

CERTIFICATE OF BENEFICIAL INTEREST

This Certifies that E. LESLIE GOODWIN

the registered owner of - - - - - - - - - - - - - - FIVE - - - - - - - - - - - - - - - - -
lly paid and non-assessable shares of the par value of $100. each in the BEVERLY LAND TR
eated by the Agreement and Declaration of Trust dated January 25, 1955, an original of which is rec
the Registry of Deeds for Plymouth County, Massachusetts and filed with the Commissioner of Co
ns and Taxation for the Commonwealth of Massachusetts, and is entitled to all the rights, int
d privileges of a shareholder as provided in said Agreement and Declaration of Trust and
nendments thereto.

This certificate and the shares of beneficial interest represented hereby are subject in all respec
e terms and provisions of said Agreement and Declaration of Trust and any amendments thereto, an
nsferable only on the books of the Trust by the holder hereof in person or by duly authorized att
on surrender of this certificate properly endorsed, to the Trustees, c/o Minot, DeBlois & Madd
4 Washington St., Boston, Mass.

In Witness Whereof the undersigned as a majority of the Truste
BEVERLY LAND TRUST and not individually, but solely on behalf of said
have signed this certificate and caused the seal of said Trust to be affixed h
this SECOND day of MAY, 19 55.

W Davis Gaylor
Stanton Deland
Truste
Beverly
Tru

In order to finance the purchase of the club's present location, the Beverly Yacht Club issued stock certificates to the members who were generous enough to contribute capital to the trust that acquired the property from the Register family who sold it to the Beverly Yacht Club. Subsequently, most of the original contributors donated their "stock" back to the club.

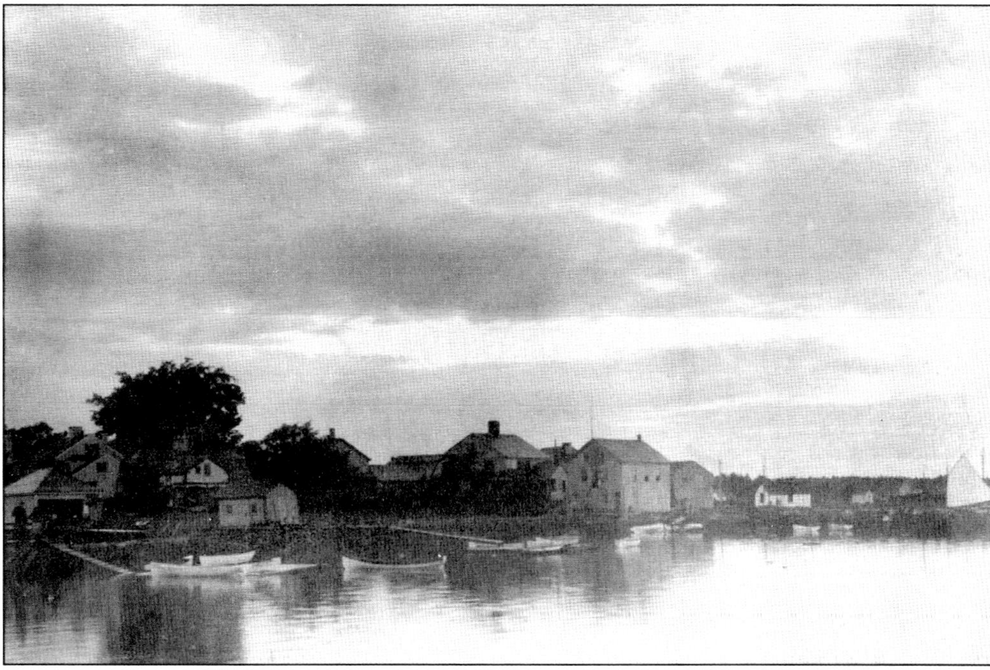

This 1886 photograph by Wilbur G. Preston, a Boston architect, shows the present clubhouse, on the left, when it was the prior home of Adm. Andrew A. Harwood, a retired Civil War veteran.

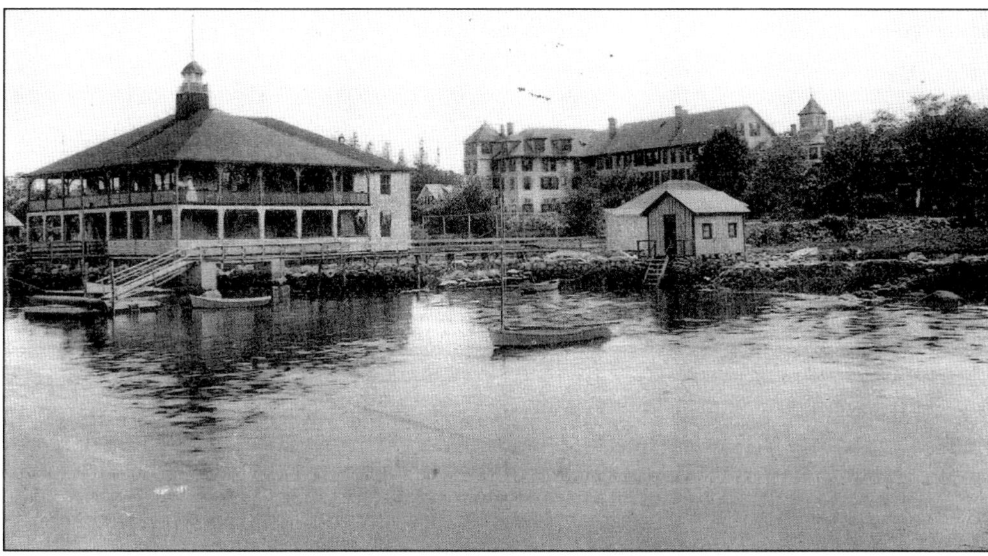

This photograph shows the Sippican Hotel (the large building in the rear middle of the photograph), which was located on Harbor Lane, now called Water Street, just steps from the present location of the Beverly Yacht Club. Many of Marion's summer visitors stayed at the Sippican Hotel. Henry James described this hotel in *The Bostonians* as a "shabby and depressing hostelry that suggested an early bed time." However, many of the hotel guests fell in love with Marion and subsequently built large shingle-style summer residences in Marion. The casino, where dances were held, is located on the left of this photograph (taken around 1900) and was next door to the Beverly Yacht Club's present location. The Sippican Hotel and the casino were torn down in the 1920s, long before the Beverly Yacht Club moved to its present location.

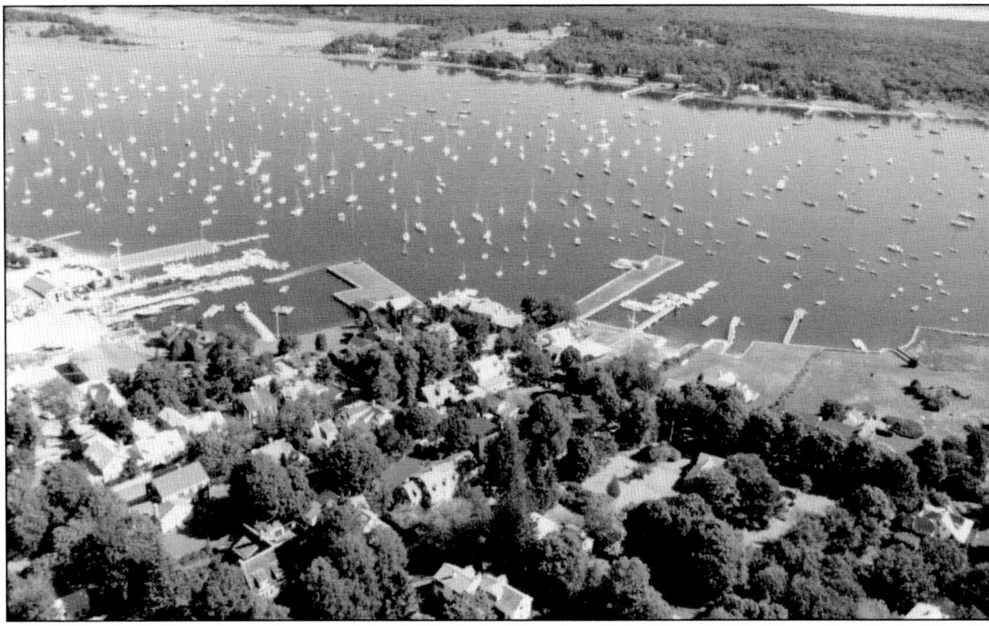

This aerial view of Sippican Harbor shows the Beverly Yacht Club's pier and floats. Because of its fine facilities at the new station on Water Street in Marion and the similarity between sailing conditions in Buzzards Bay and Melbourne, Australia, the Beverly Yacht Club was chosen as the site for races to select United States representatives in three classes for the 1956 Olympics. The elimination races started in May with two-person dinghy races, the one-person dinghies raced in June, and the 5.5-meter races brought out a large spectator fleet to follow the boats through their series in August. Because of the tremendous cooperation and interest on the part of the membership in this undertaking, the eliminations ran smoothly and efficiently, and the Beverly Yacht Club was warmly congratulated.

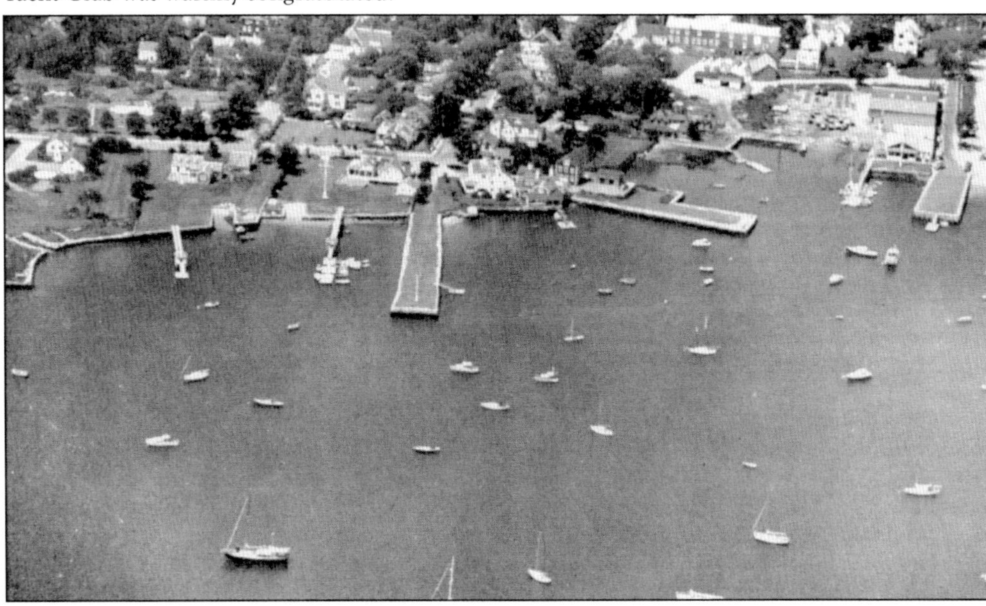

Another aerial view of Marion Inner Harbor reveals the ideal location of the Beverly Yacht Club for the past 50 years.

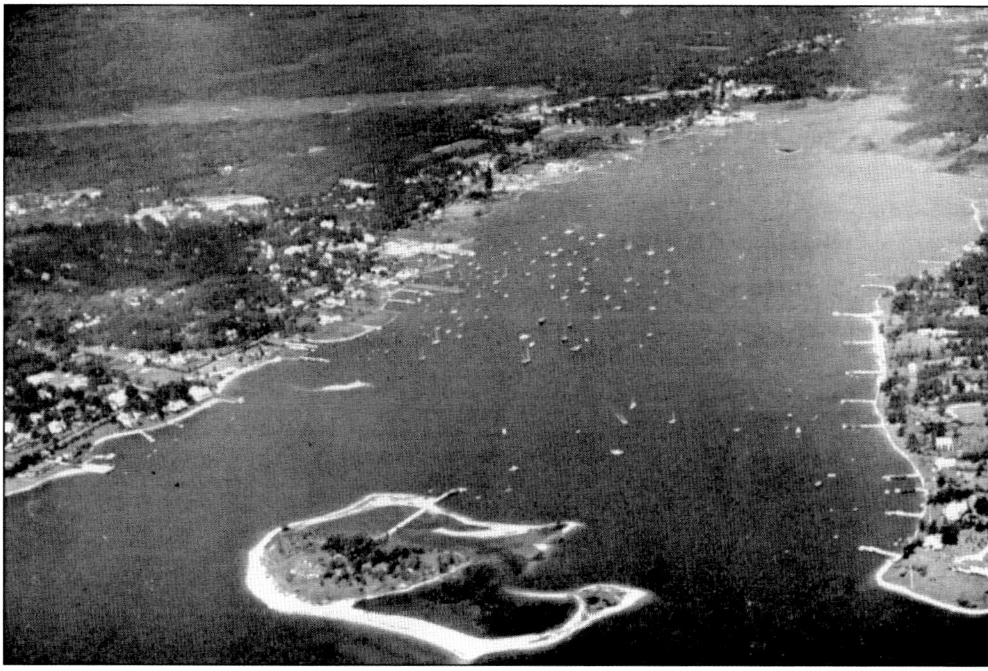

This aerial view of Sippican Harbor comes from the Beverly Yacht Club's archives. The club is located on the left side of the harbor, approximately in the middle.

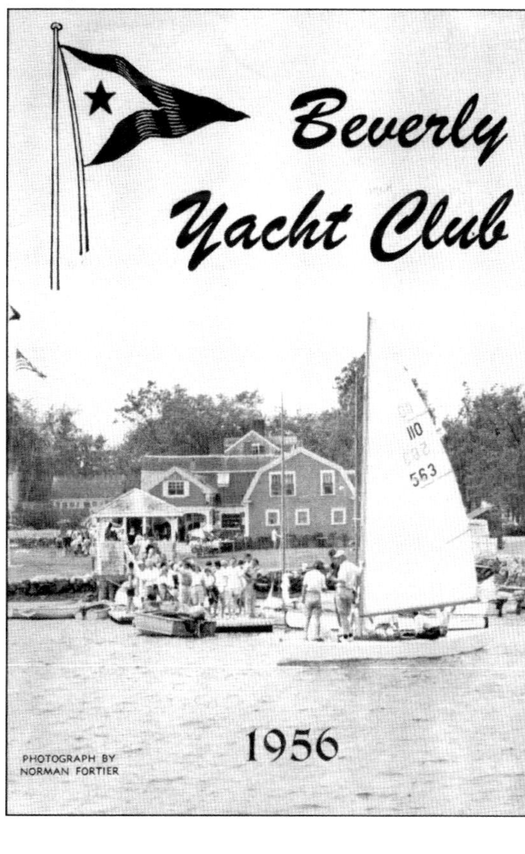

The cover of the Beverly Yacht Club's 1956 yearbook was a photograph taken by noted local photographer Norman Fortier. It shows the new clubhouse, taken from Sippican Harbor. The boat is a 110. In 1958, the club was the host for the International 110 Atlantic Coast Championship, which was won by Bill Saltonstall, a Beverly Yacht Club skipper.

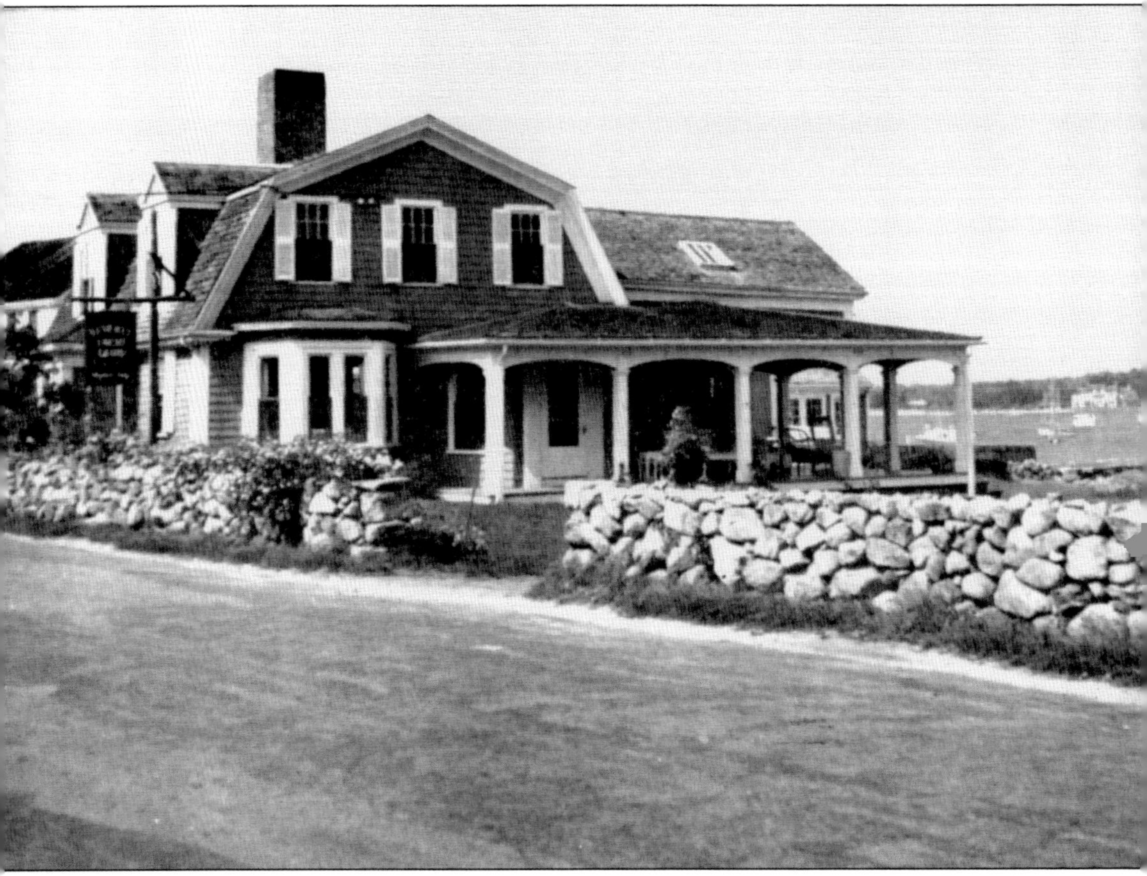

This photograph of the Beverly Yacht Club was taken before the new porch was added to the water side in 1999 to accommodate dining and club events.

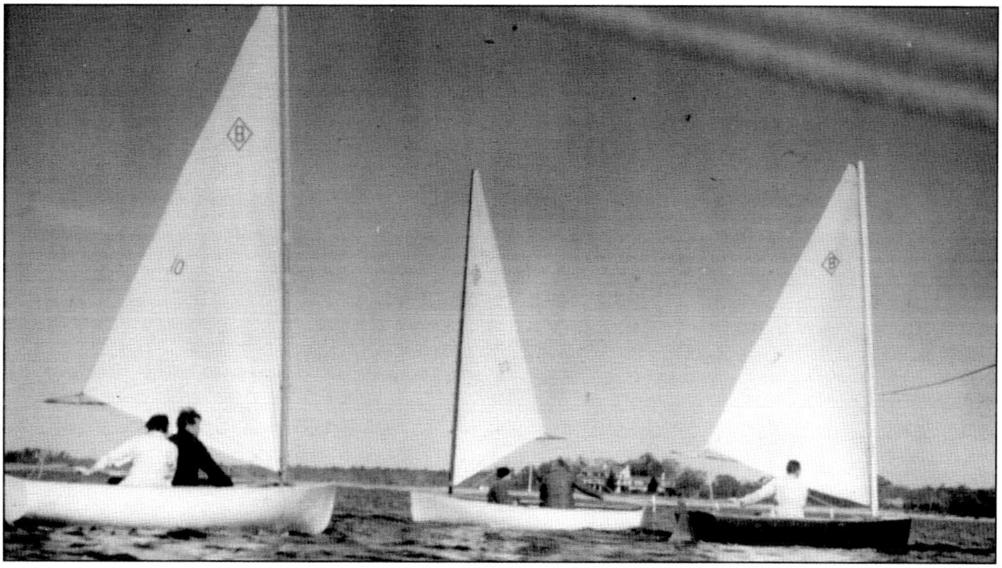

Sydney Herreshoff, the son of Nathanael Herreshoff, designed the Beverly Yacht Club dinghy, which appeared in 1951. The Beverly dinghy was the last in a long line of Beverly Yacht Club classes carrying the Herreshoff name. Because of the dinghy custom of several short races in a day, plus the advanced design of the rig and hull, the boat was especially popular to teach racing tactics, rules, trim, and weight.

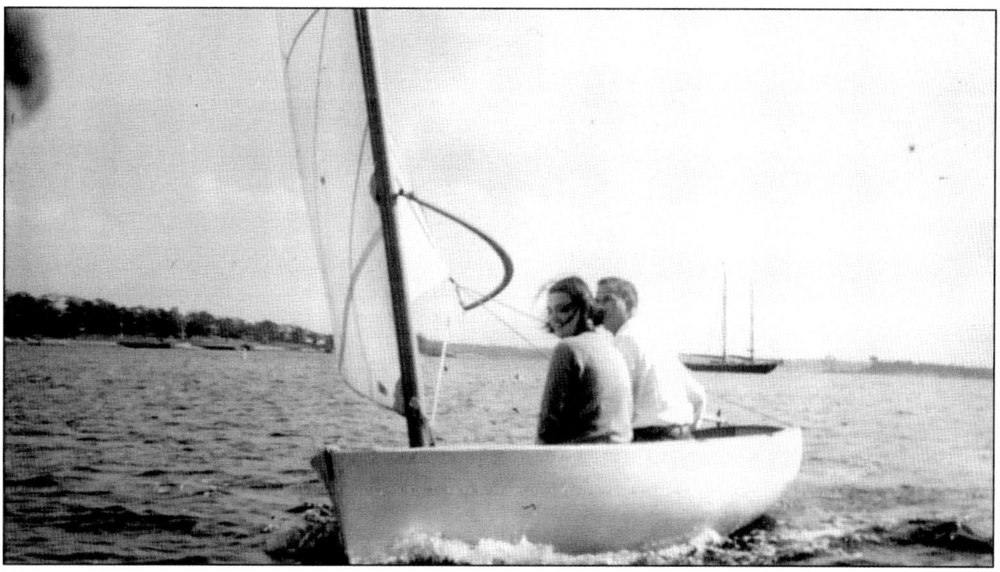

This photograph shows Beverly Yacht Club members Kitty Hill Stanton and Jack Stanton (whose family owned Berkshire Hathaway before Warren Buffet purchased it) racing a Beverly dinghy. The Beverly dinghy was adapted by the club to its training program, through the purchase of six boats, with a redesigned aluminum spar and cut-down sail area. Serving as headquarters for the little fleet was the "Clark gazebo," a combination float, clubhouse, storage and repair facility, judge's stand, diving platform, coaching base, lifeguard station, "church pulpit," and widow's walk. Anchored in a prominent spot in the harbor, this craft acted as sort of a mother hen for the dinghy racing and training program. The little dinghies, which sometimes held three small life-jacketed sailors, provided a continual round of spirited and sometimes noisy competition.

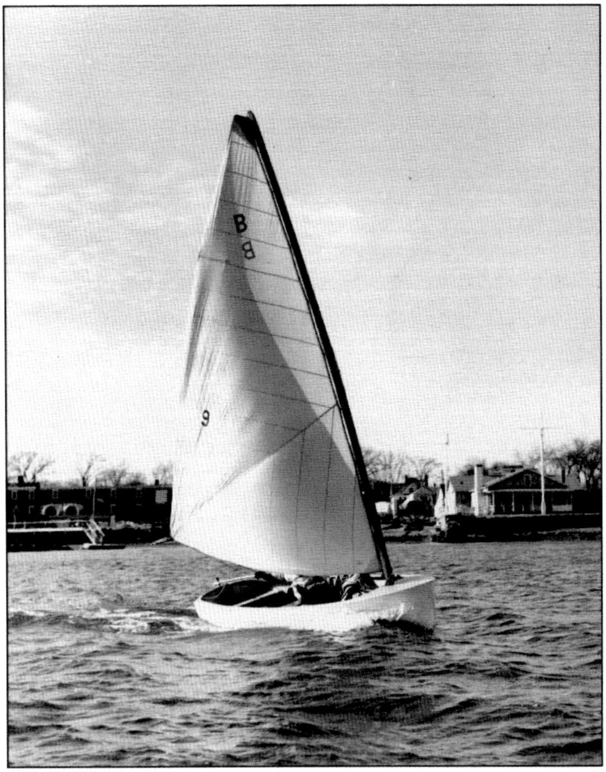

A Beverly dinghy races off the Beverly Yacht Club clubhouse in this photograph from the club's historical records.

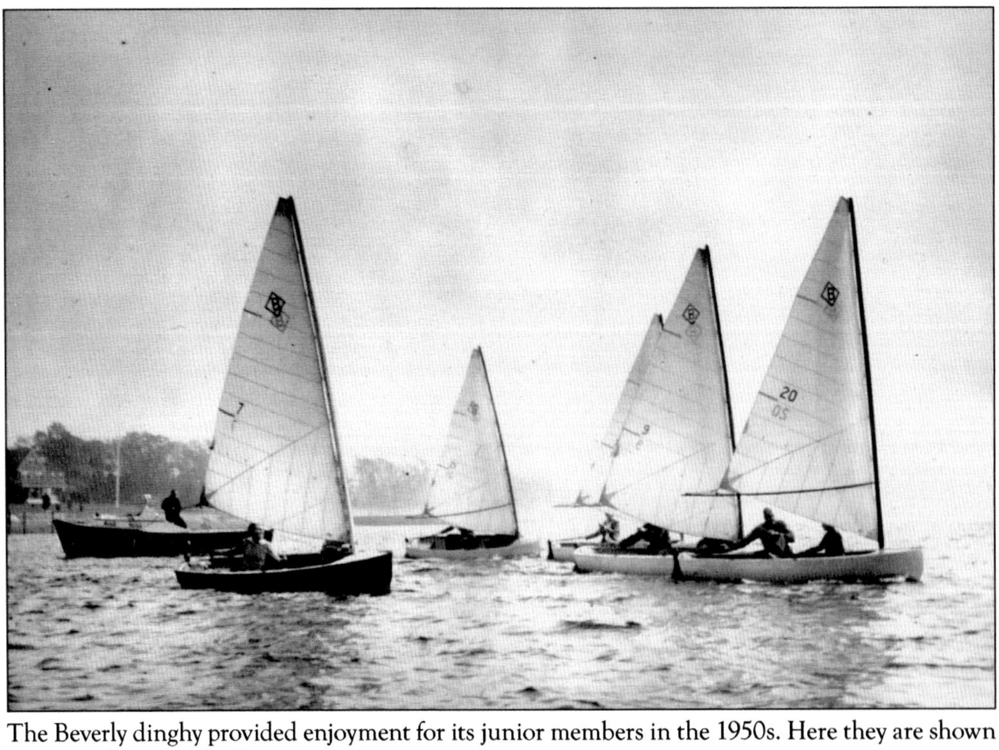

The Beverly dinghy provided enjoyment for its junior members in the 1950s. Here they are shown racing in the inner harbor.

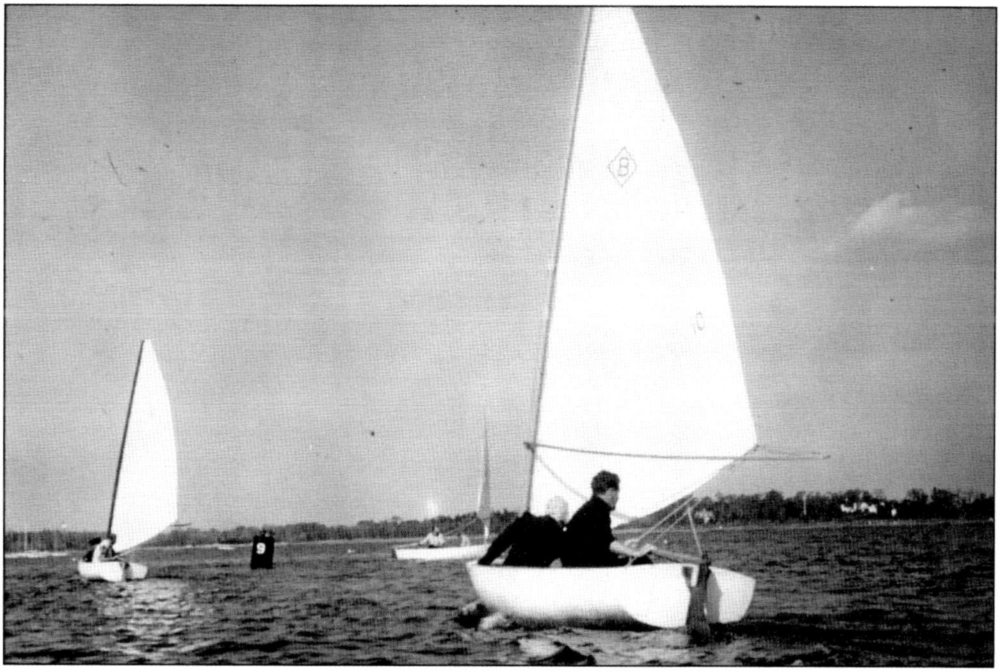

The Beverly dinghies approach a racing mark.

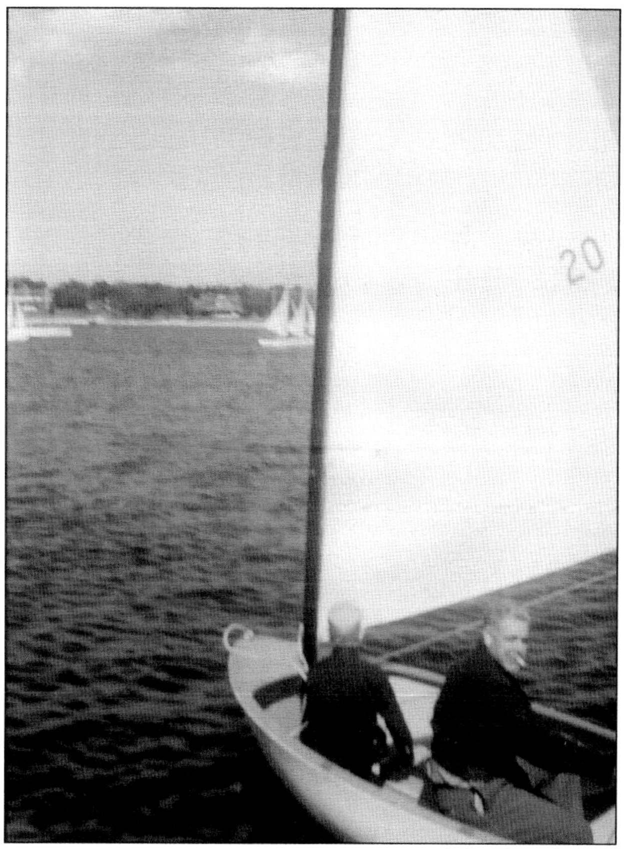

Prior commodore Rick Angle (1971–1973) races in a Beverly dinghy in 1951.

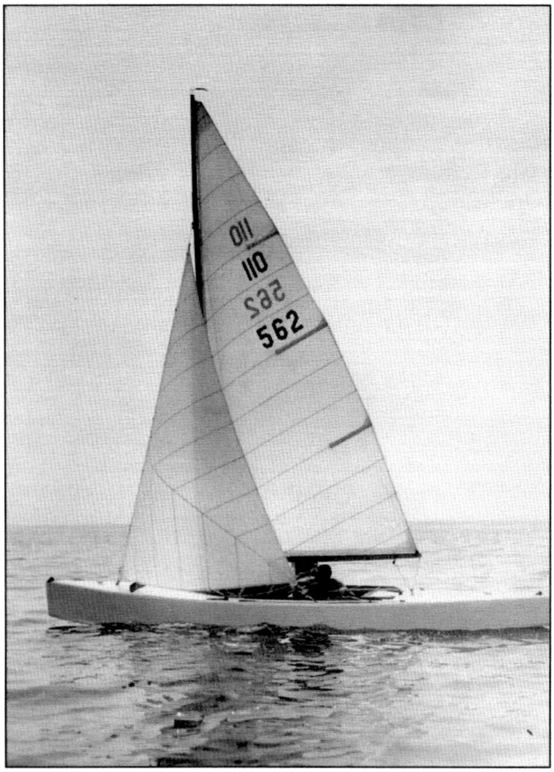

This photograph shows a 110 racing in Buzzards Bay in the 1950s. The 110s, designed by Raymond Hunt, were first raced at the Beverly Yacht Club in 1955. They proved to be an inexpensive racing machine and provided excellent training in racing tactics and the handling of light sails. They were sailed almost exclusively by younger members. They provided a class somewhat sportier than the 12 footer but were less expensive and with most of the racing characteristics of much larger craft. In 1958, the club hosted the International 110 Atlantic Coast Championship, which was won by Beverly Yacht Club member Bill Saltonstall. The 110s are no longer raced at the Beverly Yacht Club, but they served the club well.

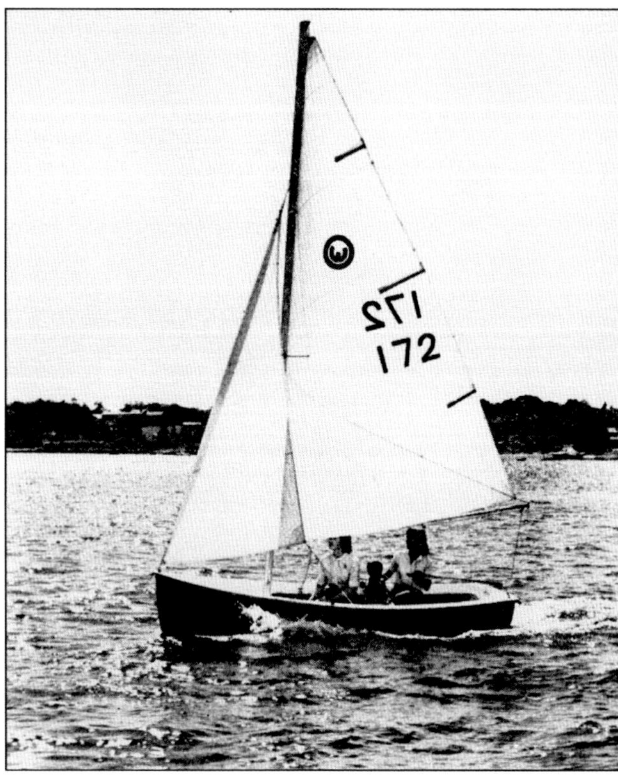

The Widgeon, a 12-foot-4-inch fiberglass centerboard boat with mainsail, jib, and spinnaker, came to the Beverly Yacht Club in 1968. There was a need for a new class of boat for juniors between 12 and 16. With the help of Liz Kowlton, the O'Day Widgeon was picked, and there were 13 of them racing in 1968 and 20 in 1969. In the first Beverly Yacht Club junior regatta in 1968, 18 out of 92 entries were Widgeons, and the first three places went to Beverly Yacht Club skippers. This class is no longer raced at the Beverly Yacht Club today.

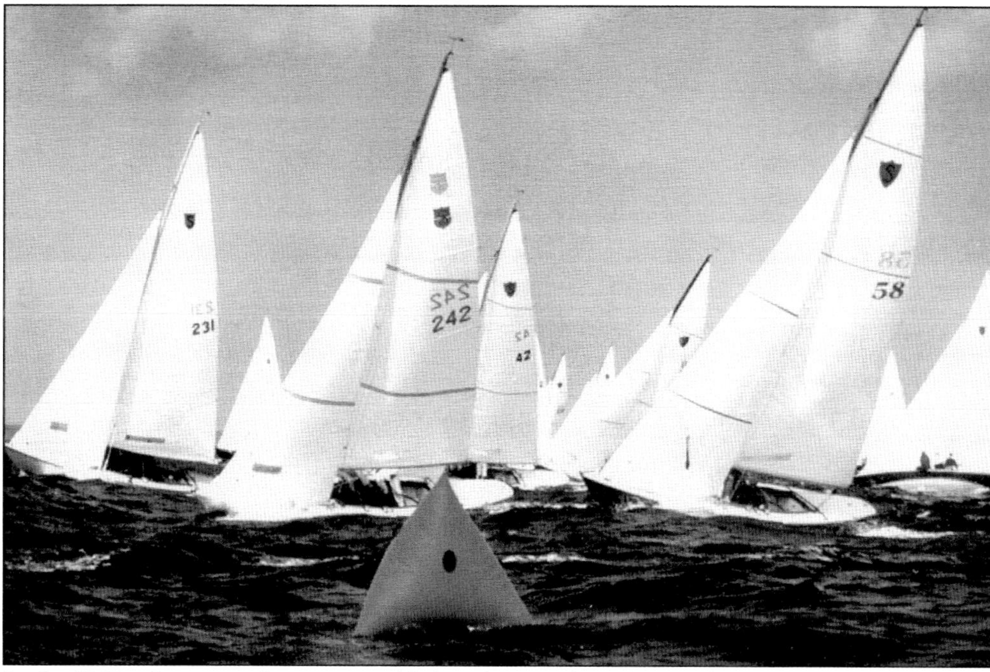

In the 1960s, three new classes were added to the Beverly Yacht Club's racing schedule: Tempests, Shields, and Widgeons. A number of club members felt that there was a need for a larger one-design class to fill the void created by the loss of the Yankees. The 30-foot Shields class first raced at the Beverly Yacht Club in the summer of 1968. The classic design of the Shields handled well in the fresh winds and steep chop of Buzzards Bay. This photograph shows Shields racing.

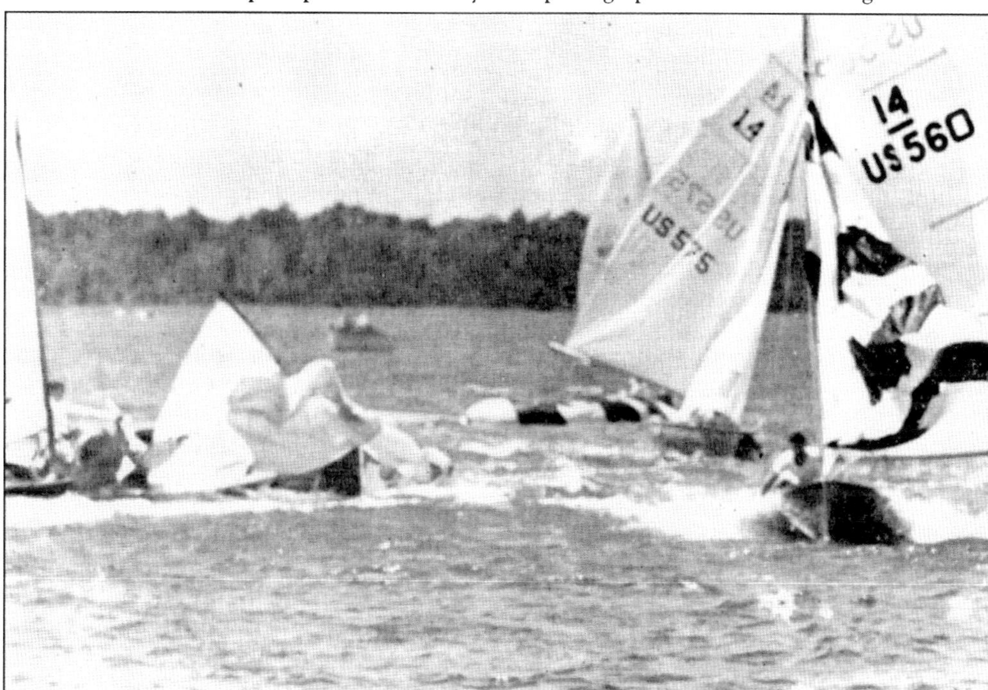

This photograph shows International 14s racing for the invitational Buzzards Bay Bowl.

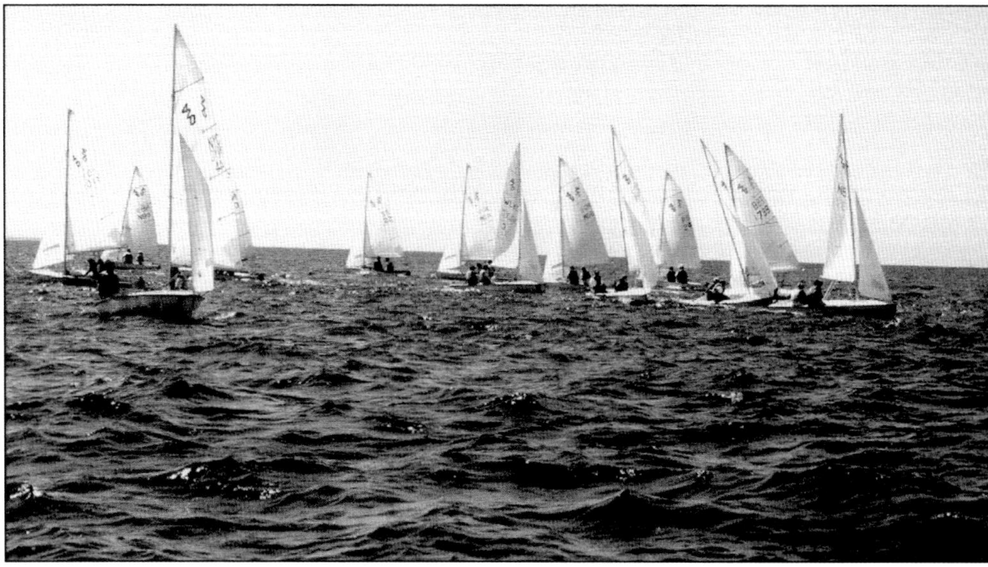

The Beverly Yacht Club junior sailing program has trained many of the club's championship sailors. The junior program hosts a junior regatta where over 200 boats participate from all over Buzzards Bay, Cape Cod, and the islands. The junior program currently trains sailors in Optimists and 420s. The 420 is fast and requires high athletic skill. The 420 is also used in collegiate sailing programs nationwide. This photograph shows 420s racing in the junior regatta held in August each summer in Sippican Harbor.

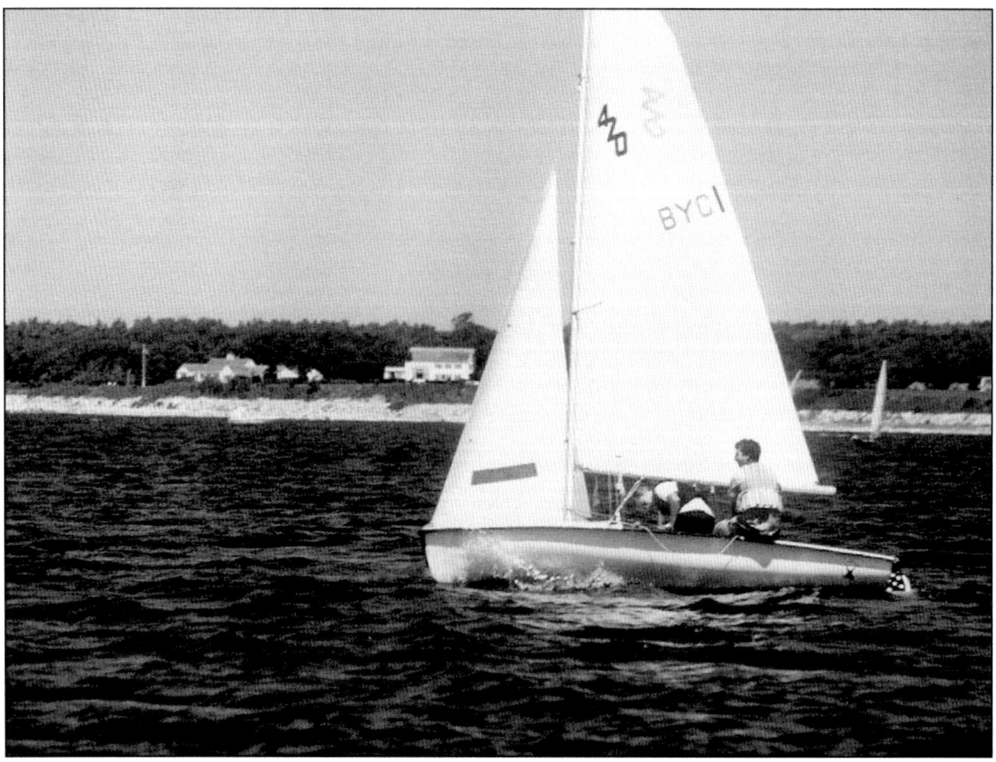

This photograph shows a 420 racing in the outer harbor.

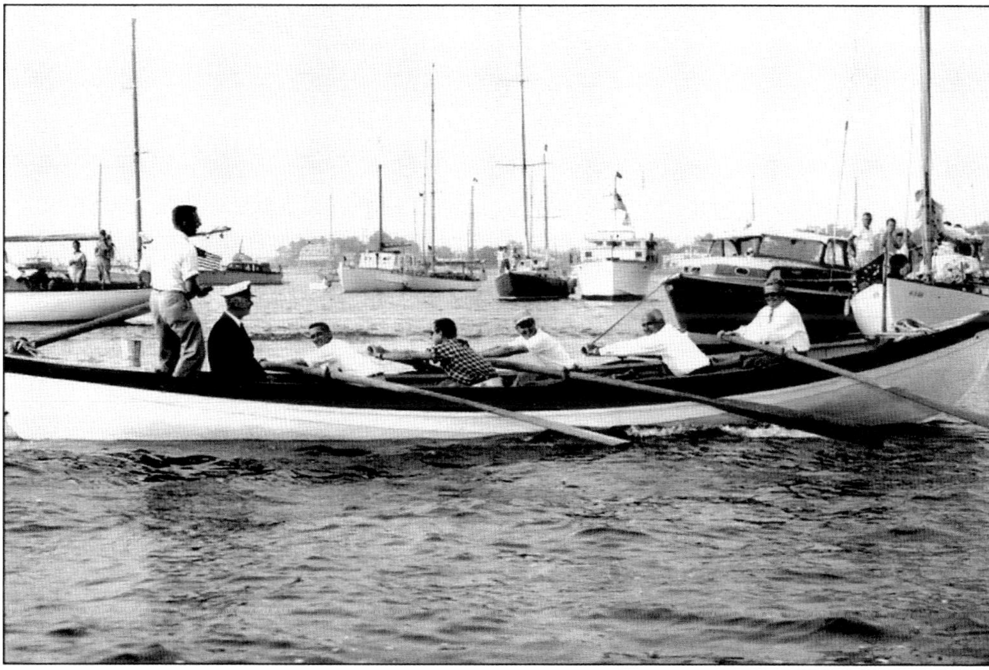

Over the years, many yacht clubs have visited the Beverly Yacht Club on their summer cruises. They are always warmly welcomed. This photograph shows prior Beverly Yacht Club commodore Lucius Hill being rowed out in the late 1950s to greet a visiting fleet.

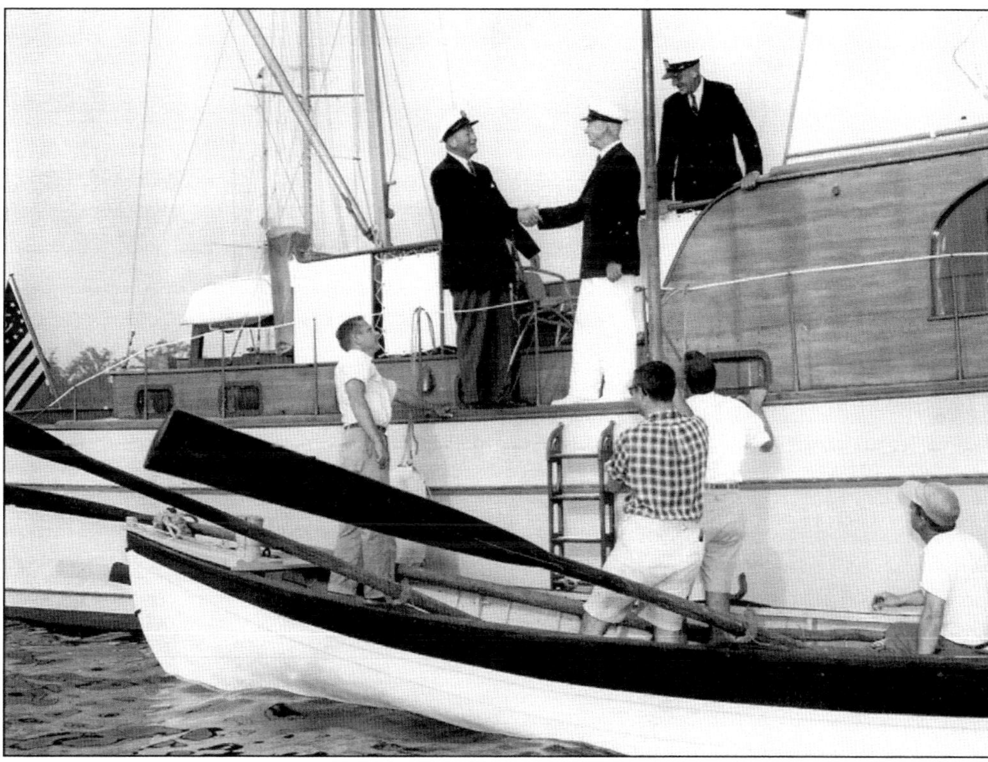

Prior commodore Lucius Hill welcomes the New York Yacht Club commodore in the late 1950s.

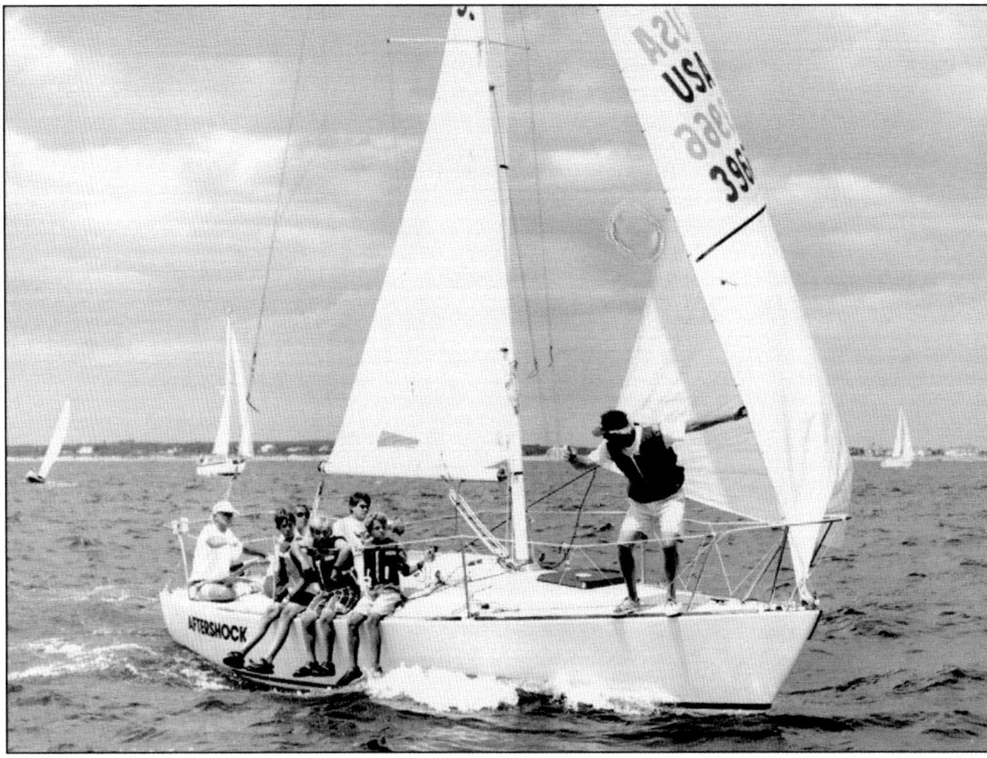

In 1997, the Beverly Yacht Club celebrated its 125th anniversary by holding a 125th anniversary regatta and celebration. This photograph shows junior members crewing on a J24 during the celebration.

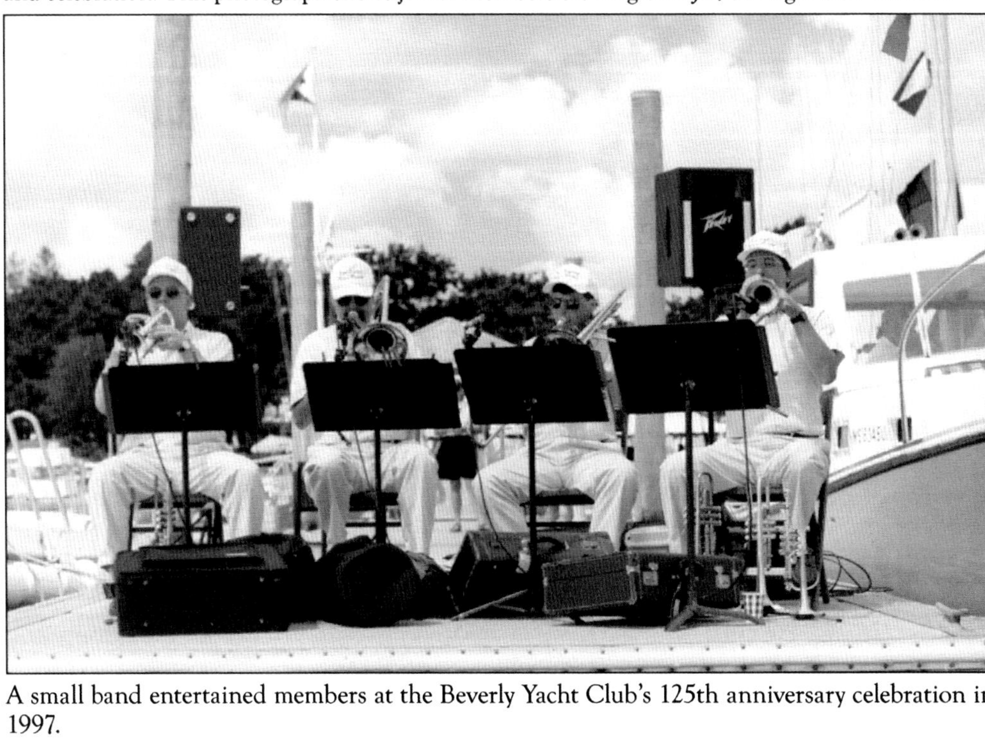

A small band entertained members at the Beverly Yacht Club's 125th anniversary celebration in 1997.

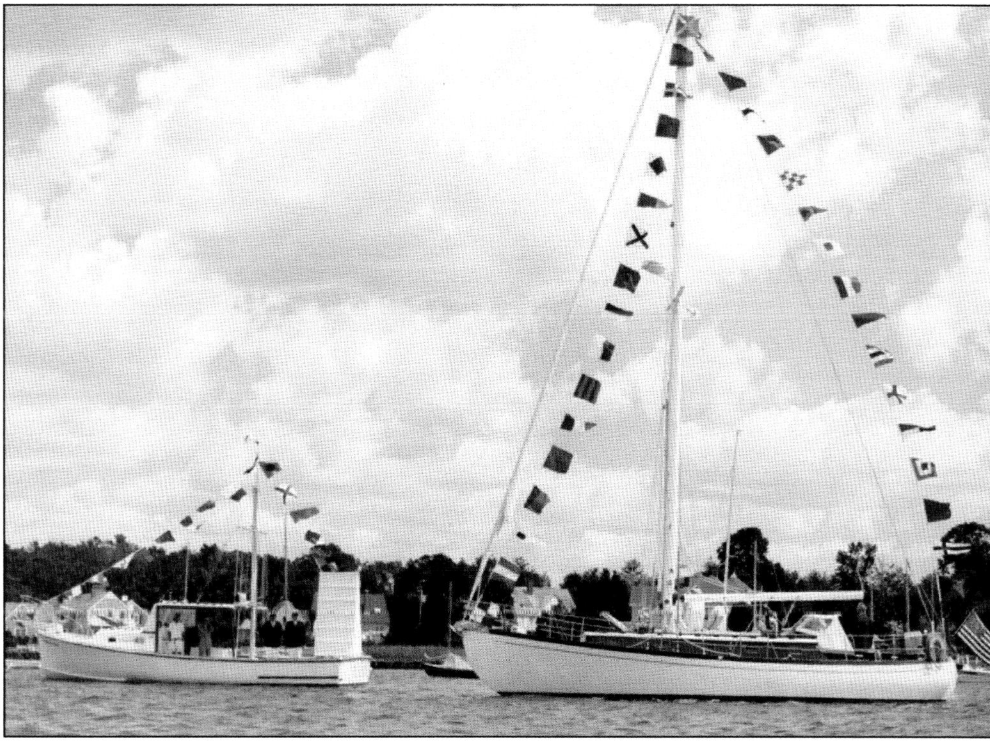

These photographs show the fleet review during the Beverly Yacht Club's 125th anniversary celebration.

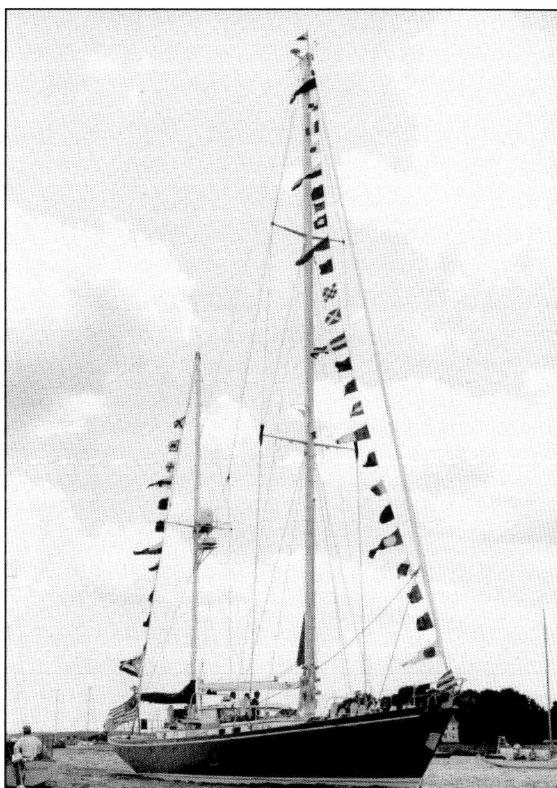

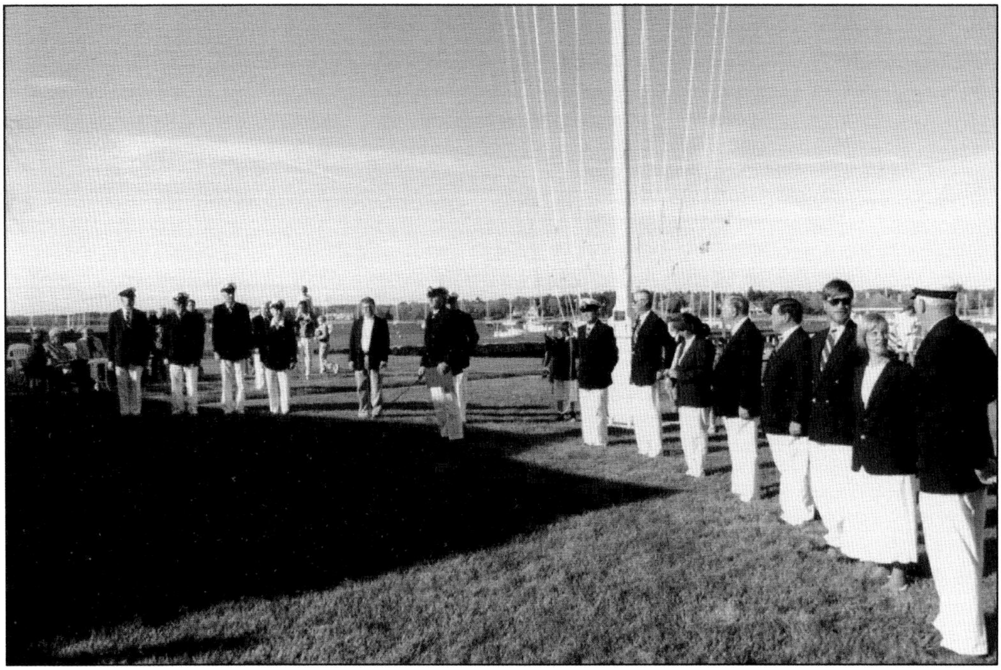

Past commodore Bill Moonan presided over the 125th anniversary celebration at the club's flag-raising ceremony in 1997.

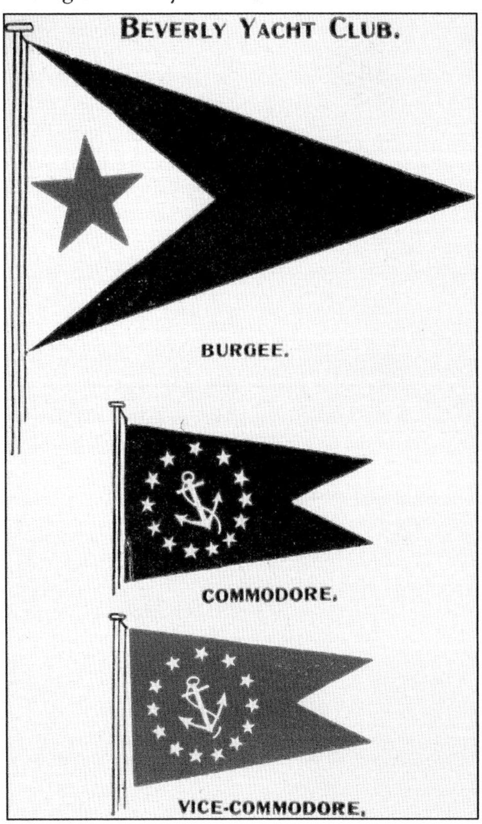

The Beverly Yacht Club's burgee was adopted in 1913.

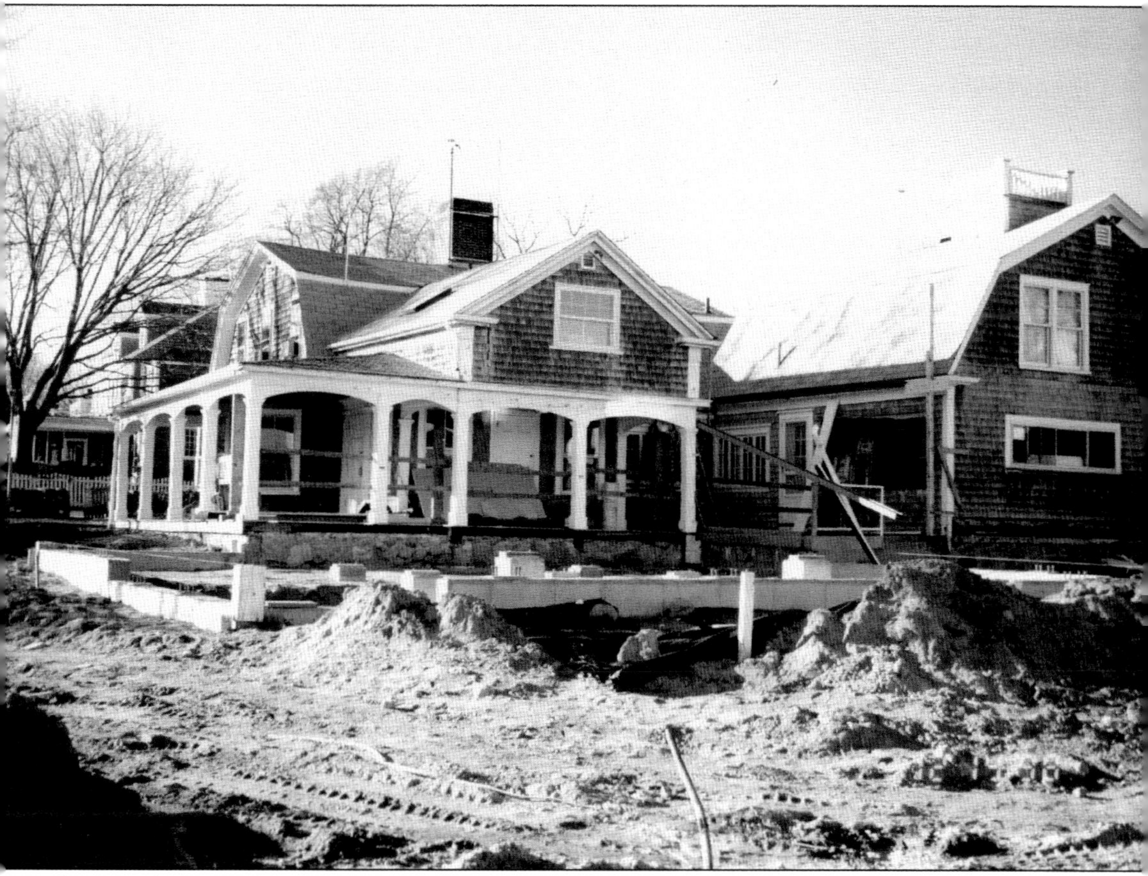

The Beverly Yacht Club added a new porch to its Water Street location in 1999 to accommodate the club's expanding activities for its members.

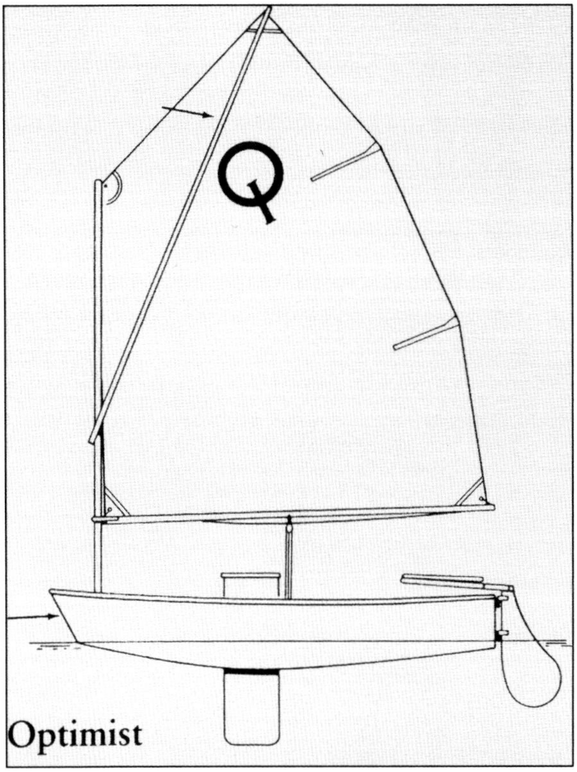

In 1989, the Beverly Yacht Club purchased Optimists for its beginning sailors in the junior program. The Optimist class, a popular and versatile training boat, is presently the fastest growing single-handed dinghy class in the United States. In 1996, the Beverly Yacht Club had the privilege of hosting the New England Optimist Championships.

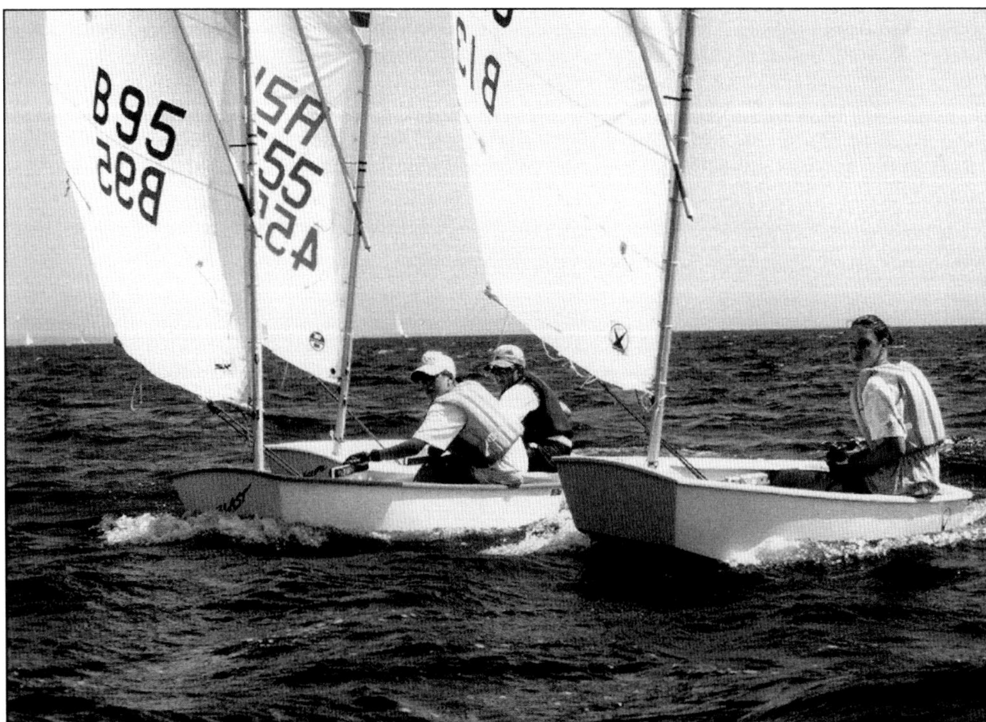

This photograph shows "Opties" racing in the Beverly Yacht Club junior program.

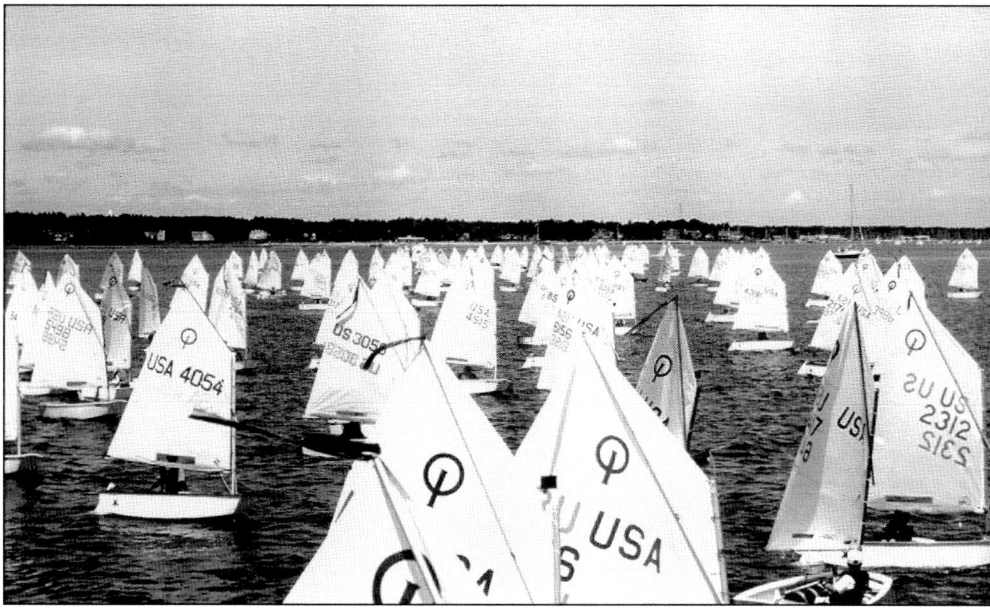

Multitudes of Optimists race in the Beverly Yacht Club junior regatta.

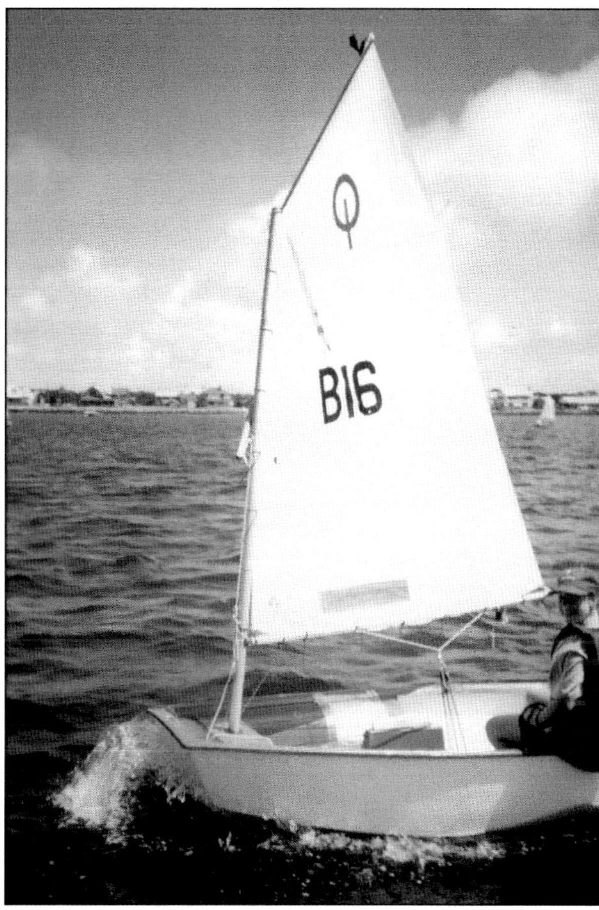

An Optimist is shown here sailing on a lovely day in the harbor.

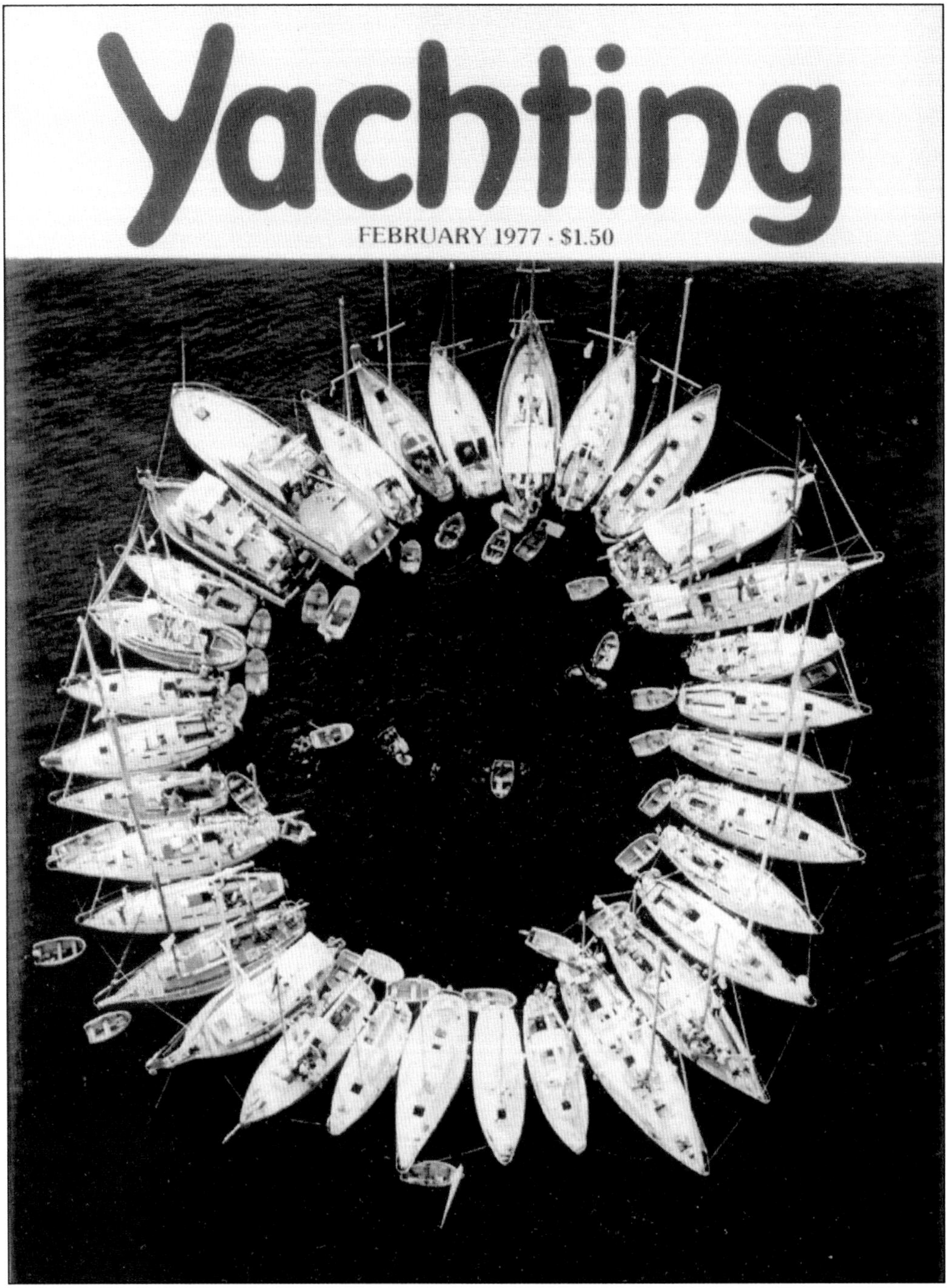

Many of the Beverly Yacht Club's members enjoy cruising, and its annual cruises frequently cruise to Maine. Harvey White, Beverly Yacht Club commodore from 1984 to 1986, and his wife, Dottie, started the annual cruising program at the Beverly Yacht Club in 1976. The boats that cruised the first year formed a "sunflower raft" when they entered Pretty Marsh Harbor in Maine on August 20, 1976. An aerial photograph was taken and appeared on the February 1977 cover of *Yachting* magazine.

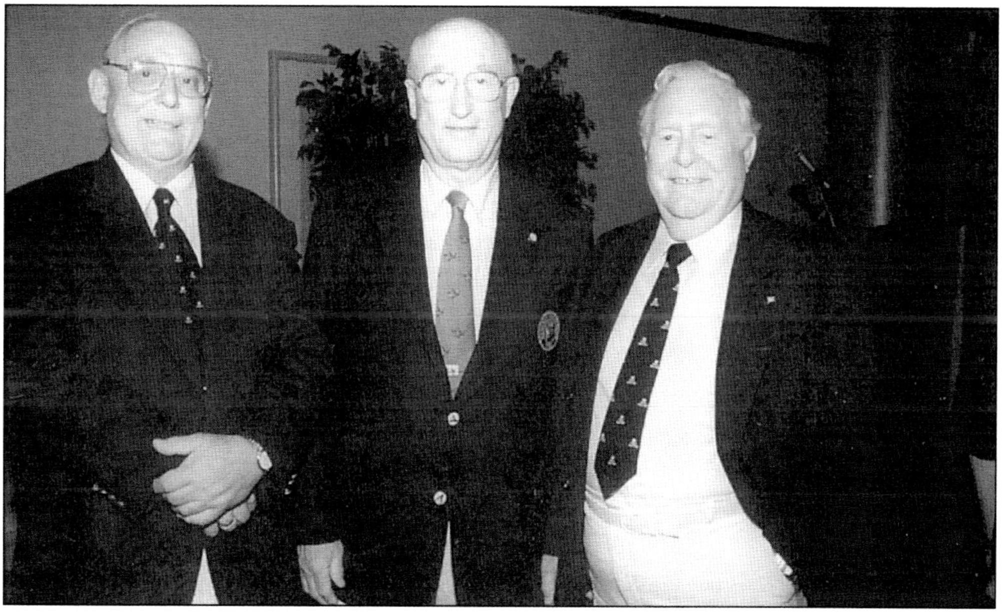

On June 25, 1977, the first Marion-to-Bermuda Cruising Yacht Race was held. This biennial race is held in alternate years from the Newport-to-Bermuda Ocean Yacht Race. Unlike the Newport-to-Bermuda race, which attracts highly competitive ocean racers, the Marion-to-Bermuda race attracts sailors who love to sail with family and friends, who want to enjoy racing, and who do not have to buy a new up-to-date competitive boat every two years to be able to stay in the sport. Shown here are founders David Kingery (left) from the Beverly Yacht Club and Geoffrey "Dickie" Bird (right) from Bermuda. Race committee chairman Jack Braitmayer (a past Beverly Yacht Club commodore) is in the center.

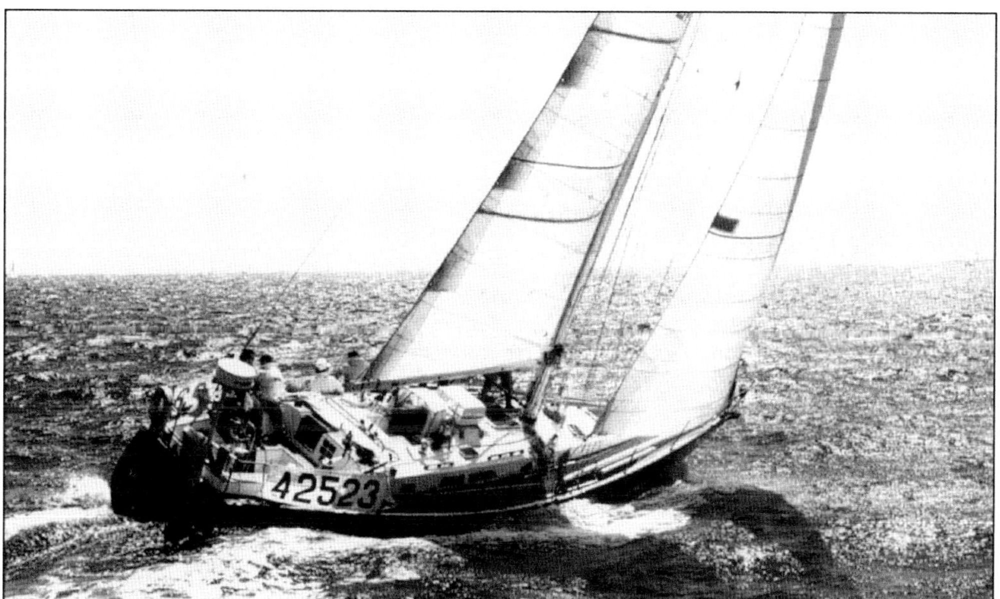

Norman Shachoy's *Volunteer* from the Beverly Yacht Club starts the 10th Marion-to-Bermuda race on June 16, 1995.

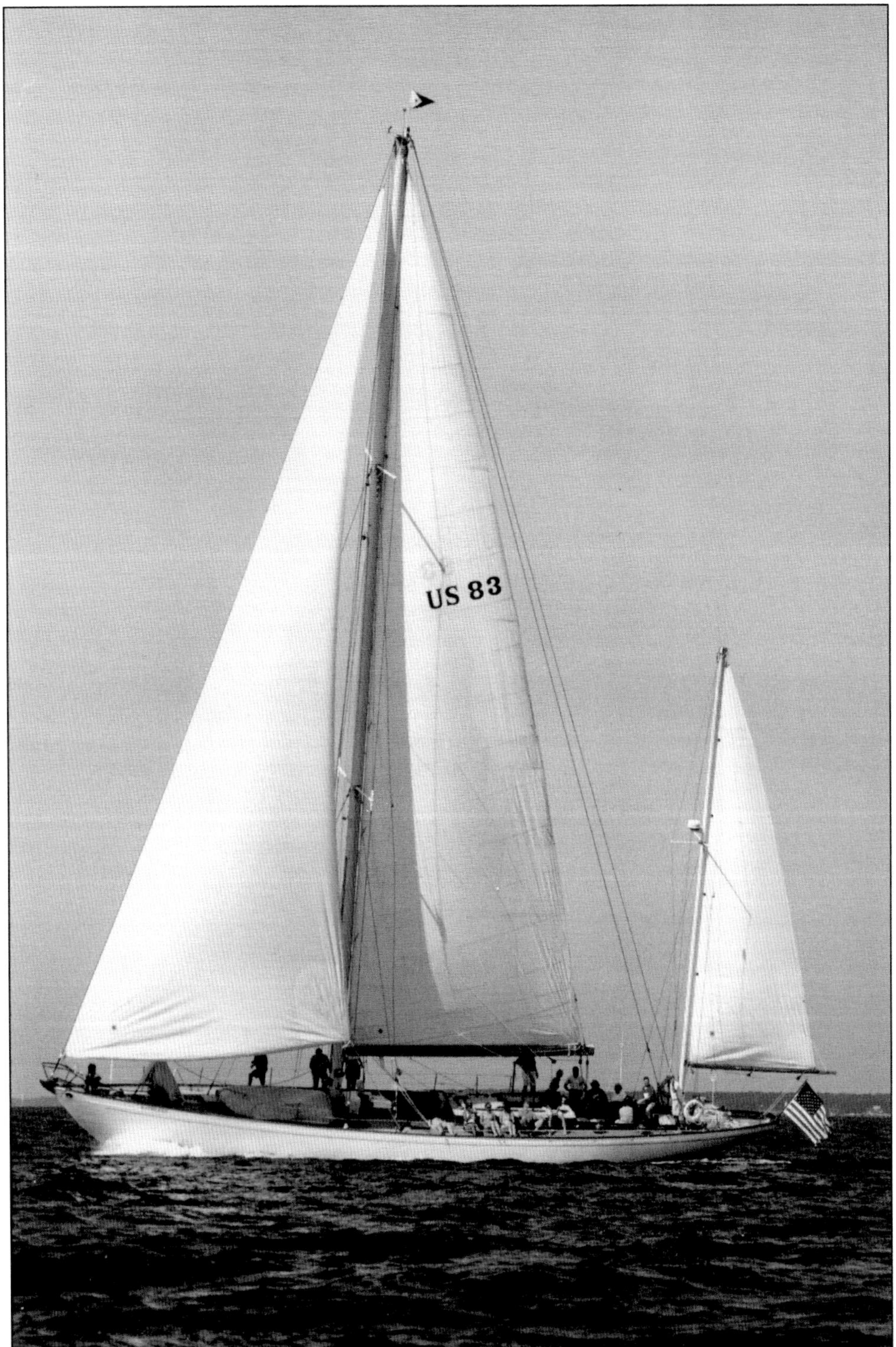

The *Kathleen*, a 72-foot yawl owned by Beverly Yacht Club members Jim and Kathy Feeney, races in the Marion-to-Bermuda Cruising Yacht Race.

Courtland B. Converse was the Beverly Yacht Club's youngest commodore ever. He is shown here in 1967 at the age of 35. He died in a tragic air accident on November 23, 1968, and members raised funds to purchase the present club launch, named the Courtland B. Converse in his memory. He is remembered for giving generously of his time, skill, and friendship to the Beverly Yacht Club. His family had summered in Marion since 1890.

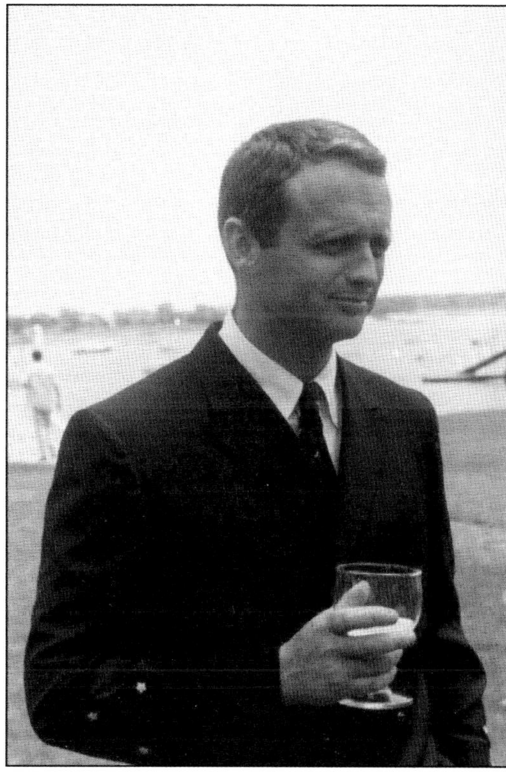

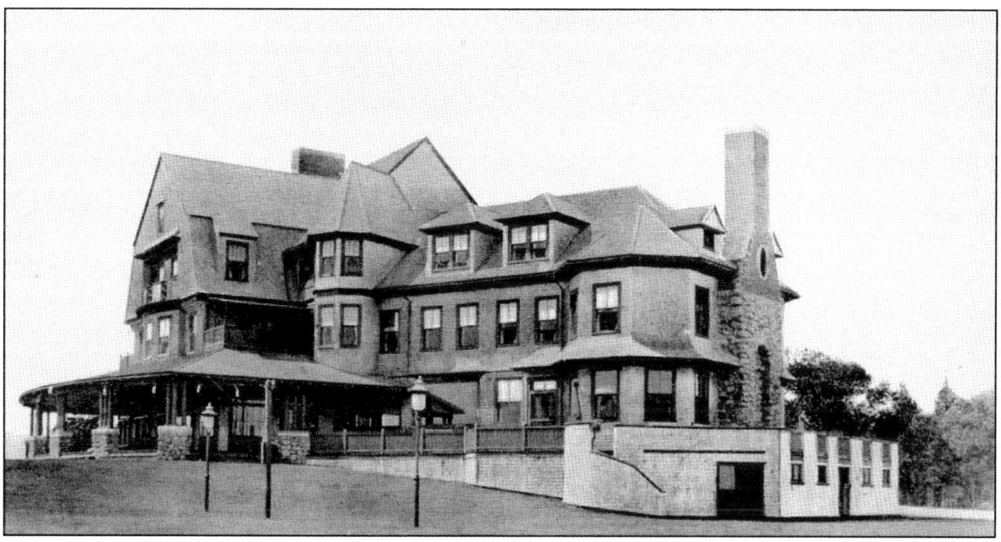

This postcard shows the Moorings, which was situated at the tip of Converse Point, the southernmost of the two necks that shelter Marion's Sippican Harbor. Converse Point was formerly called Charles Neck and was a Native American campground for centuries before the English settlement of Marion in 1679. The Moorings was built in 1890 for Harry E. Converse, who was an heir of Elisha Converse. The founder of a rubber products industry in Malden during the 1850s, Elisha Converse's rubber shoes were in great demand worldwide. Harry E. Converse was an important local philanthropist who funded many causes, including Marion's fire department. The shingle-style Moorings estate had 40 rooms.

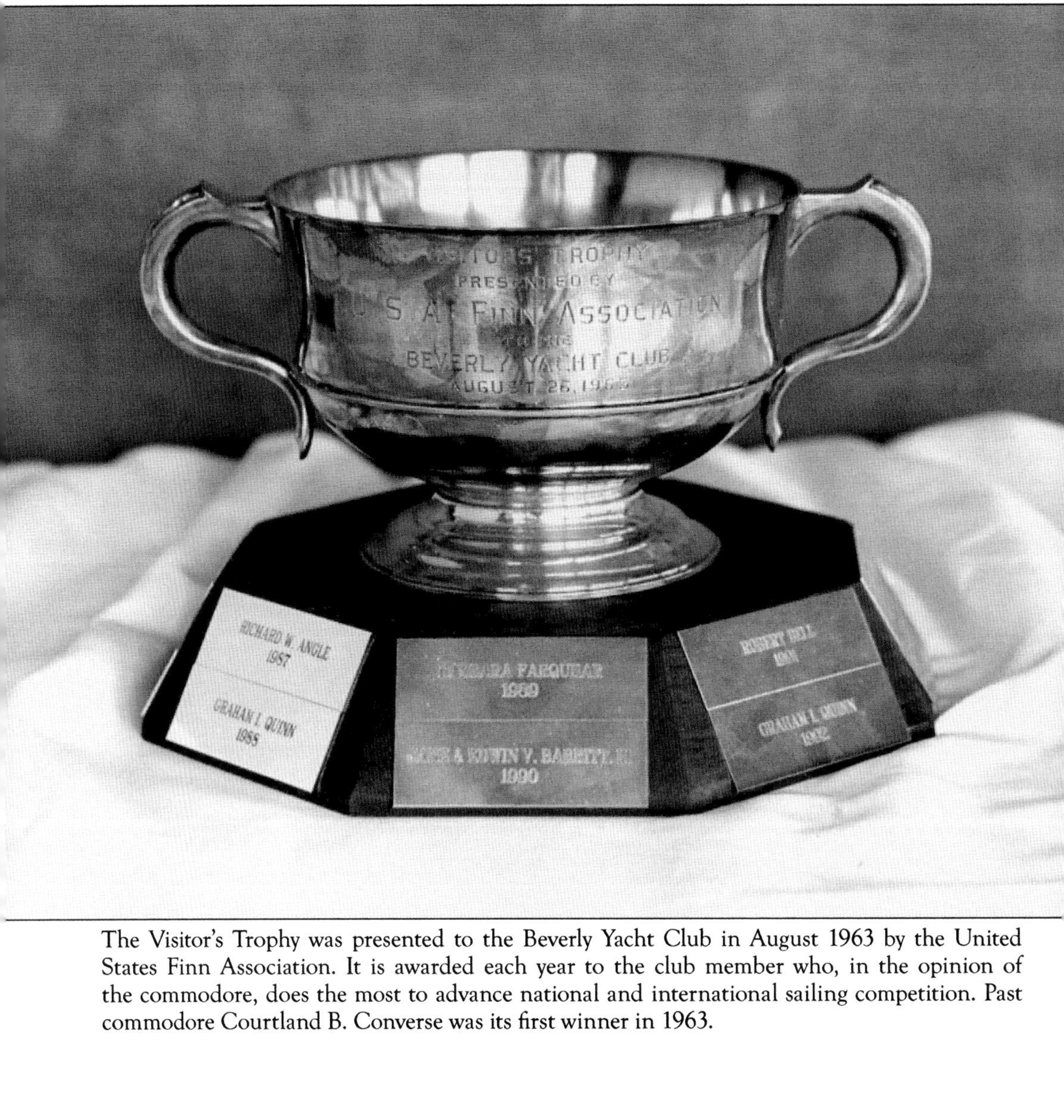

The Visitor's Trophy was presented to the Beverly Yacht Club in August 1963 by the United States Finn Association. It is awarded each year to the club member who, in the opinion of the commodore, does the most to advance national and international sailing competition. Past commodore Courtland B. Converse was its first winner in 1963.

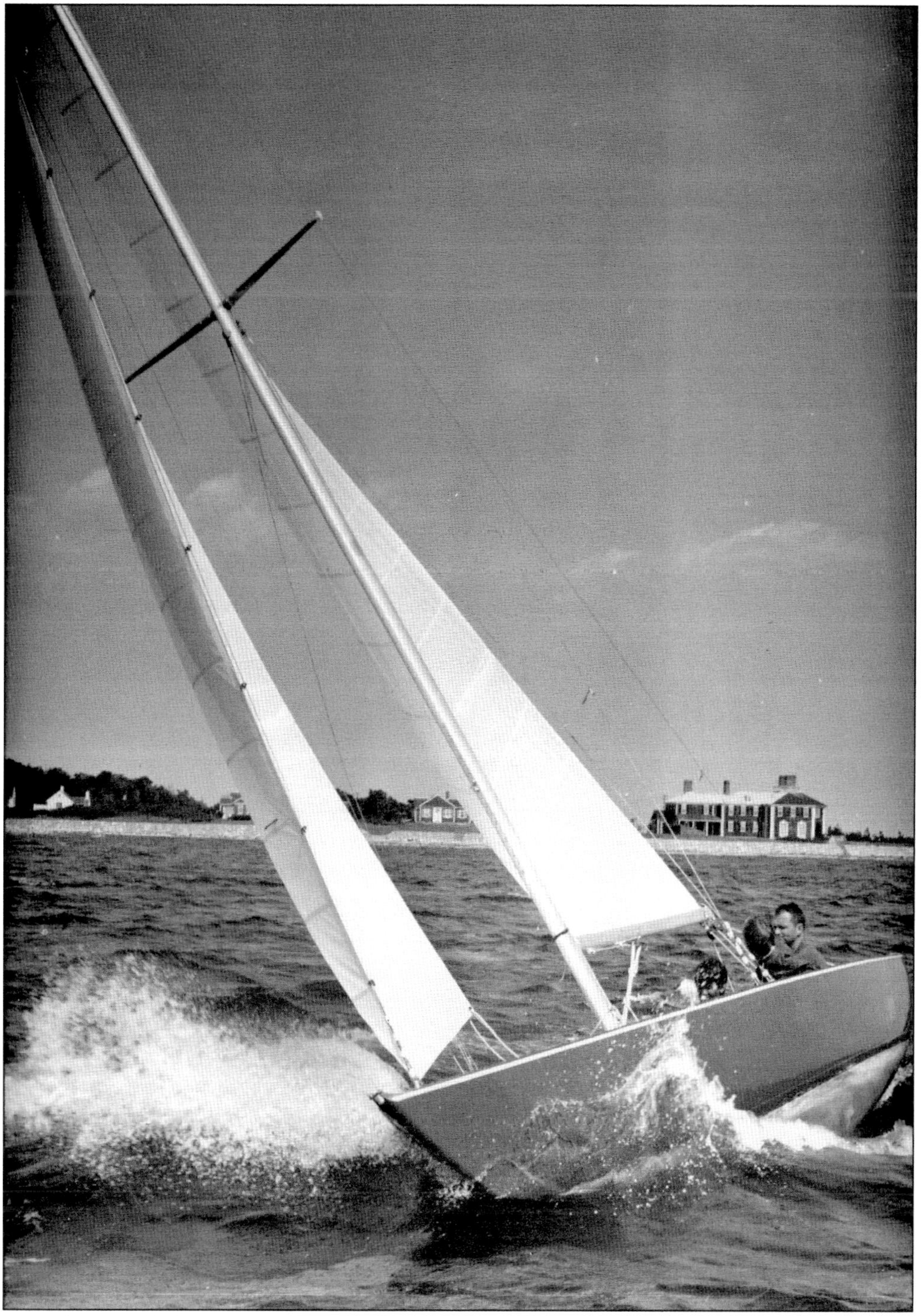

This photograph shows past commodore Courtland B. Converse racing his Shields with his wife, Joey Saltonstall Converse, and son, Chris, as crew.

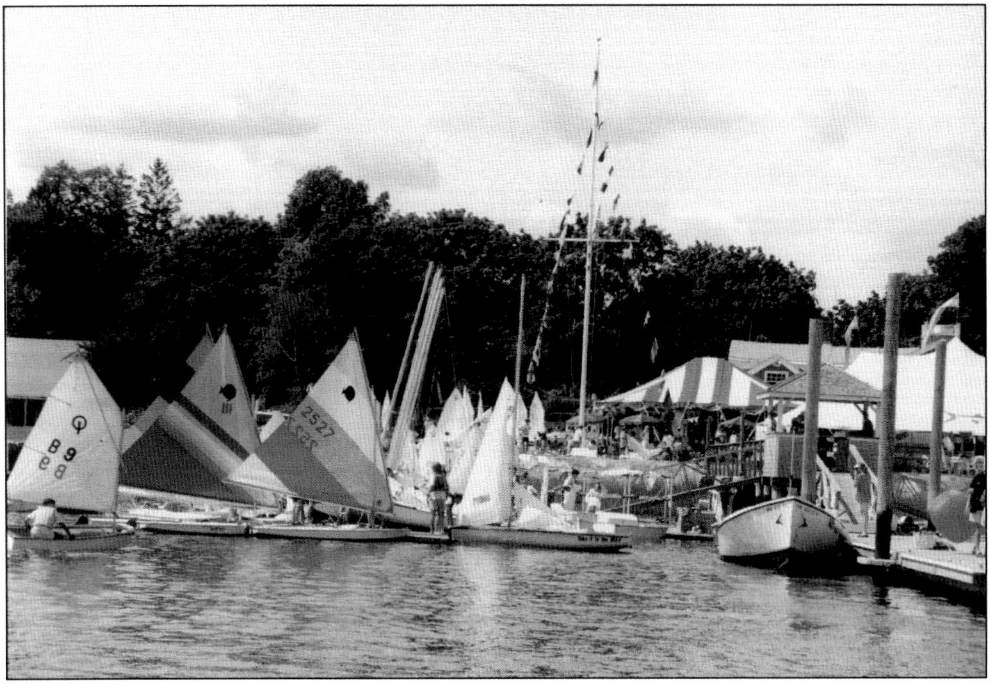

The Beverly Yacht Club junior regatta also runs races for the Sunfish class, even though the class is not raced in the Beverly Yacht Club junior program.

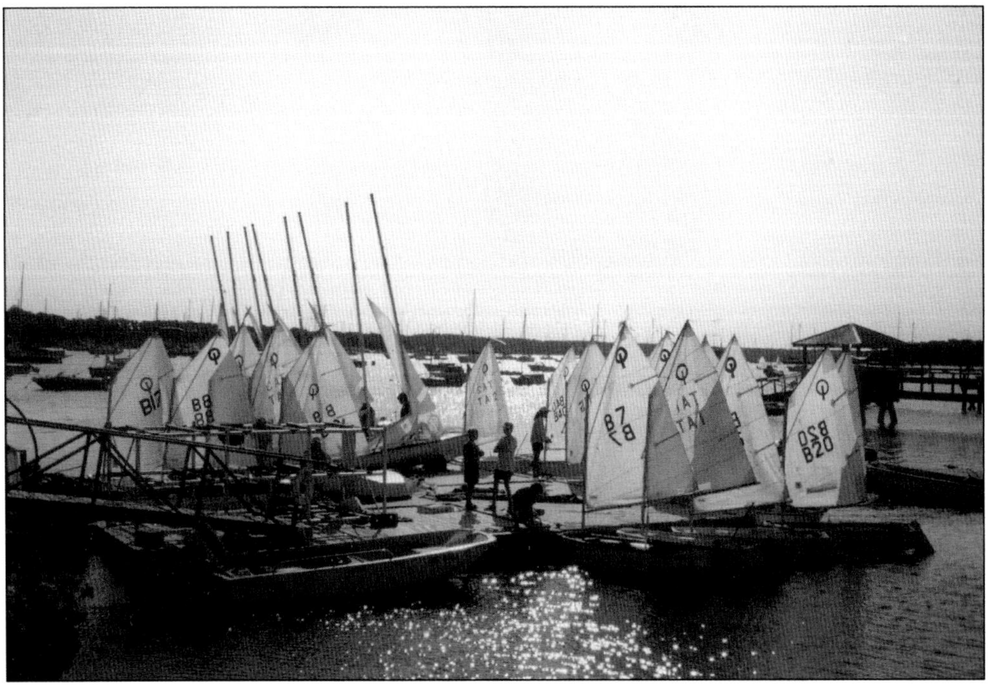

At the end of the day, the boats from the junior regatta come back to the Beverly Yacht Club dock.

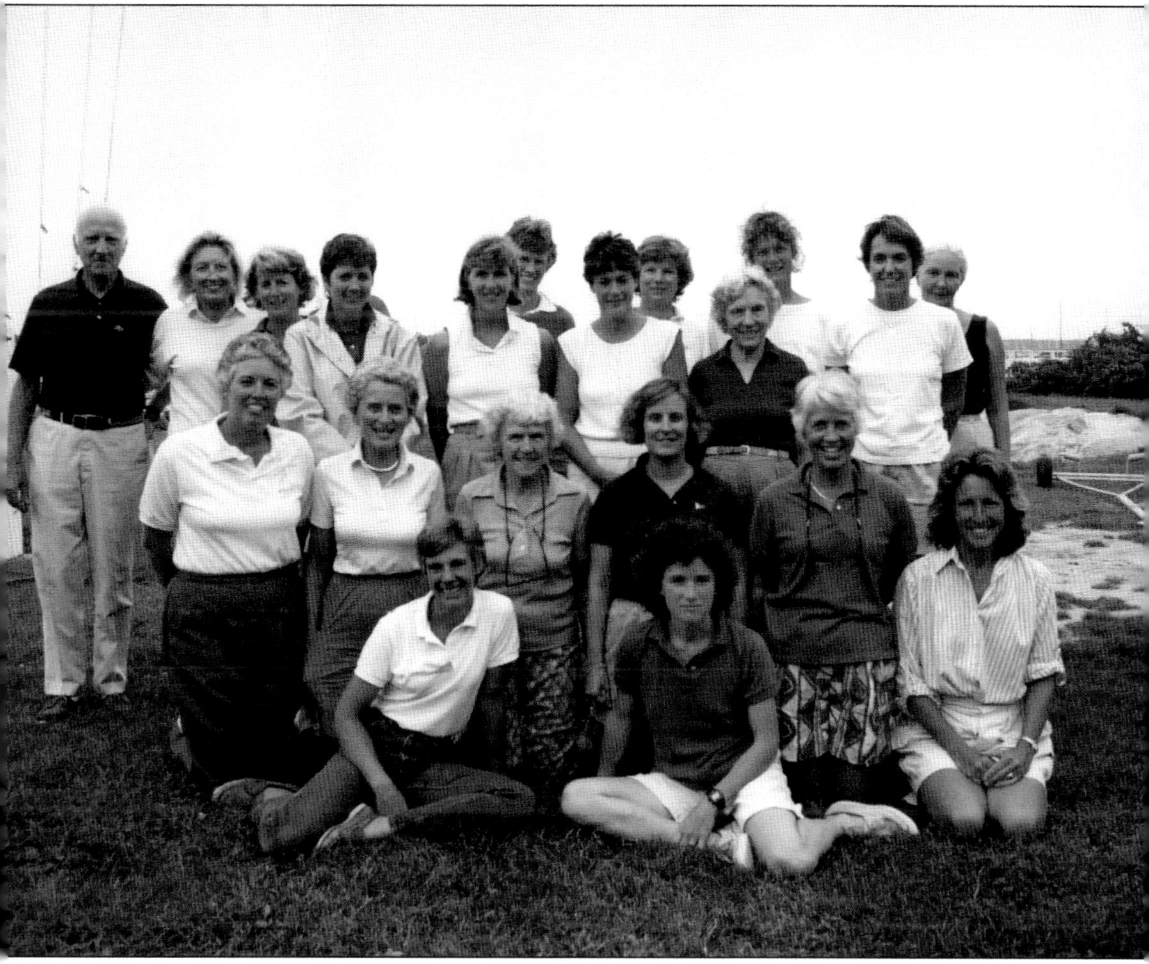

Since 1925, the Beverly Yacht Club has sponsored the Ladies' Series, which is held every Thursday afternoon. Pictured here are the Doughdish (fiberglass H12) sailors. Beverly Yacht Club women have reached the finals of the Adams Cup, the women's national sailing championship, on three occasions. They won the Prosser Cup in 1952 and 1959 and the Colt Cup in 1955 and 1959. In 1962, a Beverly Yacht Club crew skippered by Wendy Peirson won the Prosser Cup, the Colt Trophy, and went to the Adams Cup finals. Pictured from left to right are (first row) Mary Merrow and Kelli McSweeney; (second row) Barbara Farquar, Margot Foster, Virgina Nicholson, Pam Norweb, Joey Saltonstall Du Bois, and Connie Fullenweider; (third row) Carol Garey, Andrea Keene, Kitsie Howard, Kathy Saltonstall, and Carolyn Rubenstein; (fourth row) Bull Reese, Bigee Reese, Frances Russell, Sharlie Sudduth, unidentified, Liza Evans, and Joan Olson.

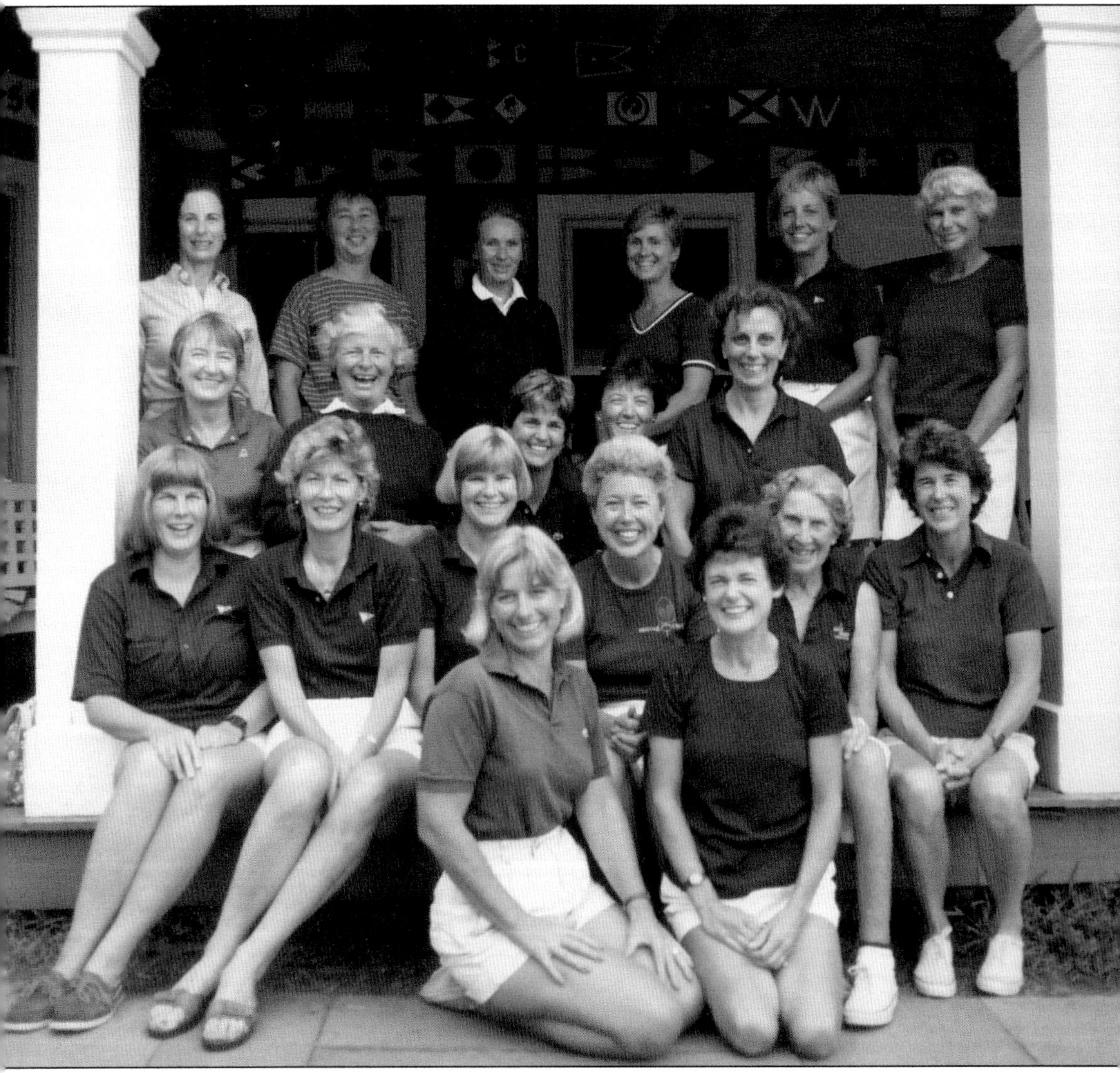

This photograph pictures the ladies' sailing Bullseye class. Pictured from left to right are (first row) Faith Thompson Paulsen and Bonnie Sorterup; (second row) Carol Rankin, Kathy Reed, Mary Pierce, Lynn Paulsen, Peggy Dyer, and Liz Brainard; (third row) Jean Briggs, Connie Shepherd, Floral Holmes, Jorie Borden, and Angela Melville; (fourth row) Janet Markel, Joan Healy, Ann TenBrook, Sylvia Strand, Doris Ludes, and Annie Bacon.

The Bullseye class (an updated fiberglass H12) is made by Cape Cod Shipbuilding Company. This photograph shows a Bullseye out for a sail in Sippican Harbor.

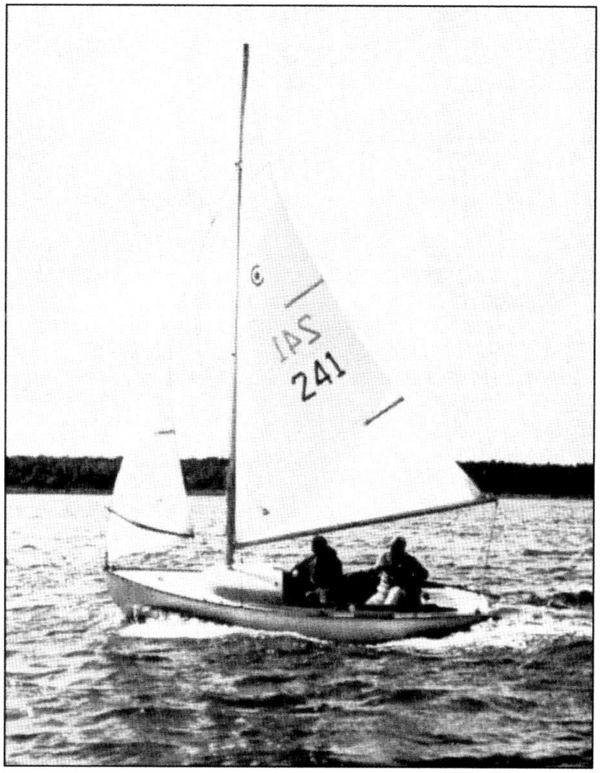

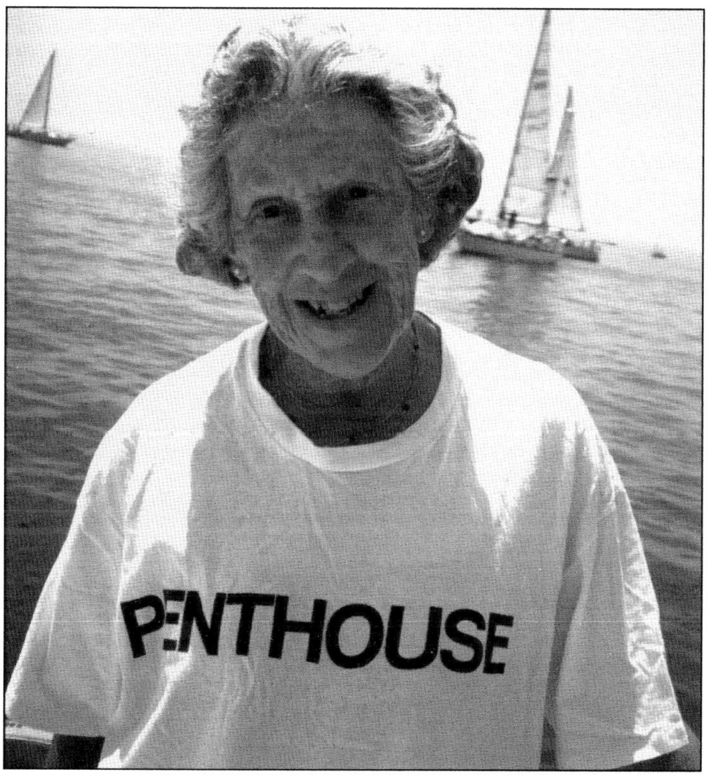

Peggy Dyer raced her Bullseye every Thursday afternoon in the Beverly Yacht Club ladies' races.

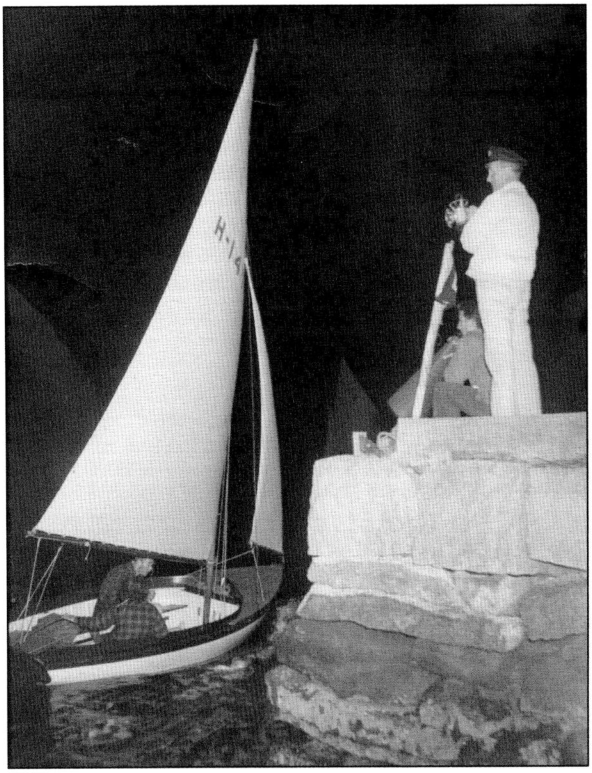

Peggs and Sam Francis near Nye's Wharf after competing in a Beverly Yacht Club Thayer Francis Moonlight Race in their Herreshoff 12.

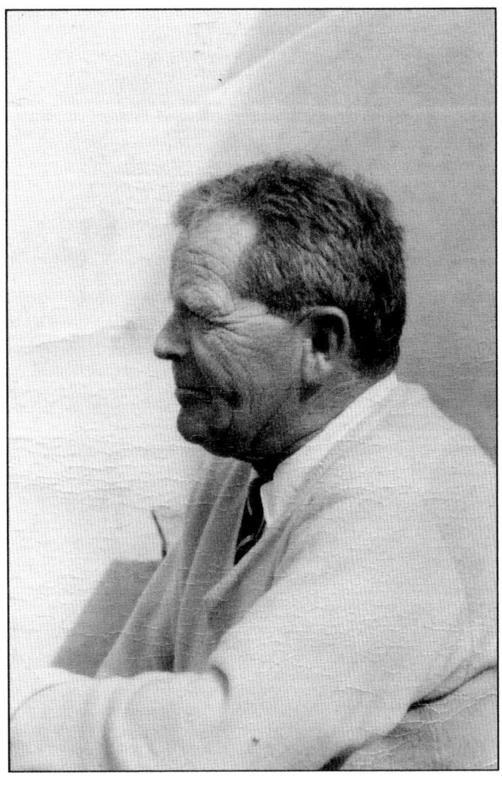

Parker Converse was Beverly Yacht Club commodore from 1952 to 1955. Converse, W. Davis Taylor, and F. Stanton Deland were the three trustees of the Beverly Land Trust, which purchased the Water Street location for the Beverly Yacht Club in 1955. An annual overnight Parker Converse Tower Race attracts a good fleet each summer.

Van Alan Clark's *Red-Herring* races in Buzzards Bay.

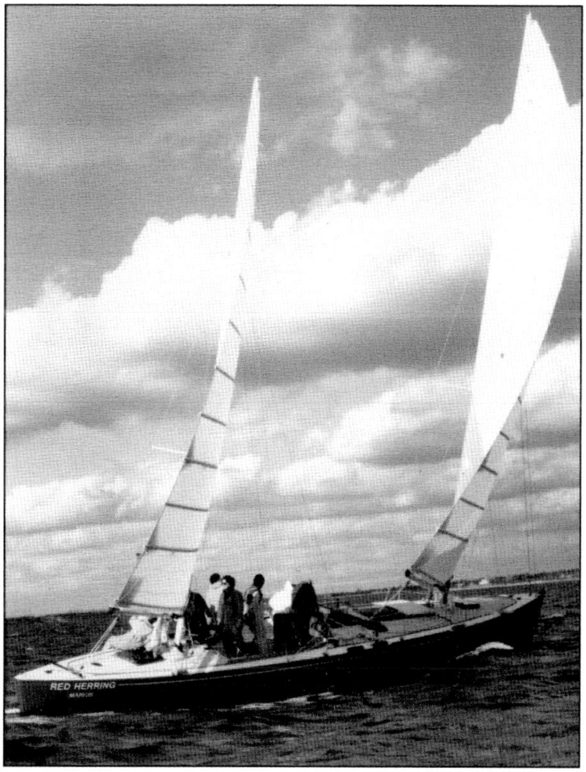

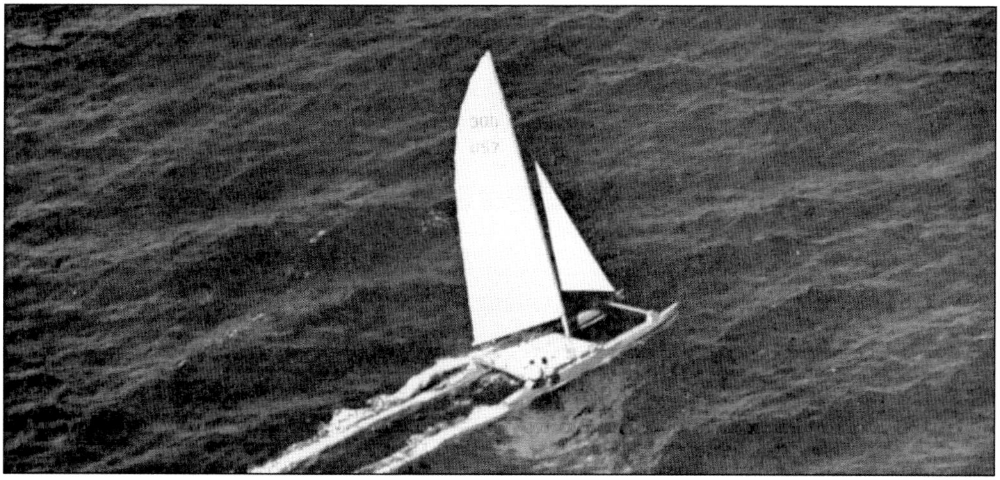

This photograph shows the catamaran *Beverly* making about 20 knots off Nye Ledge. Decisive winner of *Yachting*'s One-of-a-Kind Regatta with three firsts-to-finish and first at every mark, the *Beverly* was the outstanding performer. It was designed by MacLear and Harris, built by the Cape Cod Shipbuilding Company in Wareham, and was owned by Van Alan Clark Jr. of the Beverly Yacht Club. Its hulls were fiberglass, connected by three aluminum tubes made from standard mast extrusions. The crew sat on a nylon trampoline. Its aluminum mast rotated, its angle controlled by the gooseneck so mast and boom maintained the same relative positions. On a reach in a 15- to 20-mile-per-hour breeze, the boat's speed actually exceeded that of the wind. When beating to windward in a 12-mile breeze, its apparent wind exceeded 20 miles per hour. The *Beverly* won the North American Championship in 1962 in the 300-square-foot class.

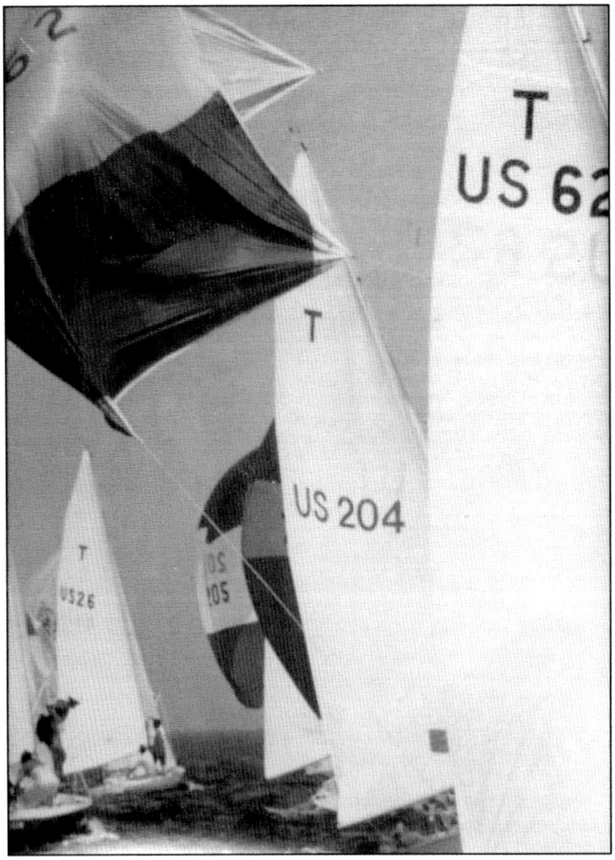

The Tempest class was adopted in the winter of 1965 by the Beverly Yacht Club, and 10 members purchased Tempests for the 1966 racing season. The boats were built by O'Day and the sails were made by Milgram and Hopkins. Tempest fleet No. 3 in Marion has since hosted the national championships once and the Atlantic championships twice, with 30 to 40 competitors in each hotly contested series. The Tempest is a 22-foot two-person keel boat, designed by Ian Proctor, which planes well on a reach in Buzzards Bay. The boat became an Olympic class in 1972.

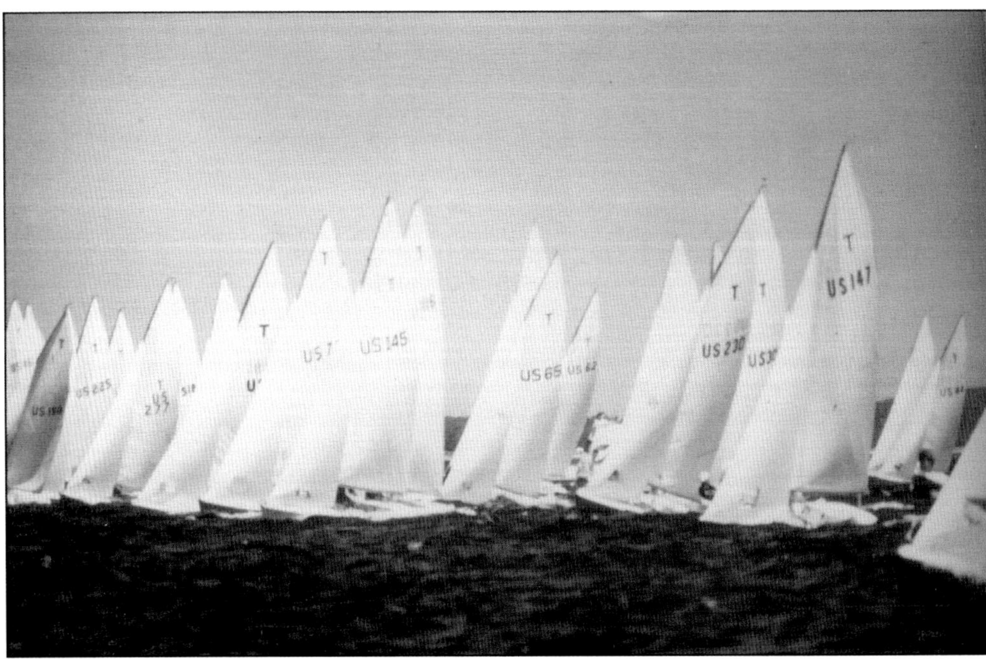

This photograph shows Tempests racing in Sippican Harbor.

This O'Day International Tempest races in Sippican Harbor. The crewman hooks himself onto the mast so that he can lean out to windward in an attempt to keep the boat flat so that it will go faster. The Tempest is 21 feet 11.75 inches in length. Its beam is 6 feet 5.5 inches, and its draft is 3 feet 7 inches. The first Tempest was built in 1965.

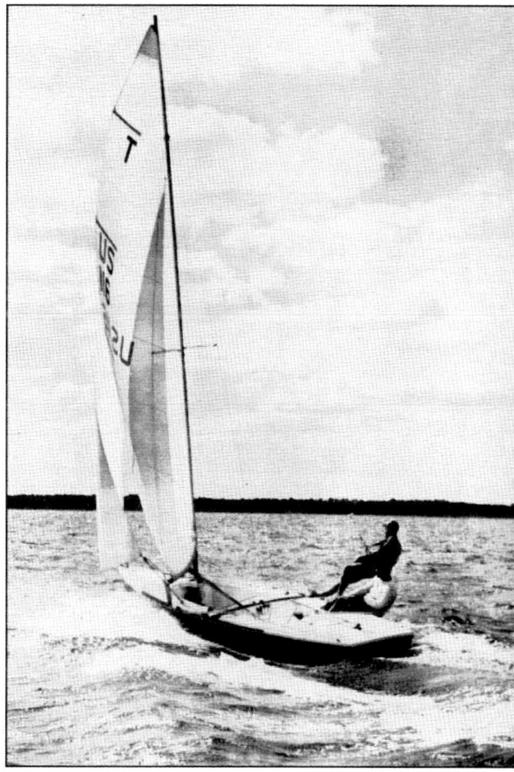

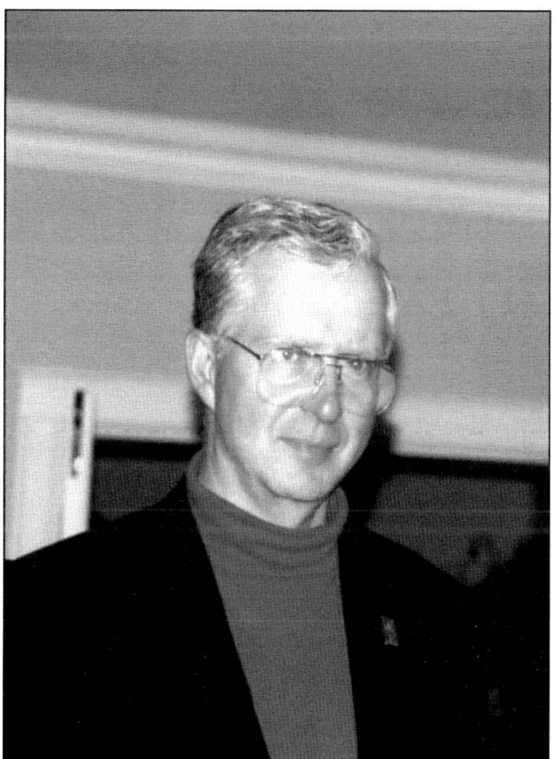

Tom Farquhar was commodore of the Beverly Yacht Club when Hurricane Bob struck on August 19, 1991. The insurance industry ranked Hurricane Bob as the second most expensive hurricane ever reported, with damage to insured property set at $780 million. It was also the earliest hurricane in the season to strike New England, thus causing severe marine losses because of its arrival at the height of the boating season.

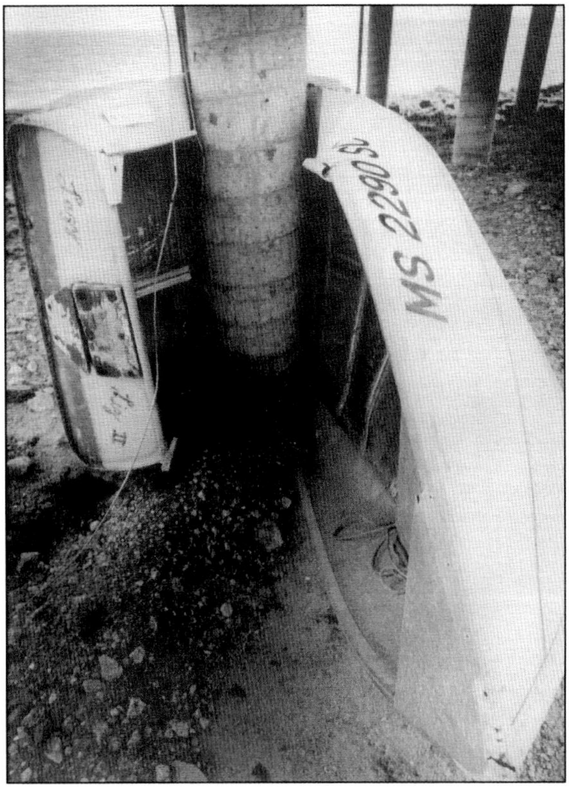

Dinghies washed up in the wreckage of Hurricane Bob.

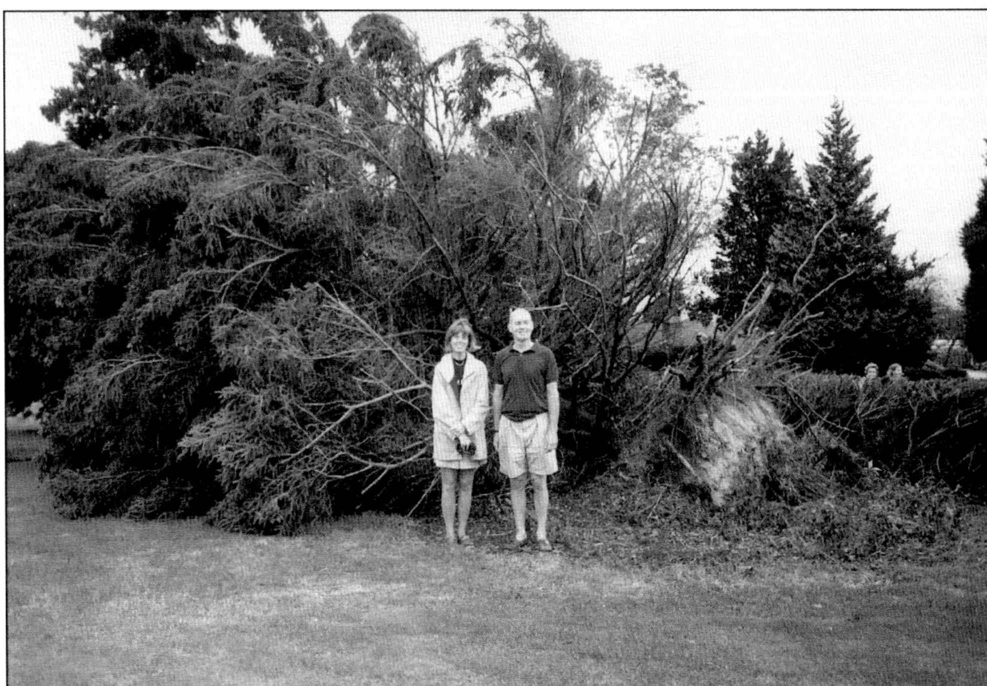

This large pine at 46 Water Street, Marion, toppled over during Hurricane Bob. Here are the owners, Judy and Bob Rosbe, standing in front of their fallen pine tree.

Nine

Buzzards Bay Regatta 1972–2006

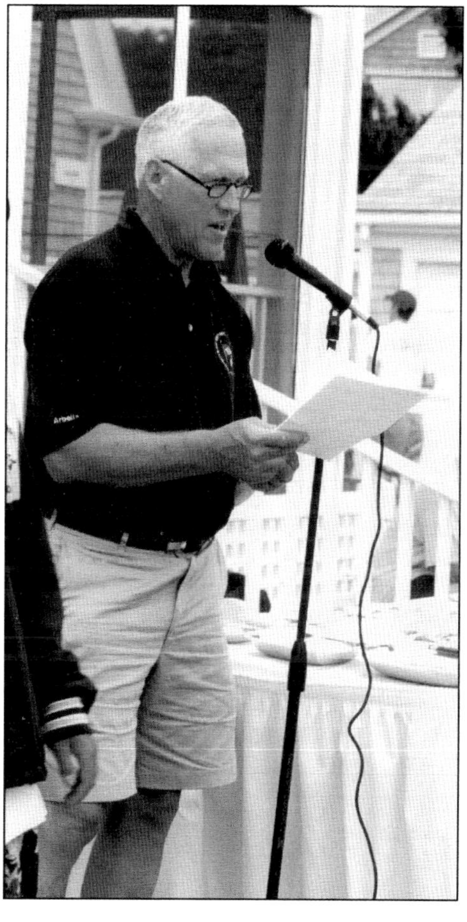

Bill Saltonstall, Beverly Yacht Club commodore from 1982 to 1984, was also a founder, along with Bob Saltmarsh of the New Bedford Yacht Club, of the successful Buzzards Bay Regatta, which was started in 1972. The Buzzards Bay Regatta is the largest multiclass regatta in North America and attracts over 400 boats and over 1,200 sailors across 15 different classes.

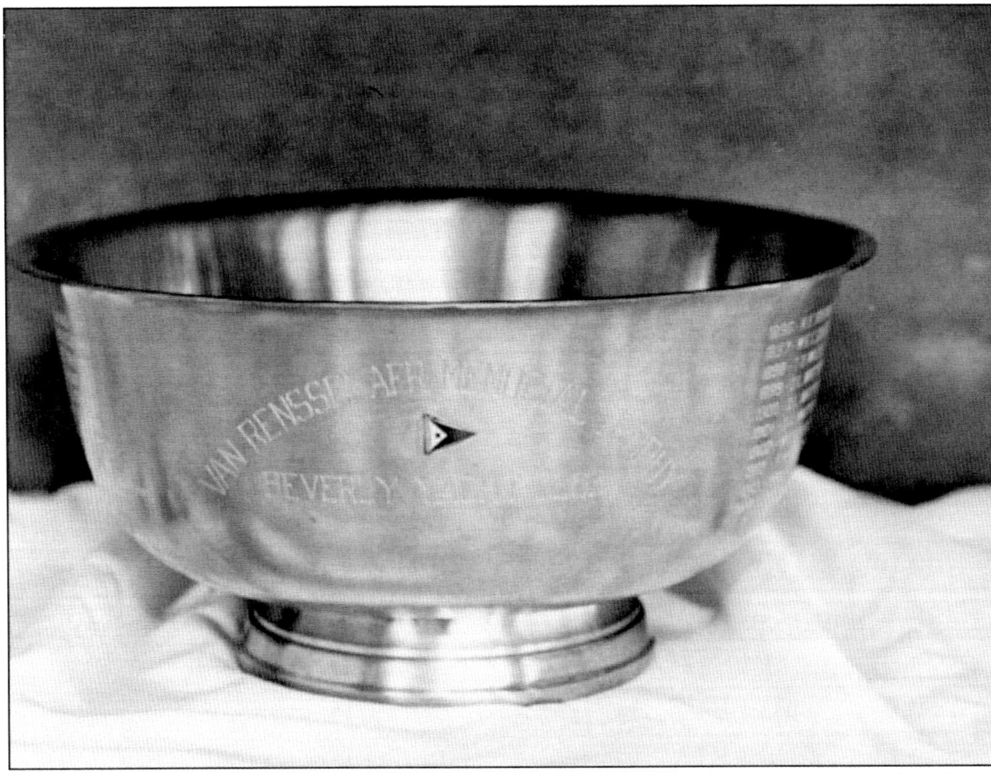

The Van Rensselaer Memorial Trophy is the oldest trophy offered by the Beverly Yacht Club. It was given in memory of George Griswold Van Rensselaer in 1896 by his mother. Prior commodore Bill Saltonstall has won this trophy many times.

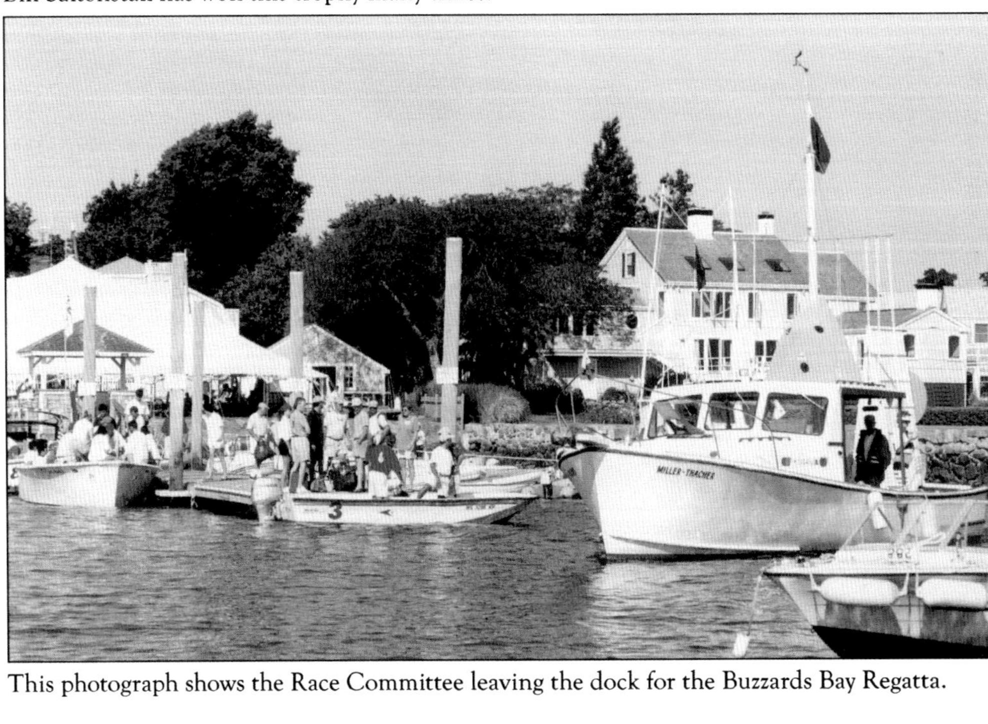

This photograph shows the Race Committee leaving the dock for the Buzzards Bay Regatta.

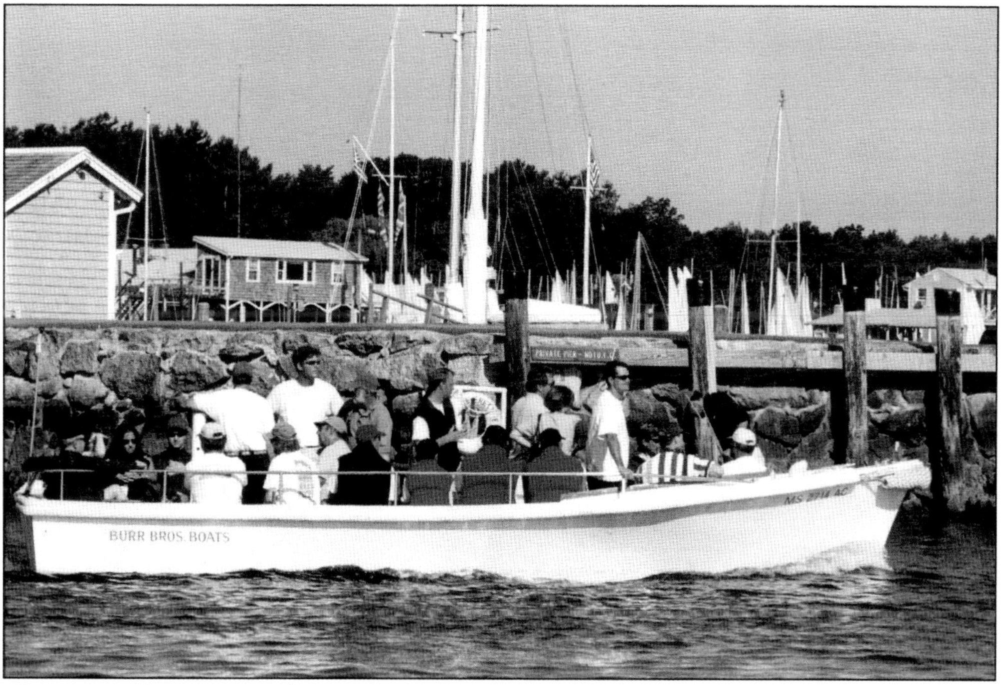

The Burr Brothers Boatyard launch assists the Beverly Yacht Club during the Buzzards Bay Regatta.

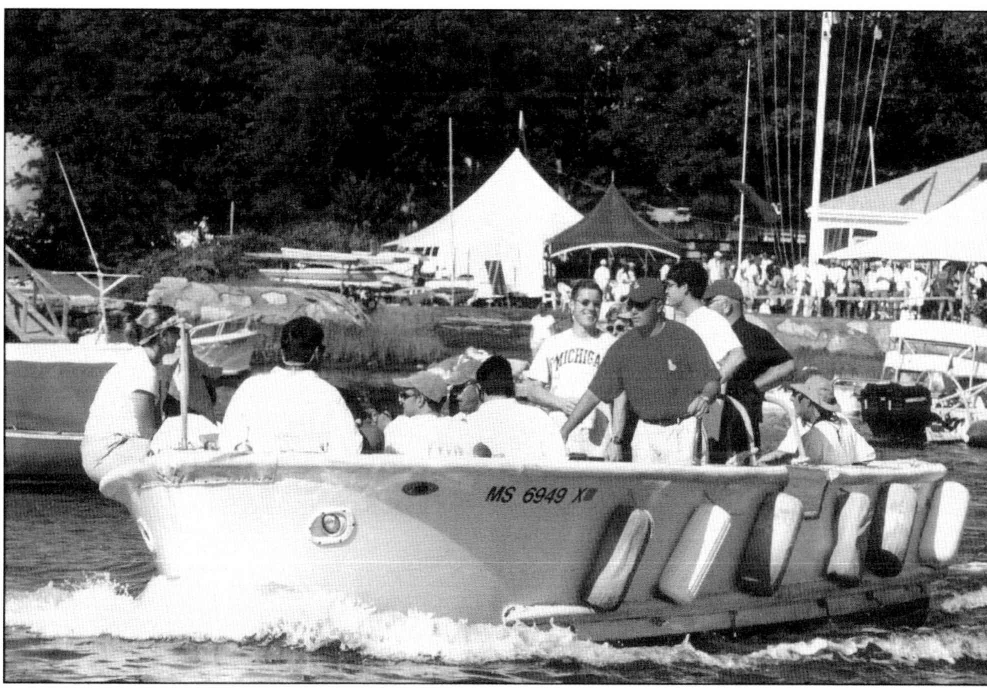

The Beverly Yacht Club launch takes members and their crews out to their boats.

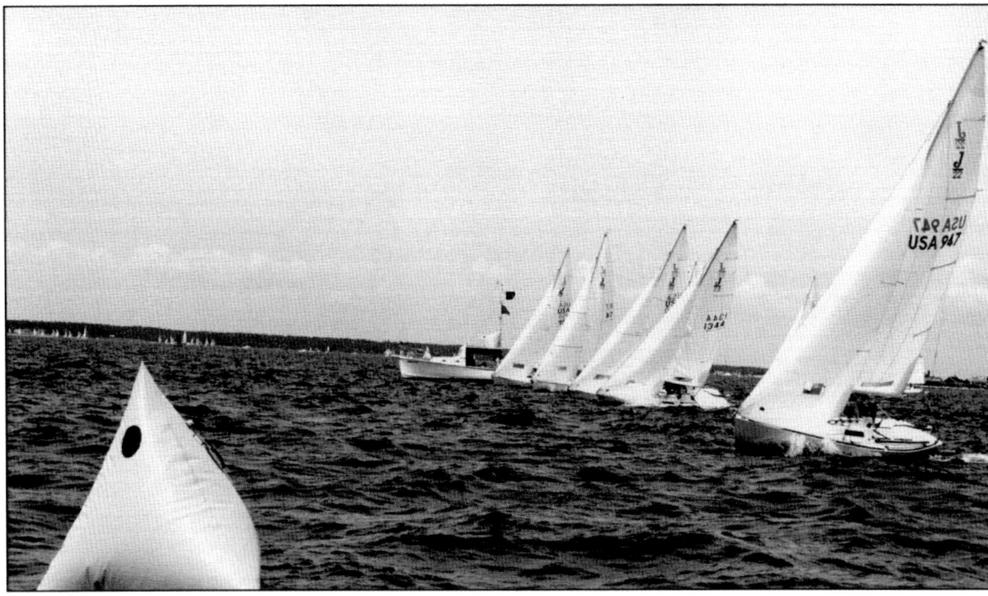

J22s cross the starting line at the Buzzards Bay Regatta in this photograph. The Beverly Yacht Club Committee Boat starts the race in Buzzards Bay off Marion.

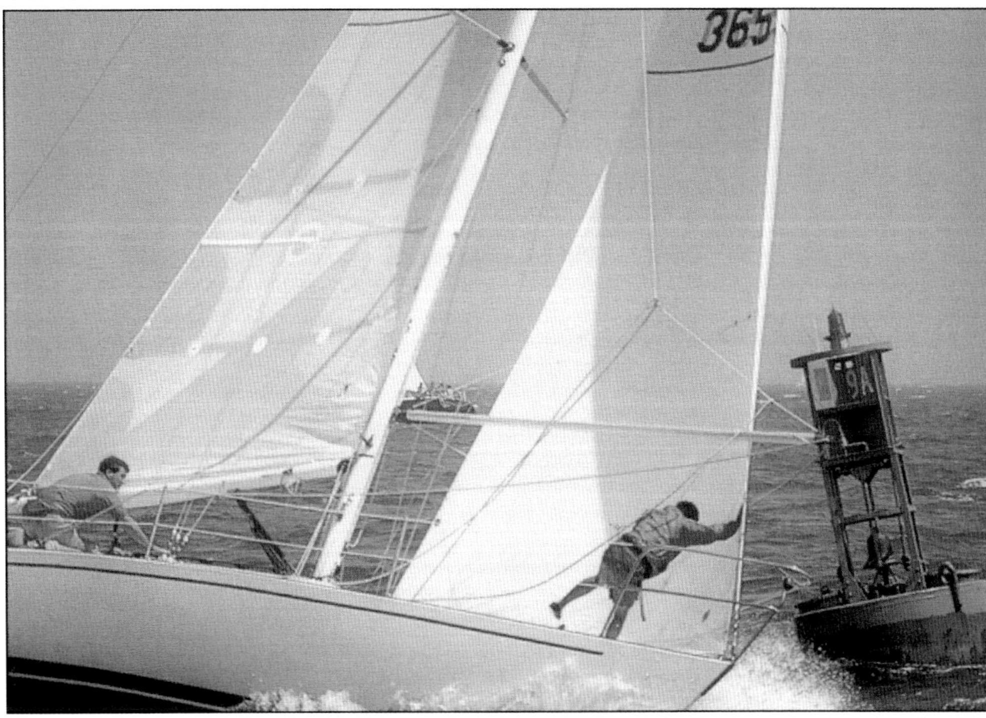

This photograph shows a mark rounding in the Buzzards Bay Regatta. In 1972, the Beverly Yacht Club joined with the New Bedford Yacht Club to initiate a large regional regatta to be held in August each year. The Low Tide Yacht Club, Mattapoisett Yacht Club, Angelica Yacht Club, and Wild Harbor Yacht Club all combined with the Beverly Yacht Club and the New Bedford Yacht Club to form the Buzzards Bay Regatta. The two largest clubs, the Beverly Yacht Club and the New Bedford Yacht Club, host the event in alternating years.

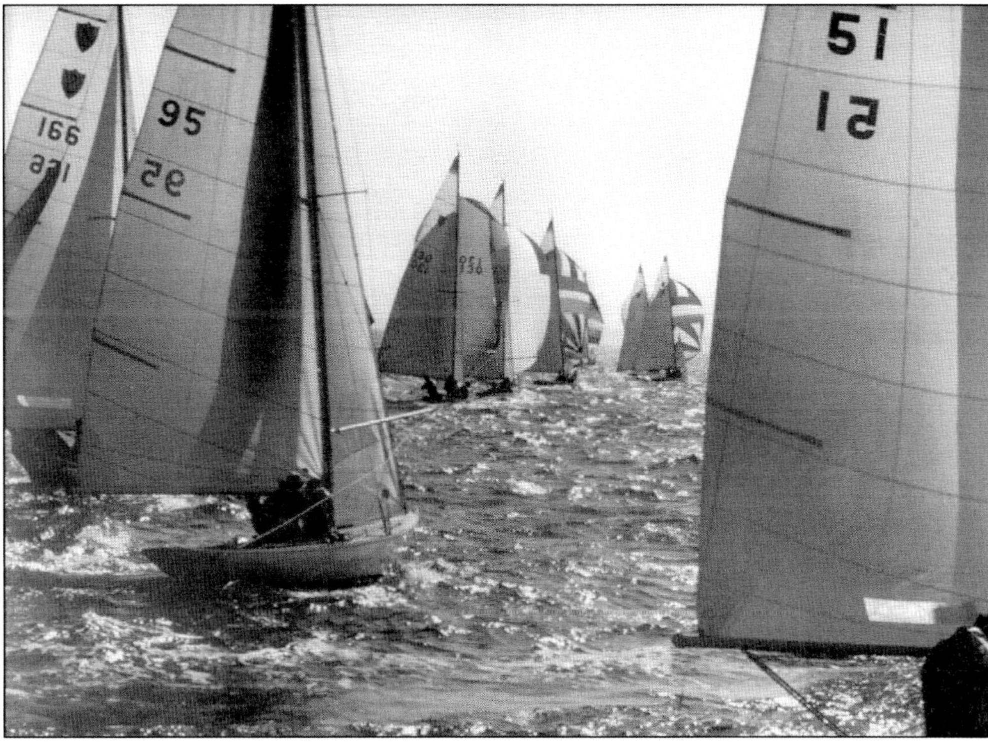

This image shows Shields racing in the Buzzards Bay Regatta.

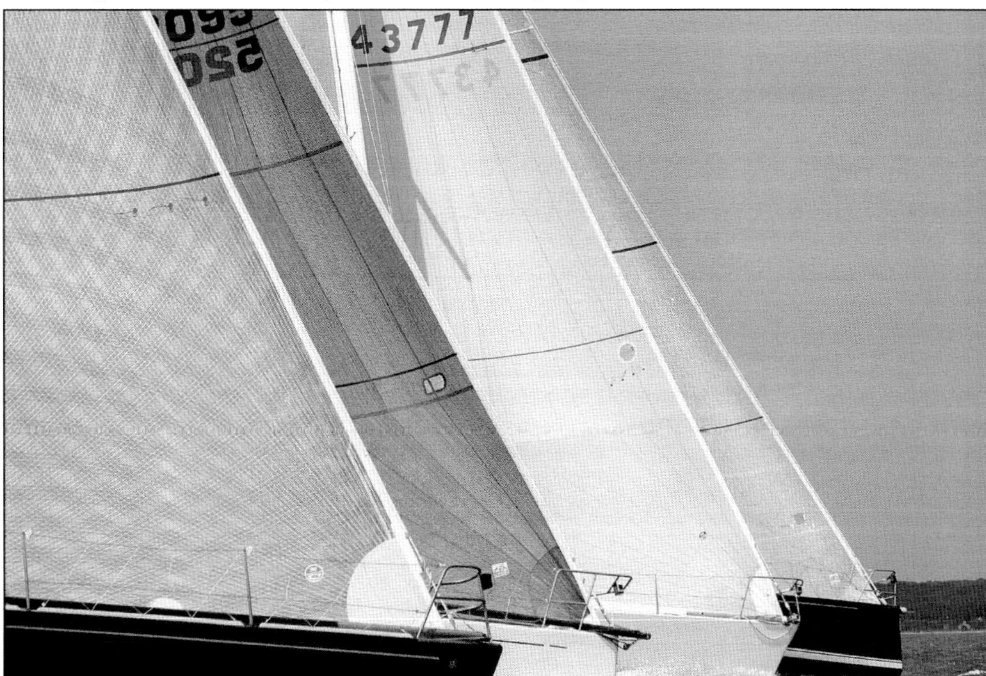

The Buzzards Bay Regatta has many closely contested starts, such as this one in the Performance Handicap Rating Formula (PHRF) start.

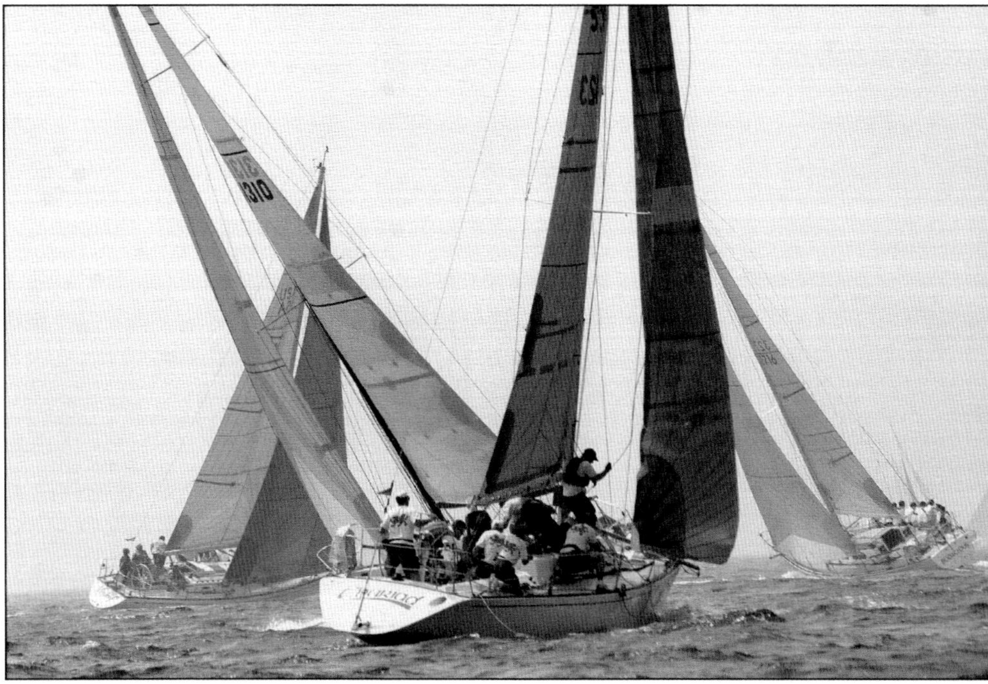

The PHRF class crosses tacks during a Buzzards Bay Regatta race.

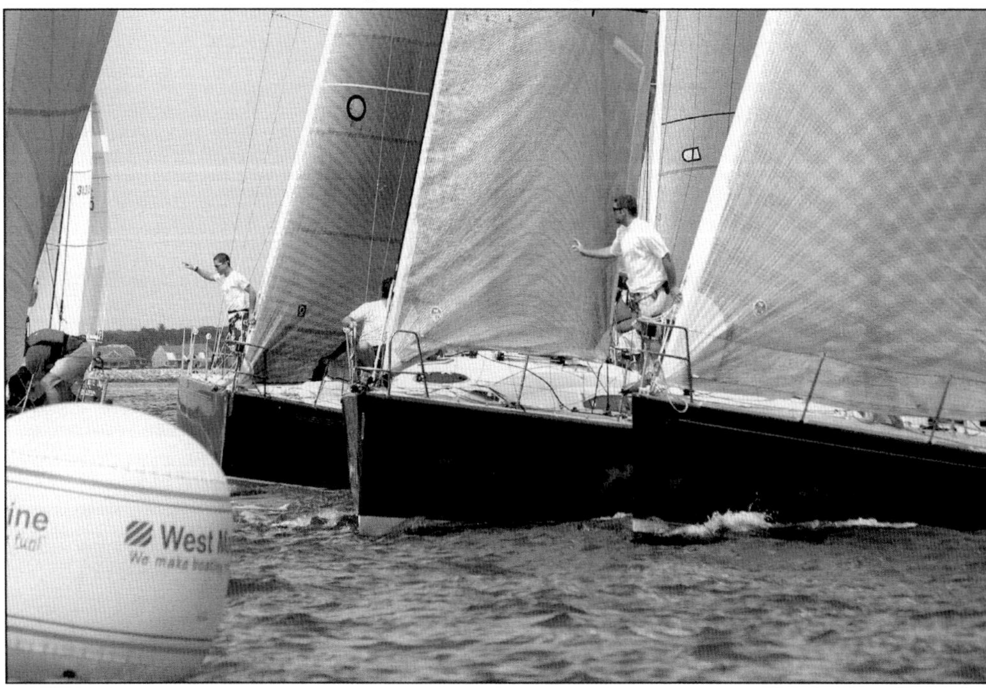

PHRF racers approaching the windward mark yell out for "room" at the mark in what appears to be an exciting rounding in this Buzzards Bay Regatta race. Foredeck crew gesture by pointing that the next windward boat must stay clear. The boat on the right of this photograph gets room at the mark to round it, and all of the other boats must stay up and out of its way. If any of the boats touch, a foul is called.

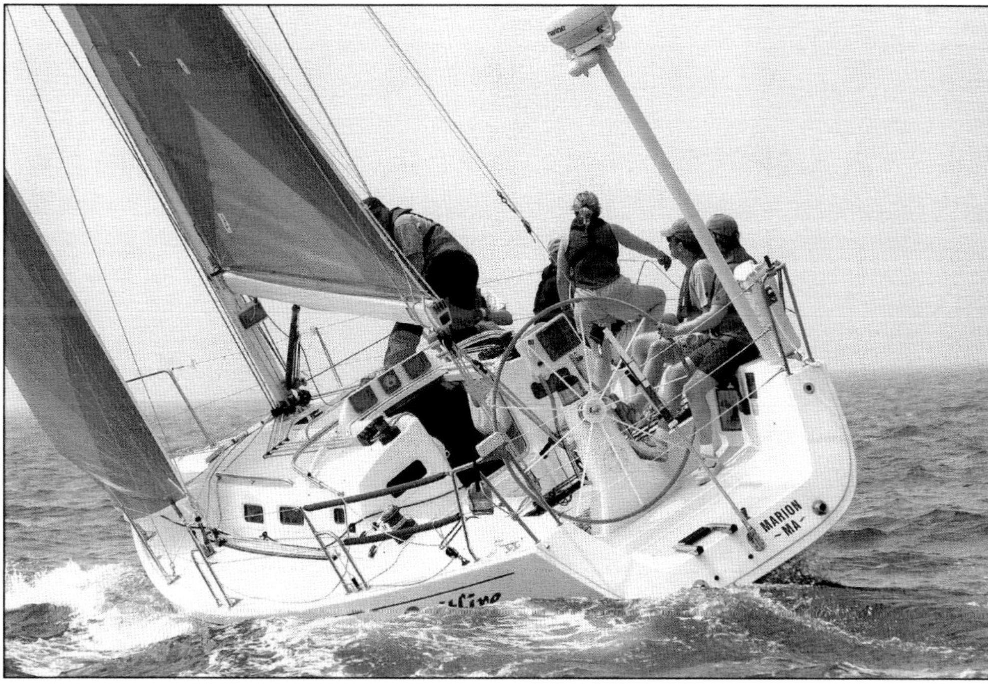

Marion boat *Spitfire*, a J109 owned by Barry Feldman, races in the Buzzards Bay Regatta.

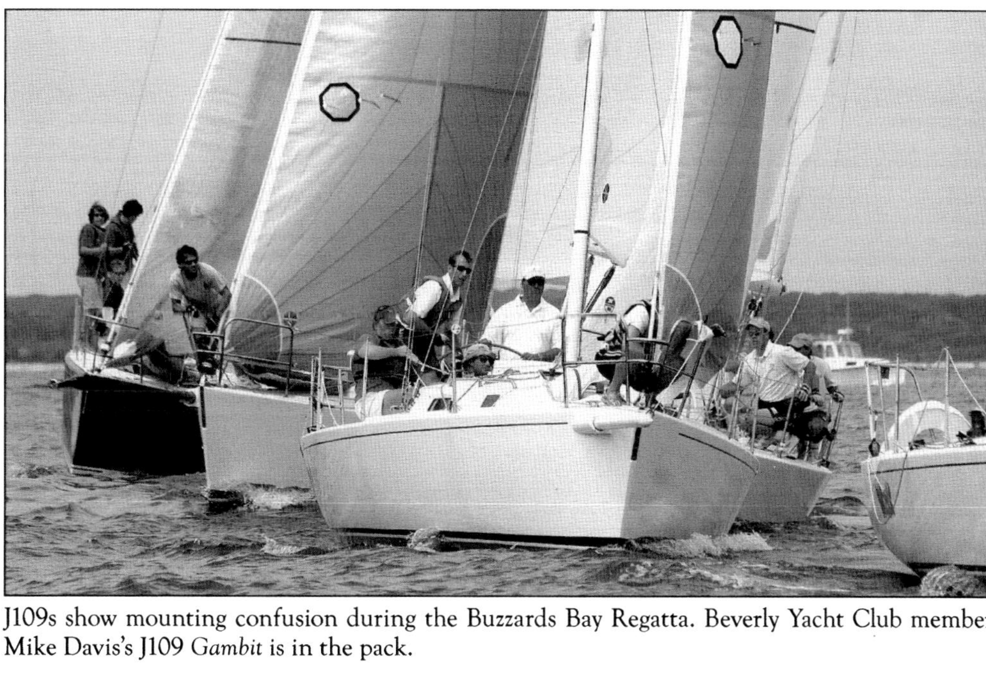

J109s show mounting confusion during the Buzzards Bay Regatta. Beverly Yacht Club member Mike Davis's J109 *Gambit* is in the pack.

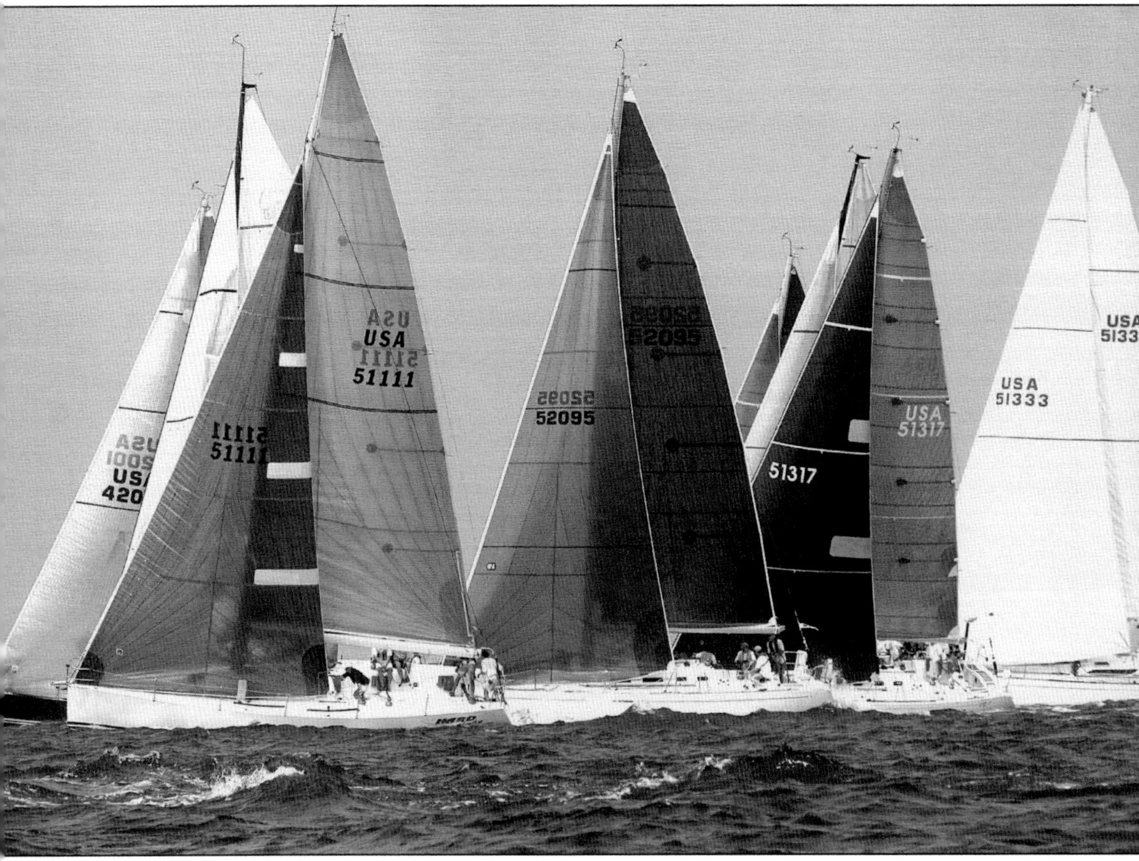

High-tech carbon fiber sails race along in the Buzzards Bay Regatta in this PHRF race. The middle two boats are J109s, 35-feet sloops.

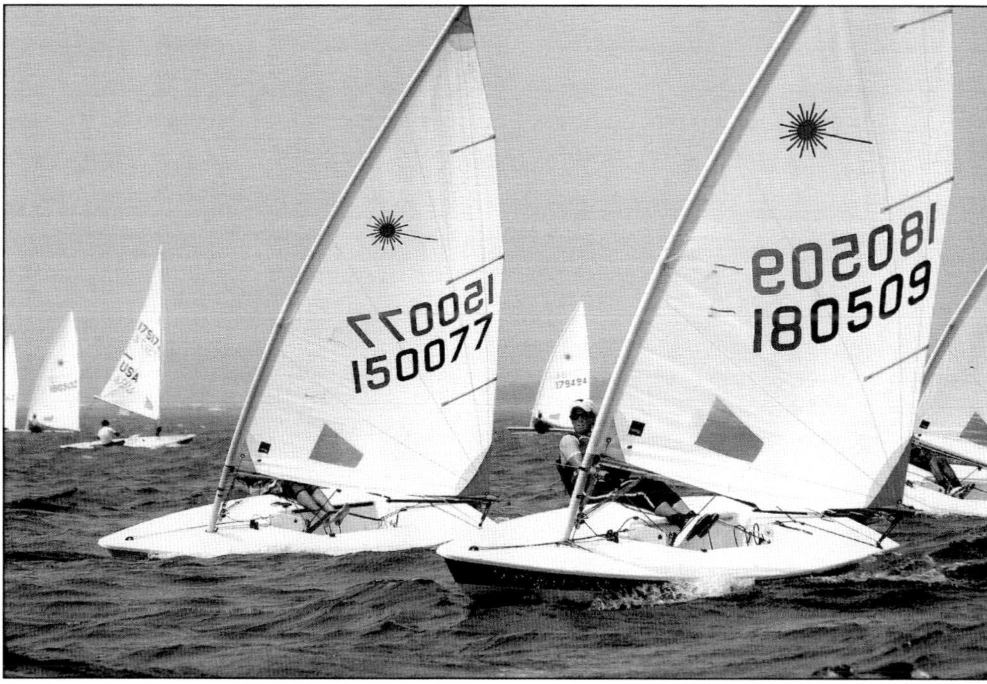

Lasers speed by in the Buzzards Bay Regatta, which provides two starts for the approximately 120 entries, most of the skippers in this one-person boat being young and athletic. The Laser is 13 feet 10.25 inches in length with a 4-feet-6-inch beam. This one-person boat was designed by Bruce Kirby and first built in 1971.

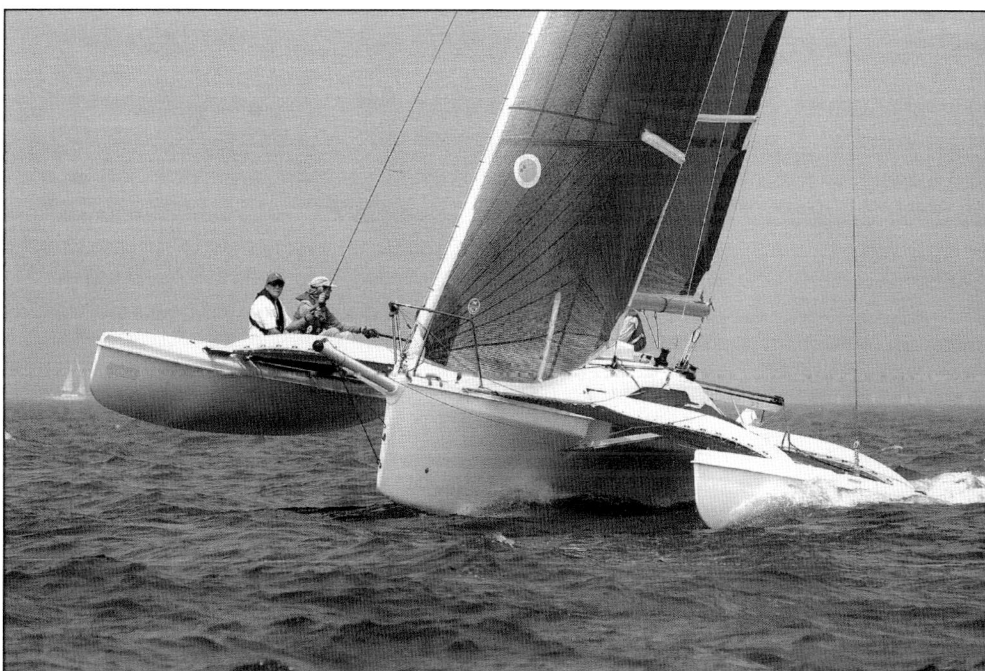

This multihulled boat tears across the bay in the Buzzards Bay Regatta.

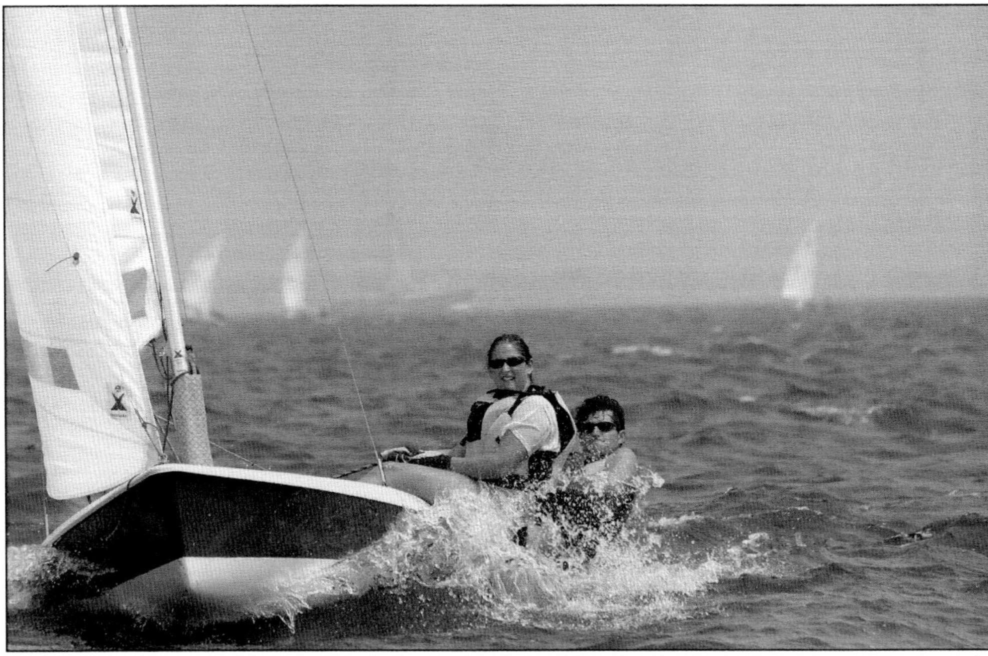

The Vanguard 15 class has two starts in the Buzzards Bay Regatta to accommodate the approximately 65 entries in this class. The Vanguard 15 is 15 feet 3 inches in length overall and 15 feet on the waterline. Its beam is five feet six inches. It was designed by Bob Ames and was first built in 1992.

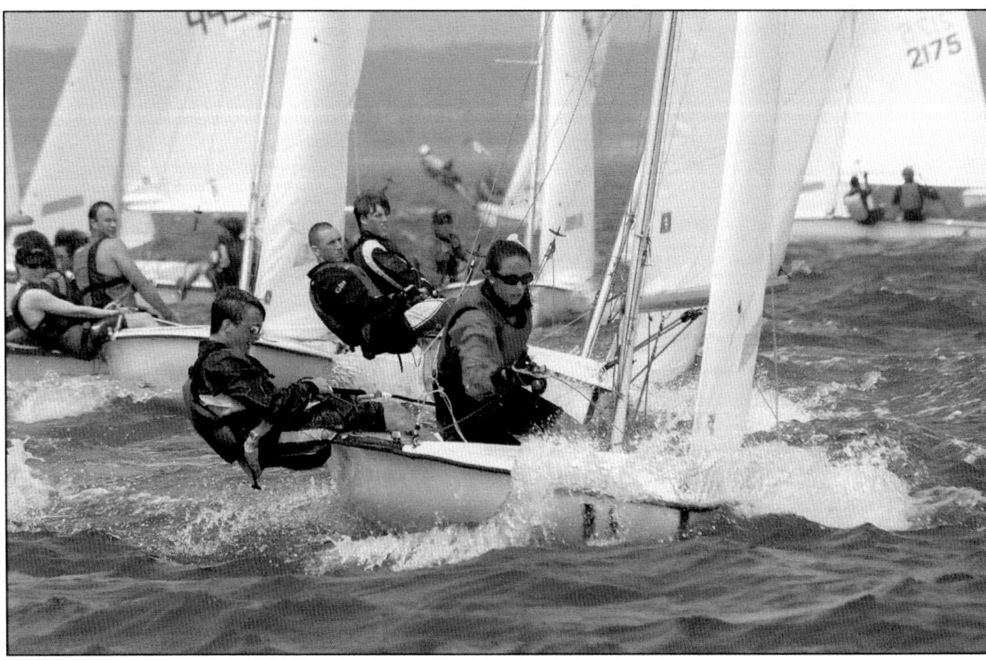

The 420s jockey for position at the start of their race in the Buzzards Bay Regatta. The 420 class is the most popular class in the Buzzards Bay Regatta with approximately 140 boats in three or four starts. The length overall of the 420 is 13.75 feet, and the length on the waterline is 13.17 feet. The 420 was first built in 1978 and is raced competitively at the collegiate level.

Ten

Jubilee Celebration 2005

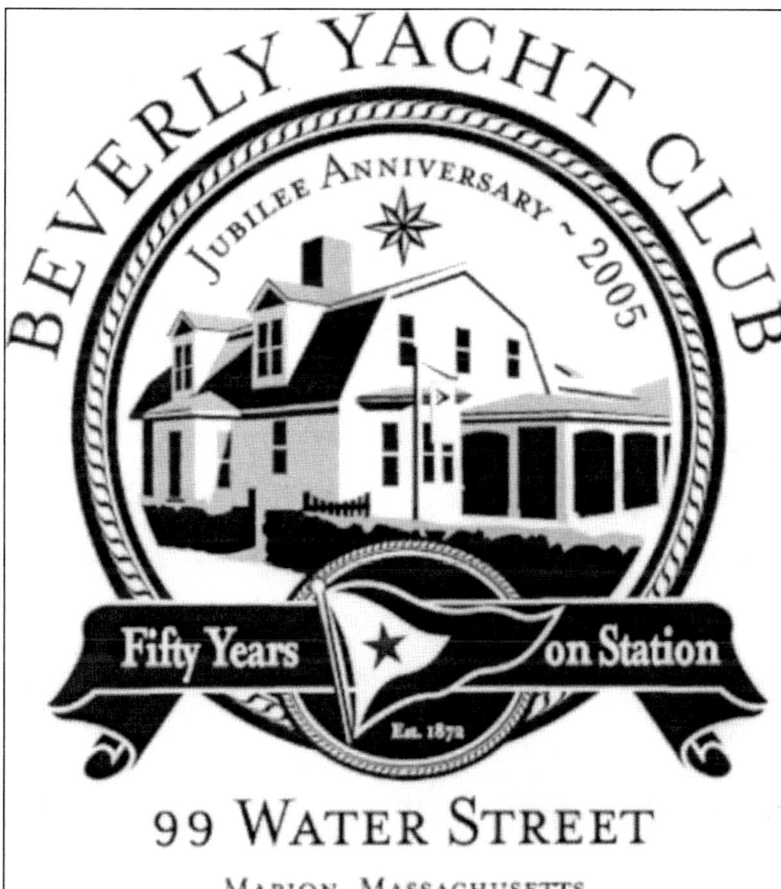

In July 2005, the Beverly Yacht Club held a jubilee celebration, celebrating 50 years on station at its Water Street location, where it moved in 1955. Over 500 members and guests danced under the stars into the beautiful night.

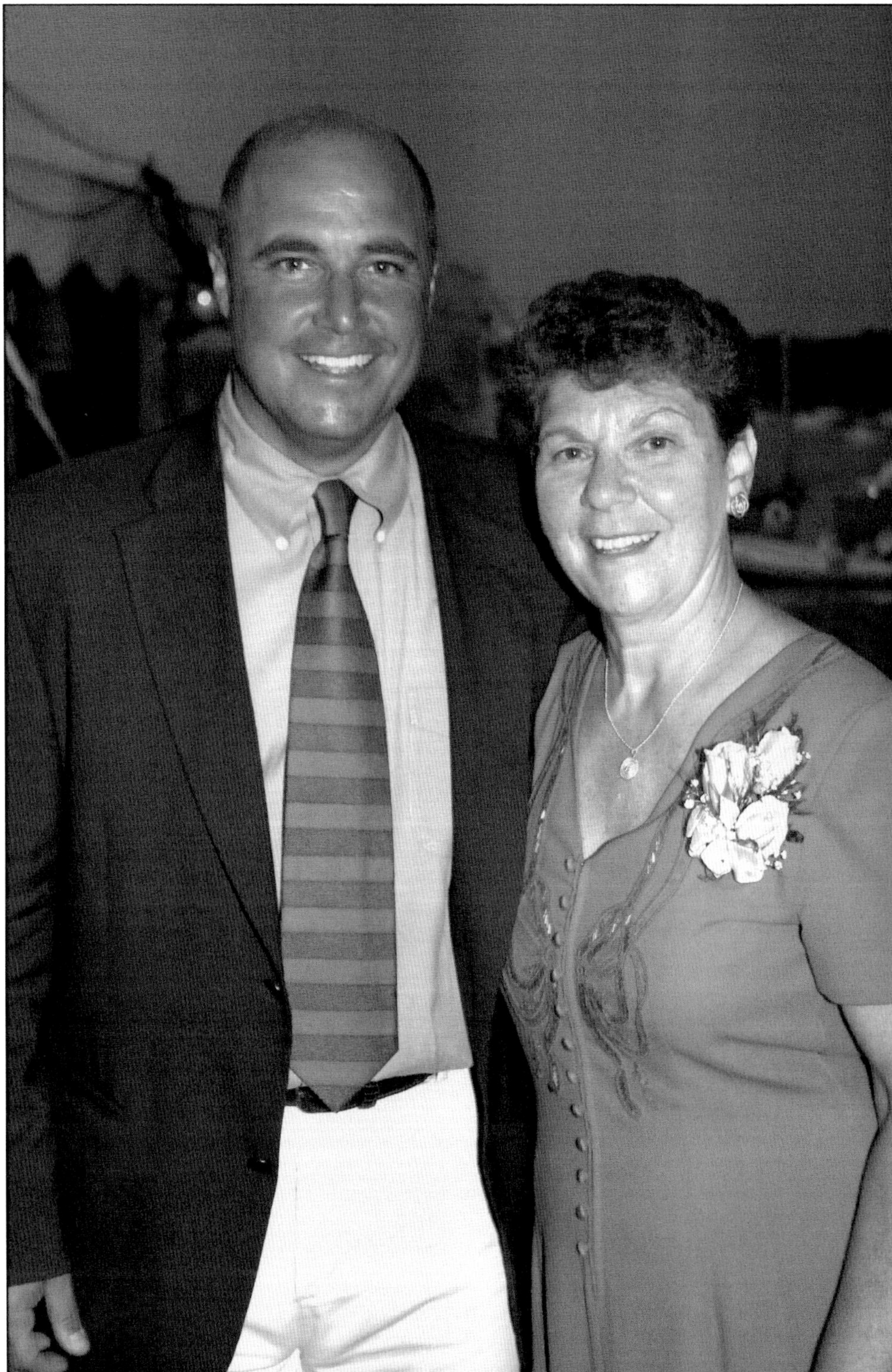

Gregg Nourjian headed up the jubilee celebration. He is shown in this photograph with past commodore Linda Goodwin at the jubilee.

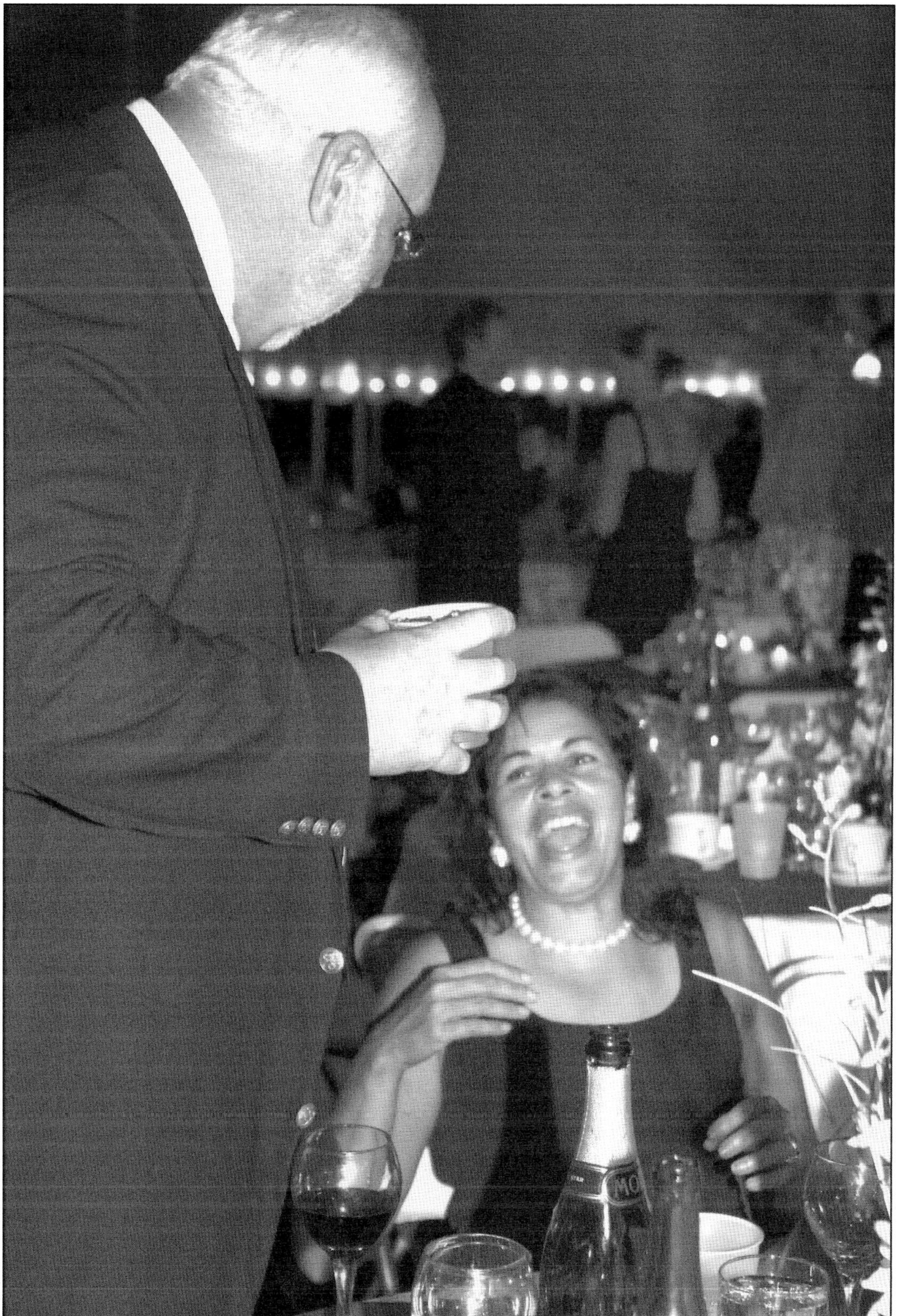

Carmen Grainger, the Beverly Yacht Club House Committee chair, who spent many hours planning the jubilee, shares a happy moment with Brian Ladouceur, vice commodore, at the jubilee celebration.

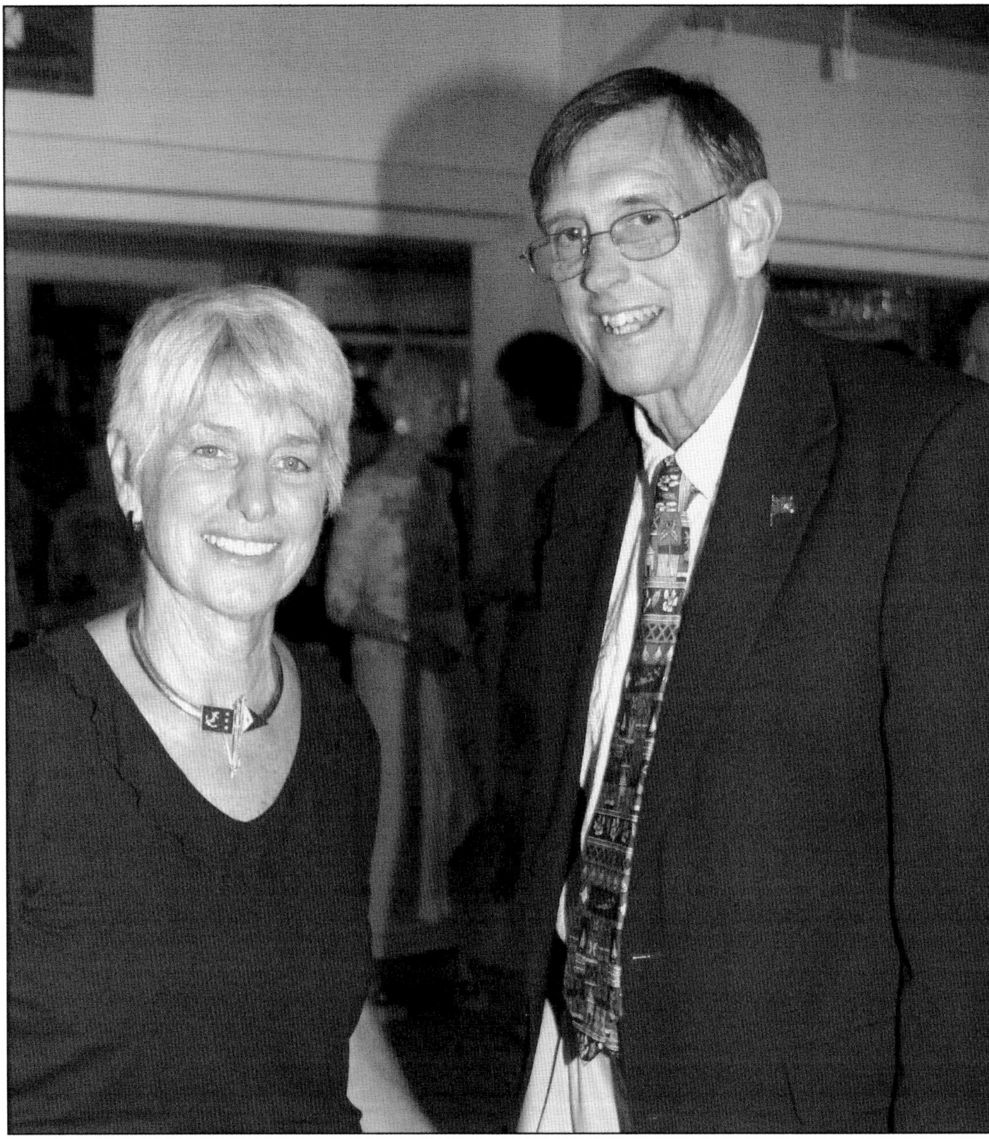

Faith Paulsen, the first female commodore of the Beverly Yacht Club (1994–1996), enjoys the celebration with her husband, Charlie. An excellent sailor, Faith has won many sailing trophies in her Bullseye, *Sandpiper*. It won the Beverly Cup in 1982, 1983, 1984, and 1985.

The Beverly Cup is a lovely trophy of antique English silver. This cup was given to the Beverly Yacht Club by Maj. Henry Forester. It is awarded annually to the boat with the highest overall score in any regular-season series.

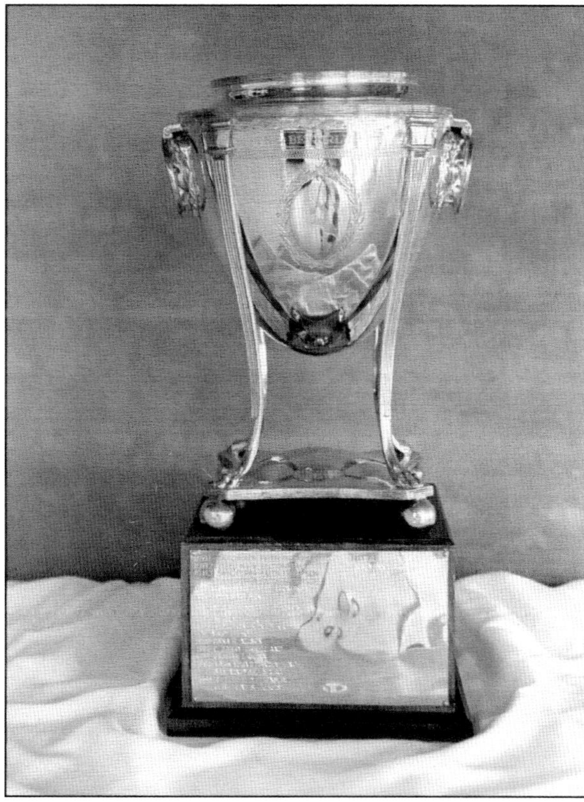

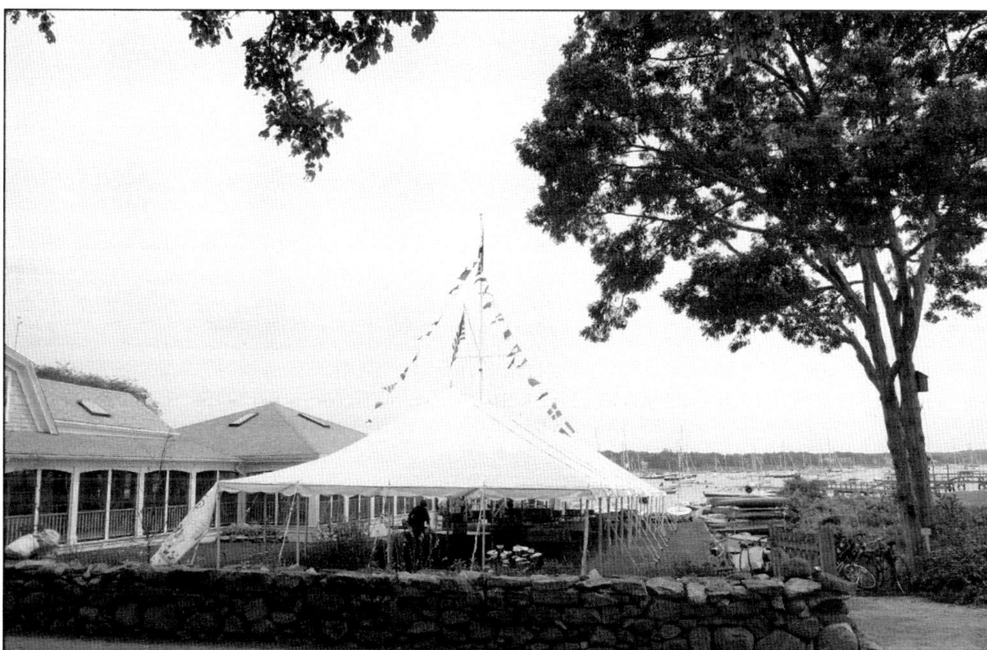

Two large tents were installed for the jubilee celebration. Members and their guests dined under the tents and then danced on the Beverly Yacht Club porch.

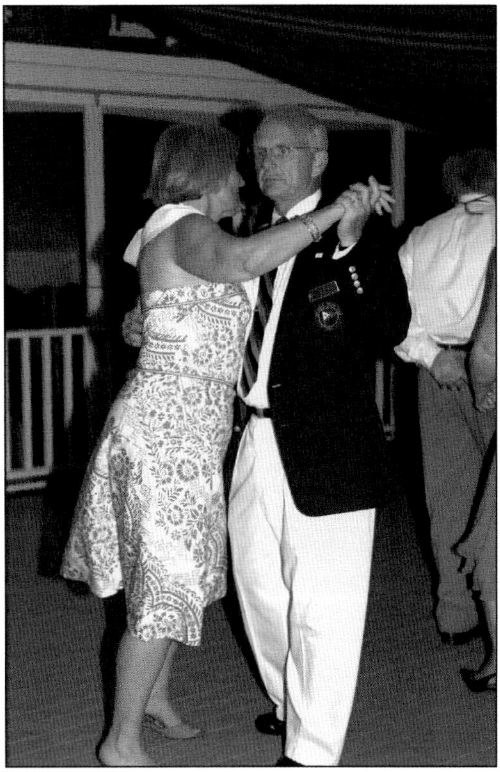

Harry Norweb, rear commodore, enjoys a dance at the jubilee celebration with his wife, Pam.

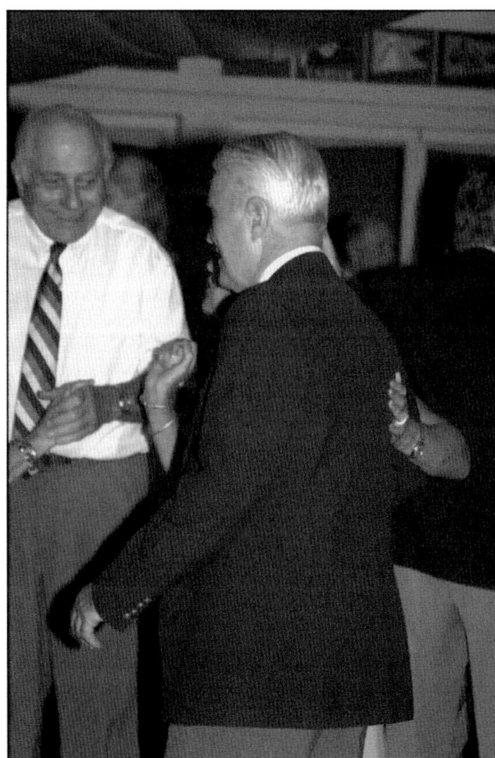

Harvey White, past commodore from 1984 to 1986, dances on the Beverly Yacht Club porch and greets veteran sailor Ron Noonan at the jubilee celebration.

Dan Cooney, council member and chairman of the Buzzards Bay Regatta, enjoys the evening with his wife, Kate.

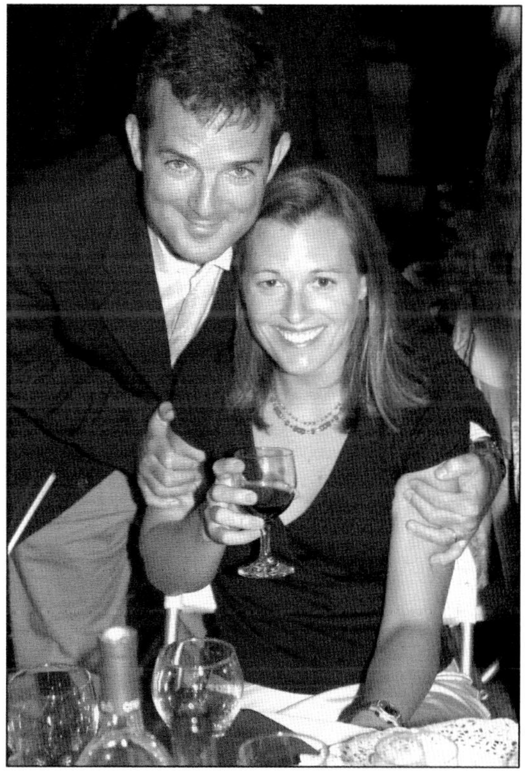

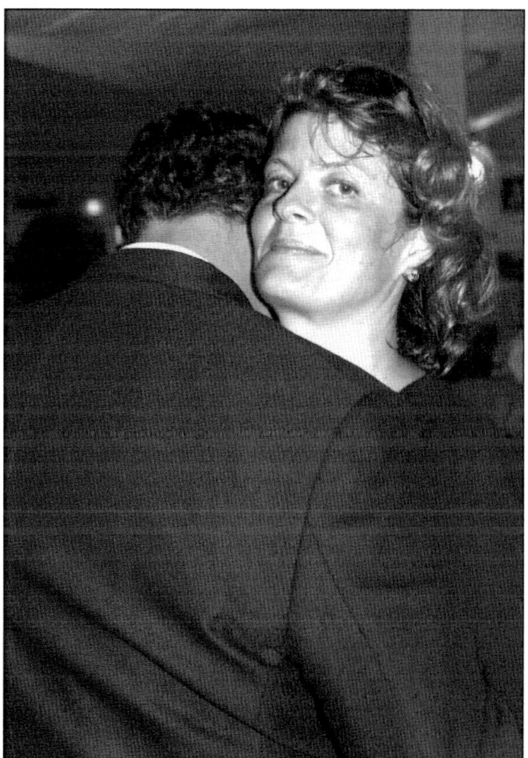

Betsy Fallon, a prior junior commodore and the head of the successful auction fund-raiser for the junior sailing program, dances with her husband, Mike, at the jubilee celebration.